IMAGES
of America

TORRINGTON

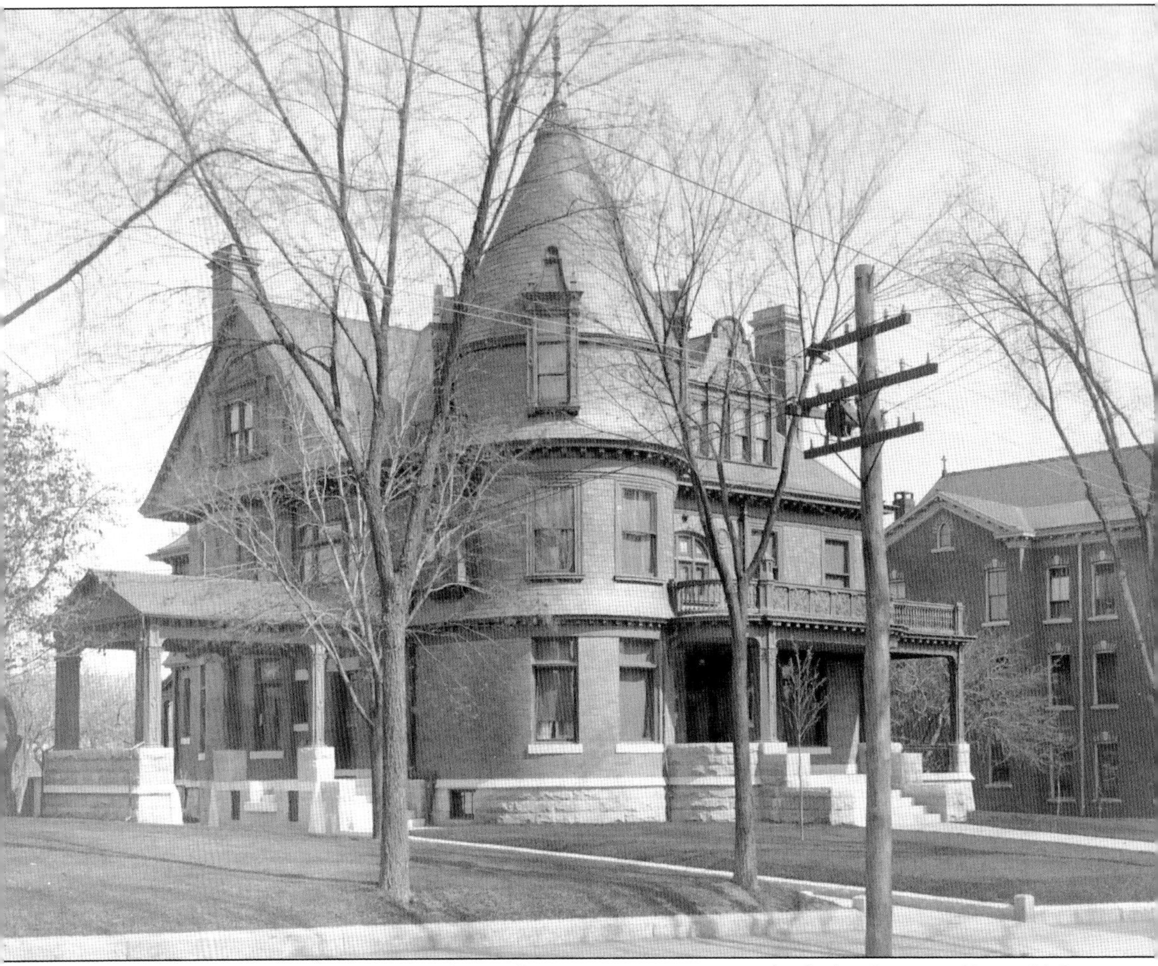

The house known as the Hotchkiss-Fyler House Museum was built for Orsamus R. and Mary Fyler in 1900. It was also home to the Fylers' daughter Gertrude and her husband, Edward H. Hotchkiss. After the death of Gertrude Hotchkiss in 1956, her will dictated that the house was to be left in trust for use as a museum operated by the Torrington Historical Society. Today, it is one of Torrington's premier cultural attractions. (Torrington Historical Society.)

On the Cover: A group of Torrington teenagers sits on the stone wall in front of the John Brown Birthplace on March 28, 1903. The house was restored by Torrington's John Brown Association in 1902, and it was operated as a museum until a chimney fire destroyed the structure in 1918. The Torrington Historical Society now owns and manages the site where abolitionist John Brown was born on May 9, 1800. (Torrington Historical Society.)

IMAGES
of America

TORRINGTON

Elizabeth A. Kaczmarcyk on behalf of
the Torrington Historical Society

ARCADIA
PUBLISHING

ISBN 978-1-4671-2781-3

Published by Arcadia Publishing
Charleston, South Carolina

Printed in the United States of America

Library of Congress Control Number: 2017944979

For all general information, please contact Arcadia Publishing:
Telephone 843-853-2070
Fax 843-853-0044
E-mail sales@arcadiapublishing.com
For customer service and orders:
Toll-Free 1-888-313-2665

Visit us on the Internet at www.arcadiapublishing.com

This book is for my parents, Betty Amrich Kaczmarcyk and Edward Kaczmarcyk Sr., and for my grandparents, who helped make their community a better place.

Contents

Acknowledgments

I would like to thank the Torrington Historical Society for offering unlimited access to its archives and photography collection, without which this book could not have been written. Mark McEachern, Gail Kruppa, and Carol Clapp welcomed me to the society; helped me locate photographs and materials; and read, reviewed, and edited the text for historical accuracy. Mark and Gail were especially knowledgeable concerning Torrington's complicated history of churches and factories as well as the society's main benefactor, Gertrude Fyler Hotchkiss. Librarian and archivist Carol Clapp helped me enormously, showing me how to use the collection most effectively and sharing my enthusiasm for archival discoveries. The entire staff, including bookkeeper Roberta Janco, along with the many volunteers and researchers with whom I crossed paths, encouraged me throughout the process and offered valuable insights and information about Torrington's history. I also want to acknowledge the many organizations and local citizens, especially church members, who took time to speak with me and share photographs from their personal collections, some of which are included in the book. Unless otherwise noted, however, all photographs are from the collection of the Torrington Historical Society.

A special thank-you goes to my husband, Peter Avenia, who offered constant support and encouragement.

I am very grateful to have had this opportunity to delve into Torrington's past and to learn more about the organizations and individuals who contributed to its success. I apologize for any errors in names, dates, or other facts contained in the text.

Introduction

Torrington was established as a township by the Colony of Connecticut in 1732 and named after a town in Devonshire, England. Only one other place in America shares its name—Torrington, Wyoming, which was christened by Connecticut Torringtonian William G. Curtis in the 1880s. For a time, neighborhood place-names such as Newfield, Burrville, Torringford, and Wolcottville (the name of Torrington's downtown from 1813 to 1881) were widely used, lending a small-town feel to each area. That sense of neighborhood identity eventually gave way to a wider sense of community as the town grew from nine families in 1740 to its current population of over 35,000 residents.

Located in the hills of Litchfield County in northwest Connecticut, Torrington might easily have remained a small rural community, like most of the surrounding towns, but for its location on the Naugatuck River, which attracted manufacturers as early as 1787. Torrington's destiny changed when Israel Coe and Erastus Hodges set up competing brass mills on the banks of the river in the mid-1830s, bringing a new industry to the Naugatuck Valley. When the Naugatuck Valley Railroad to Torrington was completed in 1849, linking the town to large population centers like New York City, industry boomed and immigrants flocked to the mills and factories, encouraging even more growth. The wars of the 20th century further stimulated factory production, especially during World War II, when local plants operated around the clock to produce a variety of items such as bearings, machine tools, and brass shell casings.

In researching the city's period of greatest growth and change—from roughly 1860 to 1960—I relied on the Torrington Historical Society's collection of photographs as well as its collection of old newspapers, church histories, scrapbooks, diaries, and interviews. I was struck by the commitment and determination of Torrington's citizens—by their efforts to make their community a better place and by their farsightedness in knowing what was crucial to Torrington's future success.

For example, when local citizens met in 1864 to establish a library, Torrington had no city water system, no electric lights, no local bank—not even a newspaper. When city services were stressed by the influx of immigrant workers, citizens raised money to build more and better schools and set up free health clinics within them. Churches welcomed the newcomers, many of whom were from foreign countries. When the 1918 influenza epidemic struck, doctors and nurses volunteered their services, and residents, sometimes at great personal risk, delivered meals and checked on the well-being of neighbors. Men and women often worked for decades at local factories and family businesses, contributing to Torrington's stability and cohesiveness.

During this period, Torrington also had the good fortune to attract factory owners and entrepreneurs who chose to live in the town where they ran their businesses. Because they had such personal stakes in the town, their philanthropic efforts extended to all facets of city life—education, public health, recreation, religious worship, and many other areas of civic engagement.

Many persons, places, and institutions that played an important role in the town's history are, unfortunately, not represented here. Space limitations have forced me to make painful choices among equally valuable topics deserving mention. And because this is a photographic history, I could only include subjects for which a suitable photograph was available.

Given these limitations, I have tried to capture a sense of Torrington's progress over two centuries and to highlight some of the people and institutions that supplied the driving force for that progress. Many of them are lost (or nearly lost) to time and memory, but I hope this book helps to illustrate how thousands of hardworking citizens, whether forgotten or remembered, produced so many enduring civic benefits while striving to improve their lots and their community.

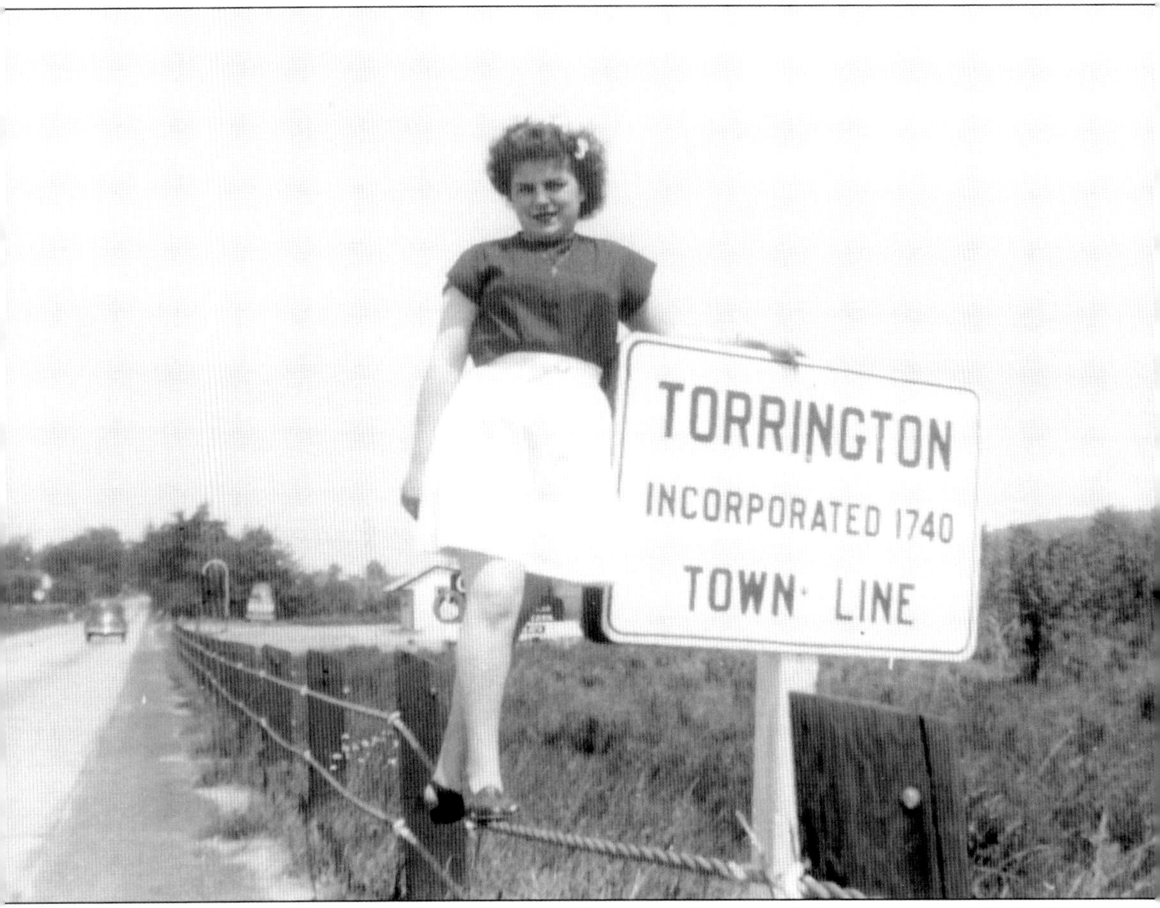

Mary Angieri Pellegrino is shown here performing a low-wire balancing act while holding on to a street sign marking Torrington's town-line boundary. The photograph is undated, but the car in the distance suggests it may have been taken in the 1940s, some 200 years after the town's incorporation.

One

IMMIGRATION

If one looks carefully, traces of Torrington's immigrant past are still visible all around town. Cameron and Pulaski Streets, the Germania Singing Society building, Fuessenich Park, and Besse Pond are just a few of the places that remind locals and visitors of the immigrants who came to Torrington in the 19th and early 20th centuries. The first big wave of 19th-century immigration occurred in the 1830s when the English arrived after being recruited to work in the brass mill. They were followed by Irish, German, Swedish, and Scottish immigrants, among others. By the late 1890s, German immigrants had created a prosperous downtown business district on lower East Main Street that included saloons, restaurants, a high-class hotel, and a performance hall.

But it was the massive influx of Poles, Italians, Slovaks, Lithuanians, Hungarians, and others that most shaped Torrington's future. With a force as powerful as the Naugatuck River, these immigrants came by the thousands in the early 1900s, doubling Torrington's population and then doubling it again, at first threatening to undermine wages and overwhelm infrastructure, but soon leading to a sharp increase in overall prosperity.

Torrington's religious organizations offered support and guidance to the newcomers. Center Congregational Church set up missions and provided meeting space for Italian, Hungarian, French, and Syrian Protestants. Directly across the street, the Irish St. Francis Catholic Church and parochial school welcomed all Catholics, hosting visiting priests who spoke multiple languages.

With ample factory work and steady wages, the new immigrants quickly reestablished family life in their new homes. They married or brought their families from the Old Country and bought or built the two-family homes that characterize Torrington's neighborhoods, sharing them with relatives and friends. In the process, they created vibrant ethnic enclaves that flourished for decades.

The immigrants also built their own churches, established fraternal organizations, and set up the small grocery stores and meat markets that anchored their neighborhoods. Over time, work, sports, military service, dances, and English classes drew them out into the larger community—and drew the outside community to them. For nearly 100 years, Torrington was a true ethnic mosaic that exemplified prosperous, industrious small-town America at its best.

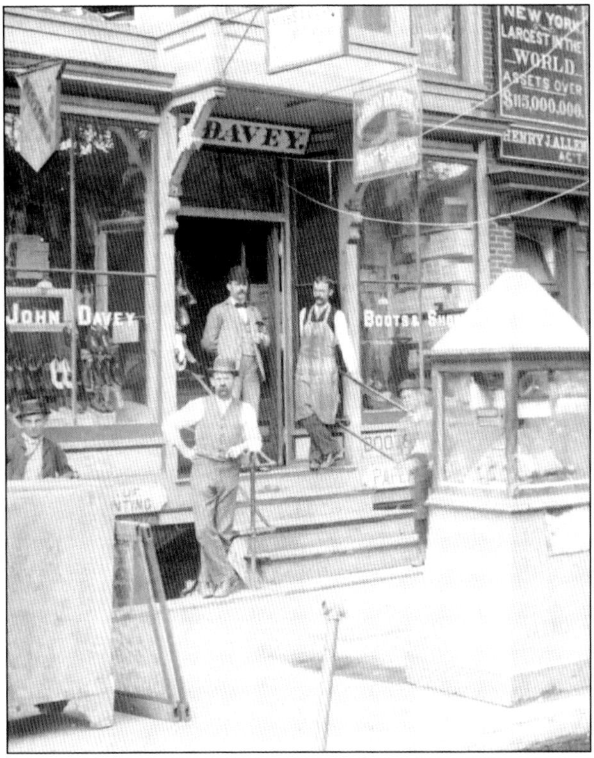

John Davey, born in England in 1830, opened Torrington's first shoe store in 1867 in a small frame building in downtown Torrington. A custom shoemaker by trade, Davey added ready-made shoes to his inventory in 1875. The store, "neatly and admirably stocked," according to the *Torrington Daily Register*, sometimes employed as many as six clerks. Davey's son John, who took over the business from his father, retired in 1920.

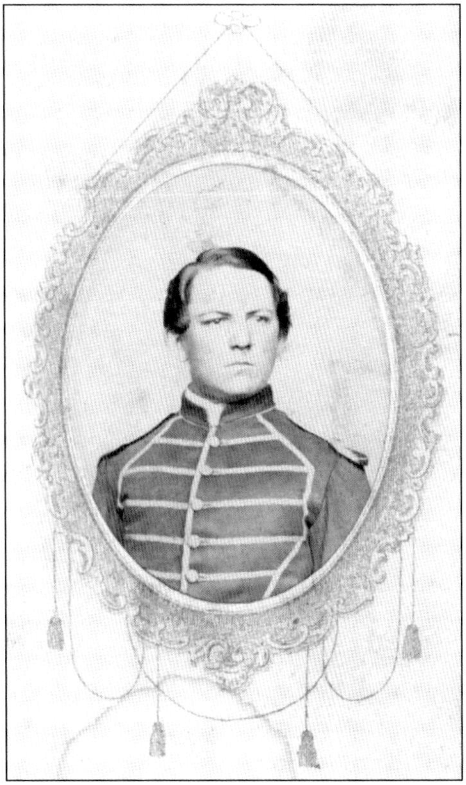

Andrew Workman came to Torrington from England as a child with his family in 1851. During the Civil War, Workman enlisted with Company C as a musician and served for three years as a fifer in the drum corps. After his discharge in 1865, he returned to Torrington, where he joined the Wolcottville Band. Workman was employed by the Coe Brass Company for over 40 years, spending 30 of them as foreman of the annealing department.

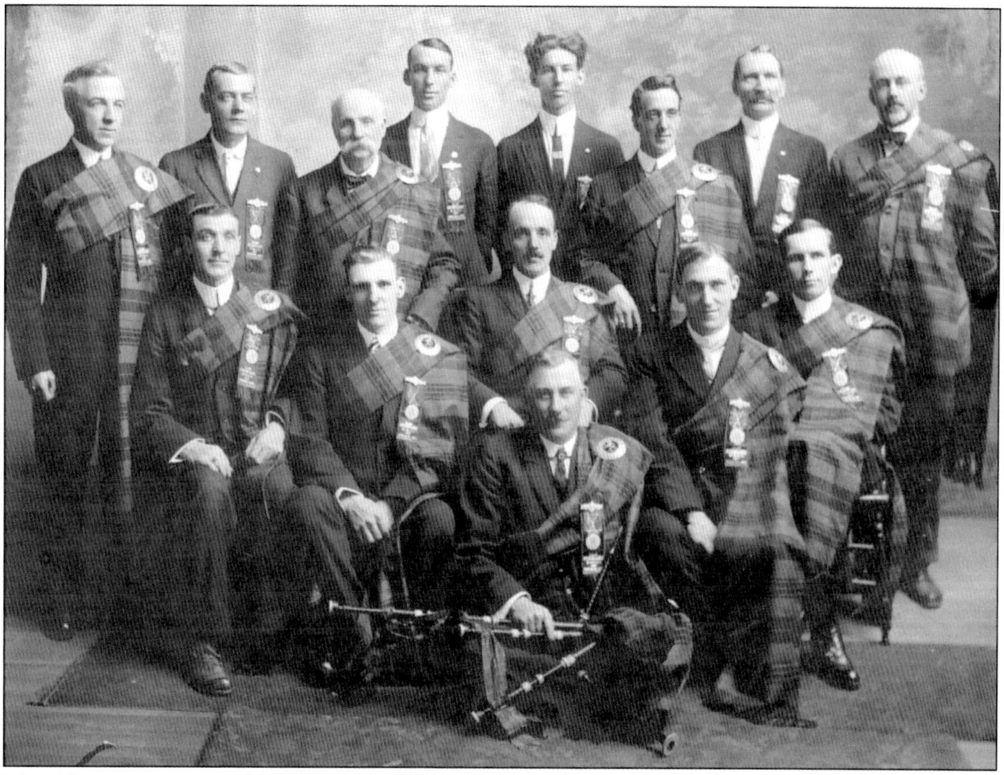

The Clan Stewart, Number 145, Order of Scottish Clans, included talented vocalists and musicians who enjoyed entertaining Torrington's Scottish community. In 1902, the *Evening Register* noted that the group "tripped the light fantastic until an early hour" at Torrington's Ashborn Hall. Daniel Cameron Sr. (standing third from left in the back row) was one of the singers.

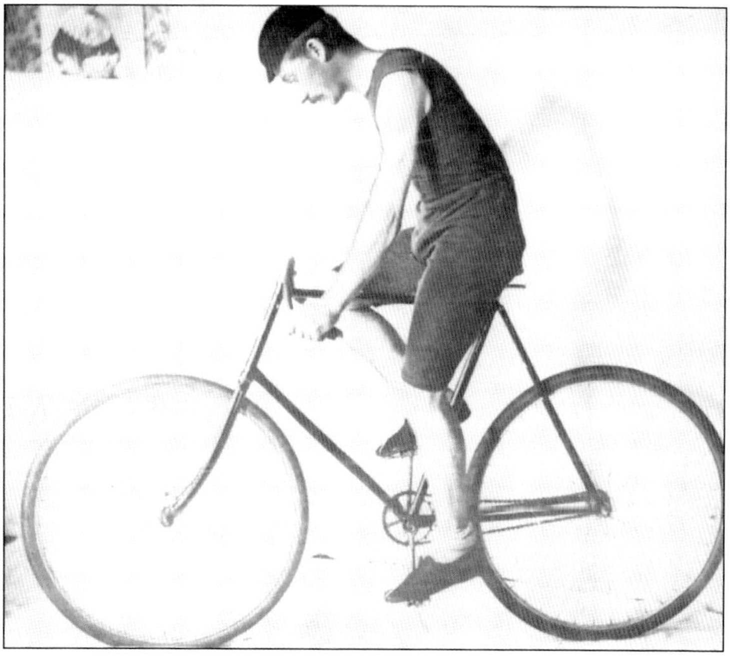

Scottish immigrant John M. Cameron was a champion bicyclist in the 1890s. After his Eagle bicycle frame collapsed during a race, Eagle rebuilt the bicycle and offered him a replacement. Cameron poses here on his new bicycle, which was later donated to the Torrington Historical Society. In the early 1920s, Cameron formed the Cameron Pipe Band, casting the band members' belt buckles by hand and making their bagpipes.

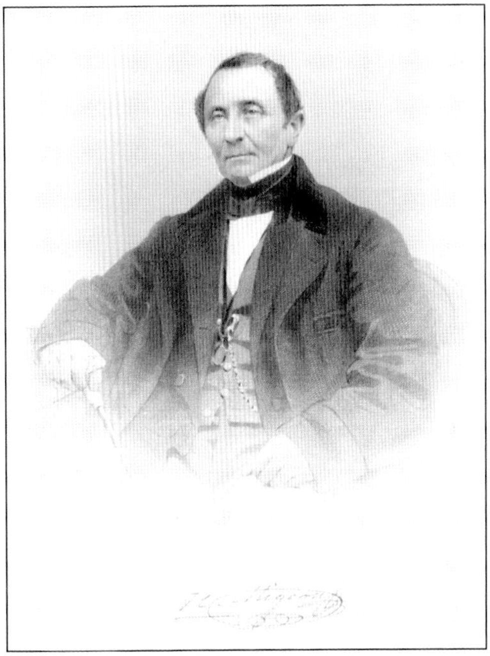

Born in France in 1799, Henri Migeon came to the United States in 1828. When Migeon died in 1878, he was one of the oldest French residents of the country. A self-made man with little formal education, he arrived with a letter of introduction from General Lafayette and extensive knowledge of the wool industry. Migeon eventually settled in Torrington and purchased and improved considerable property along what is now Migeon Avenue.

This Shingle Style residence of Achille Migeon, son of Henri Migeon and also a prominent local businessman, was built at the corner of Forest Street and Migeon Avenue in the 1890s. The Migeon house is one of several elegant homes on Migeon Avenue, a portion of which has been designated as a historic district.

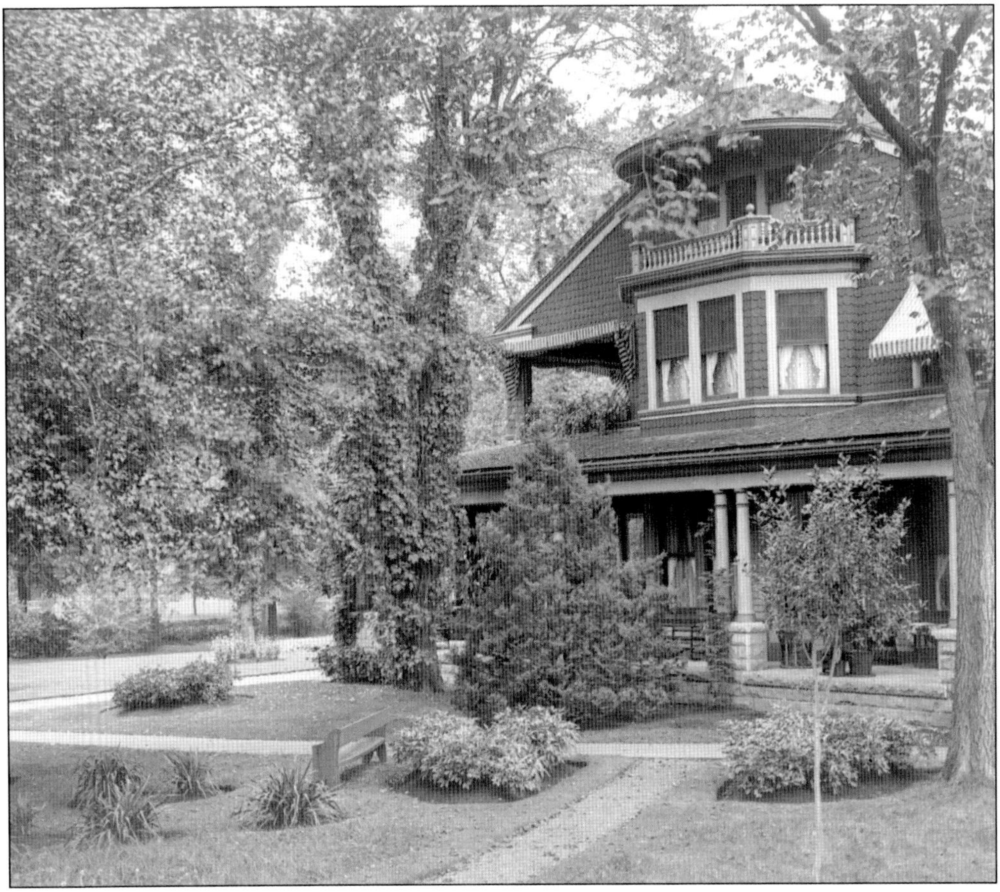

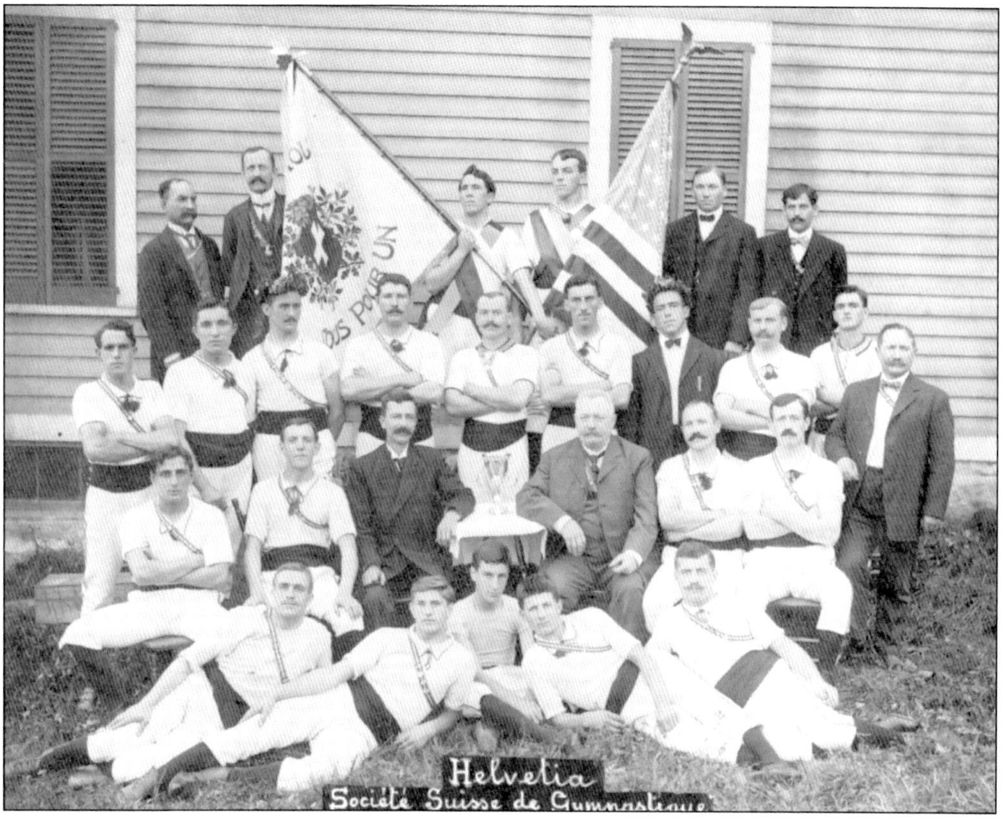

This photograph of the Helvetia gymnasts was probably taken at the dedication of the Swiss and American flags in 1908. The gymnasts formed human pyramids and swung their lighted clubs at the Opera House in "one of the finest as well as unique events ever held in Torrington," according to the *Evening Register*. Gymnastic groups, which were formed to enhance physical and mental well-being, were common in the early 20th century. (Elizabeth Kaczmarcyk.)

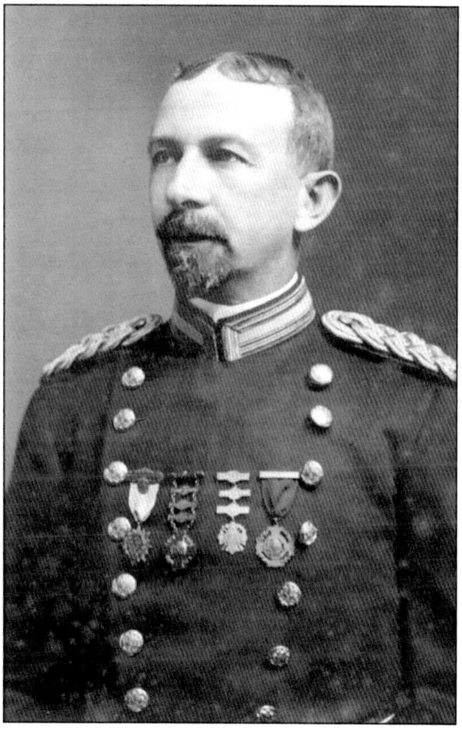

Swiss immigrant William E. Besse remembered arriving in Connecticut in the 1880s without gloves or boots and hiking through deep snow from Cornwall Bridge to his uncle's farm knowing only one English phrase: "Where is the road to Goshen?" Besse worked his way up from day laborer to superintendent of the American Brass Company. He donated the Besse Pond property to the city as well as land in West Torrington.

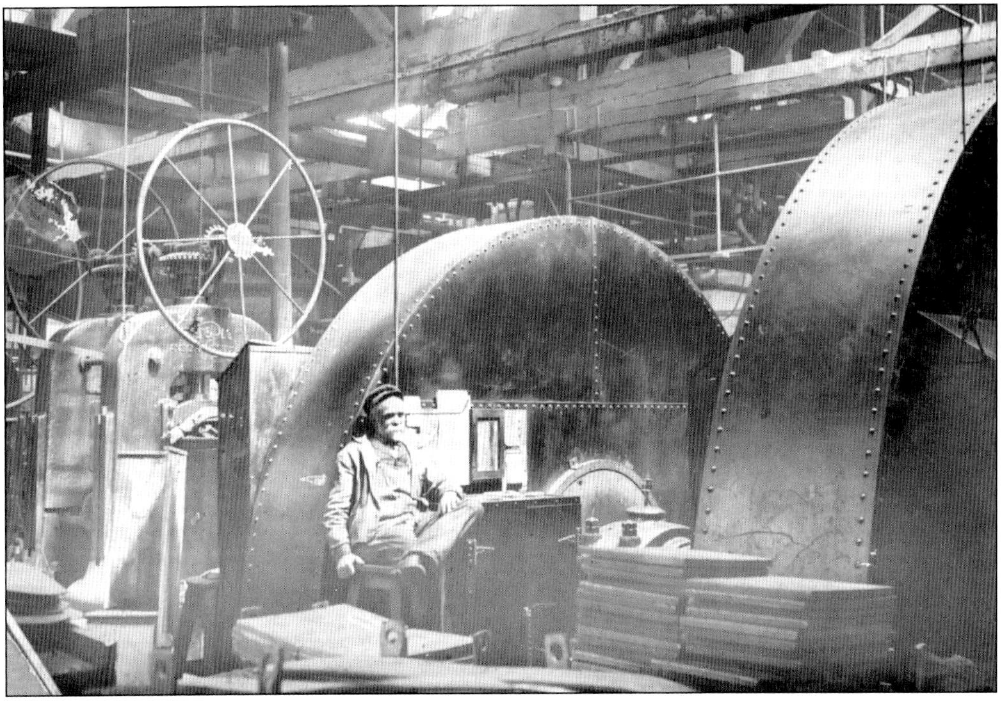

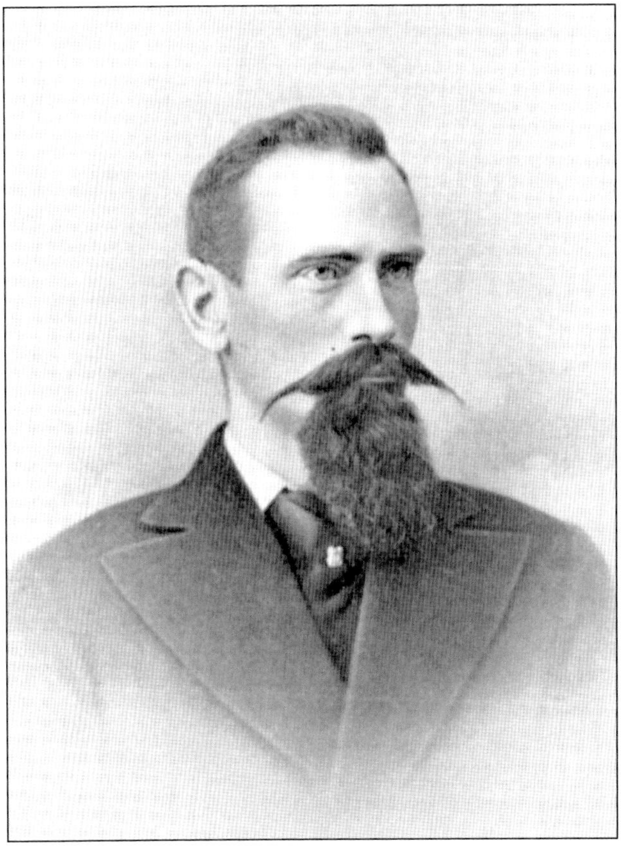

Brothers Charles and Carston A. Janssen came to Connecticut from Germany in the early 1880s. Carston, known as Andy, is shown here dwarfed by equipment at the American Brass Company, where he worked for more than 40 years. In his early years, he walked back and forth from Burrville to his job. Loyal and hardworking, Andy could write upside down and could also draw with both hands simultaneously.

Charles Janssen used his artistic talents to build a successful architecture and construction business in Torrington in the 1880s and 1890s, when German immigrants were starting to put their stamp on Torrington. One of his most significant projects was St. Paul's Lutheran Church, which was completed in 1895 on South Main Street. He also designed the Batter's Building on Church Street and the Berkshire Café on Albert Street.

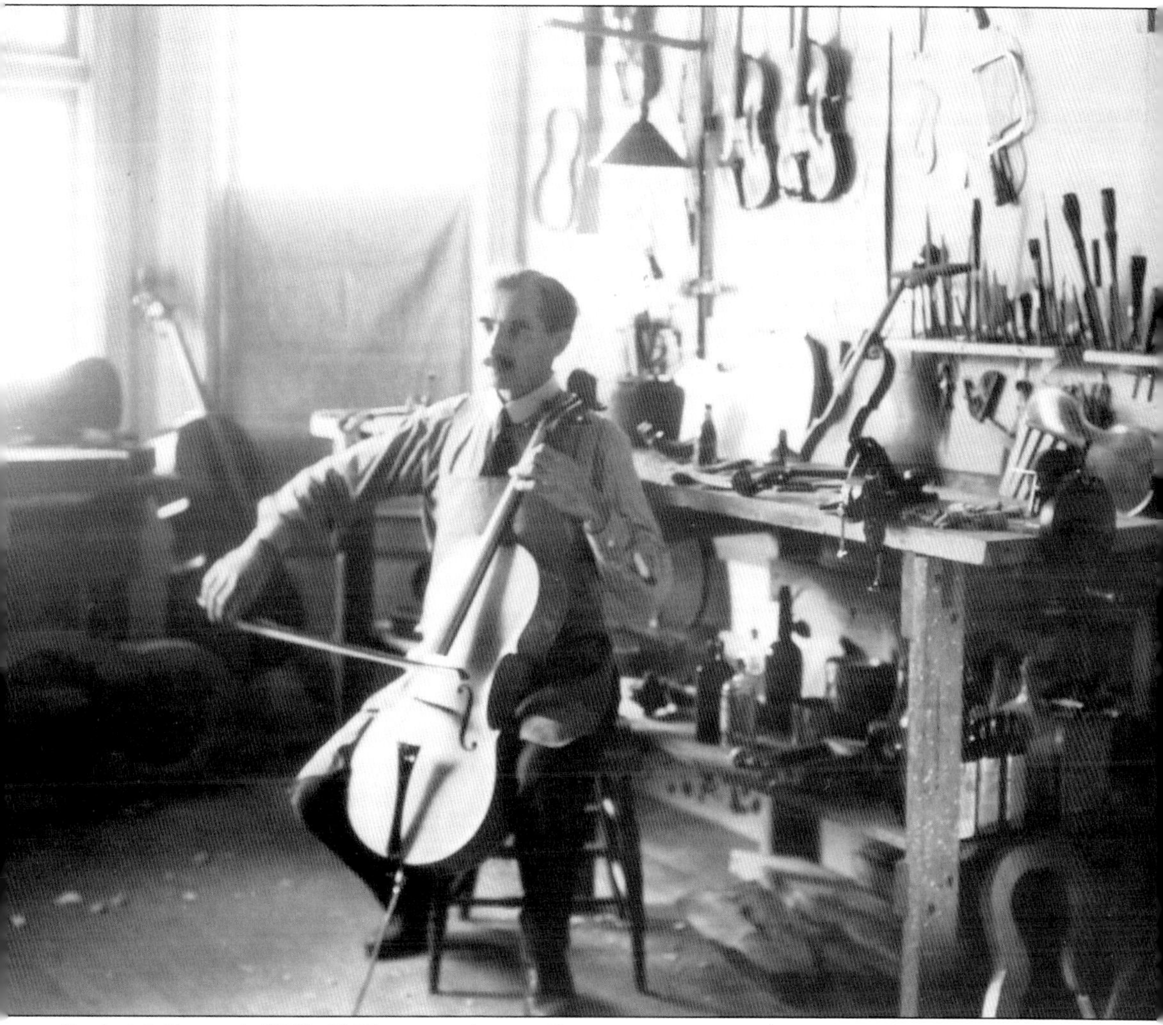

Frederich Dautrich (1875–1942), pictured, was a German immigrant who came to America in 1891. After first working as a patternmaker at the Turner and Seymour Company, he later studied fine arts at a school of art and design in Los Angeles. Dautrich was first a fine arts painter, but his love of music led him to instrument-making. He returned to Torrington, where he set up a shop to build and repair violins. He is noted for the invention of three new stringed instruments that, together with the standard violin and bass, comprise the Dautrich Quintet. Dautrich's new instruments were the vilonia (slightly larger than a violin), the vilon (slightly smaller than a cello), and the vilono (slightly larger than a cello). These new instruments never achieved wide popularity, but during his lifetime, music was written for them and performed by a quintet that included his son, Jean Dautrich, and daughter-in-law, Helene Halabe Dautrich. The elder Dautrich's instruments are in the collections of the Metropolitan Museum of Art and the Torrington Historical Society.

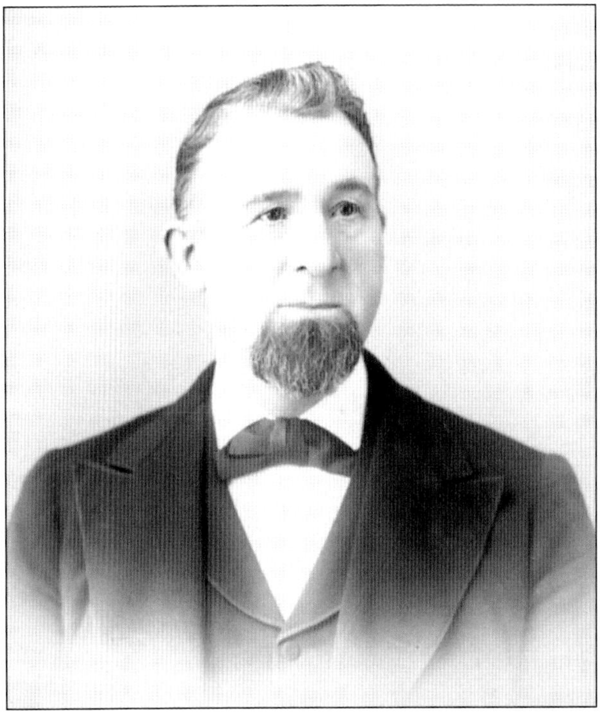

According to the *Torrington Register Souvenir Edition*, Richard Carroll, born in Tipperary, Ireland, came to Torrington in 1851 when it was "a comparatively insignificant place." He started out at Wooding's pocketbook and trunk lock factory (later the Union Hardware Company). Carroll worked there until the age of 72, when a grinding wheel hit him in the head. He also served as collector of taxes and borough burgess.

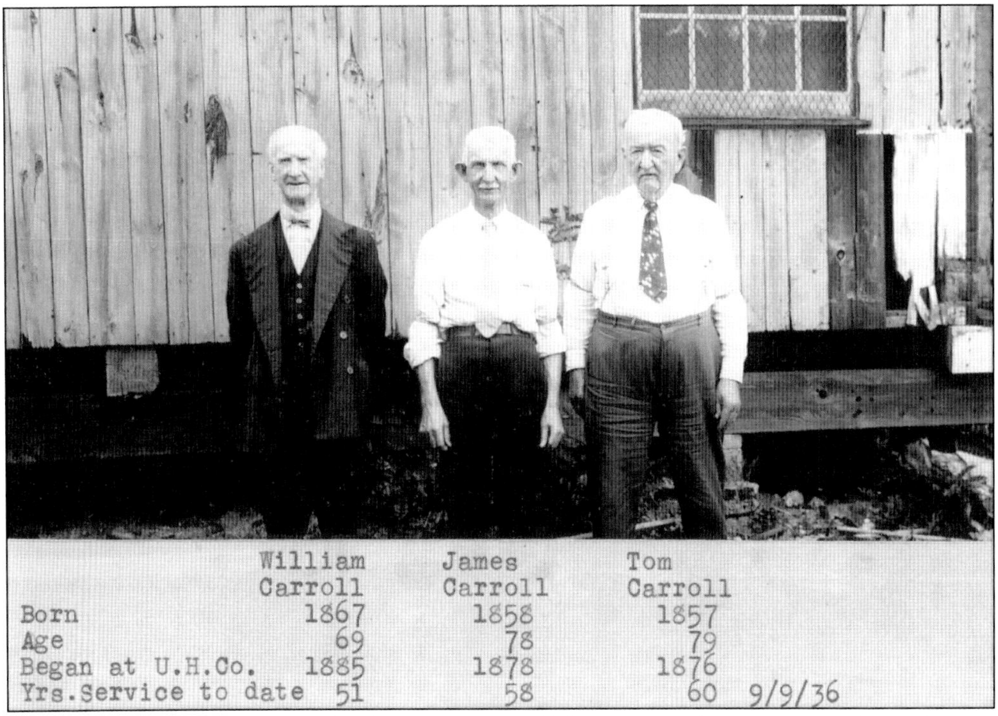

Richard Carroll's three sons—William, James, and Thomas—followed their father to Union Hardware. This photograph commemorates each brother's employment for more than 50 years. When 84-year-old William retired in 1947, he had missed only one week of work in his 61 years at the company.

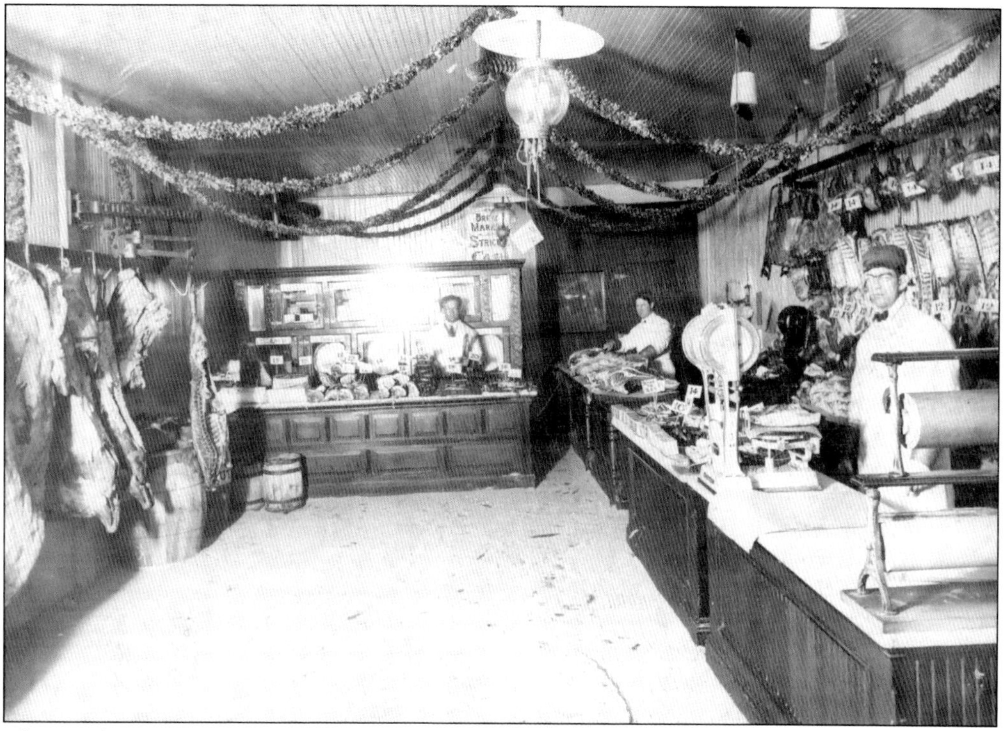

This market, Meara Bros., on the west side of Center Bridge was owned and operated by James and William Meara, members of one of Torrington's earliest Irish families. Described as "all-capable and wide-awake" in the 1896 *Biographical Review*, the brothers began selling meat and fish sometime in the mid-1880s. In 1896, they opened a men's furnishings store in a brick building they erected at 22 Main Street, where Howard's Shoes later did business for decades.

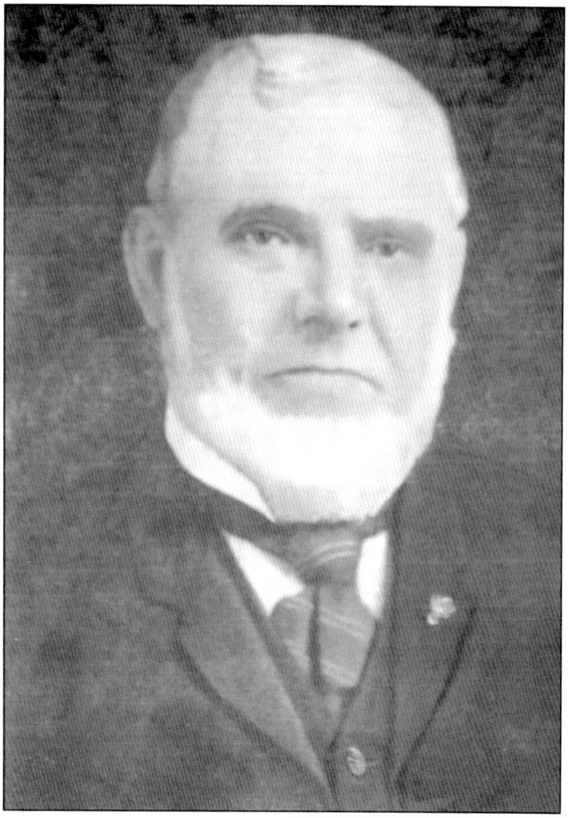

Irish-born Patrick Gleeson made Torrington his home in 1871. As a general contractor, he did extensive work on the city's streets, including grading and excavating. In the early 1890s, Gleeson studied embalming in New York City and became Torrington's first Catholic undertaker. His son William continued the Prospect Street funeral business and, as city clerk, organized the town's records.

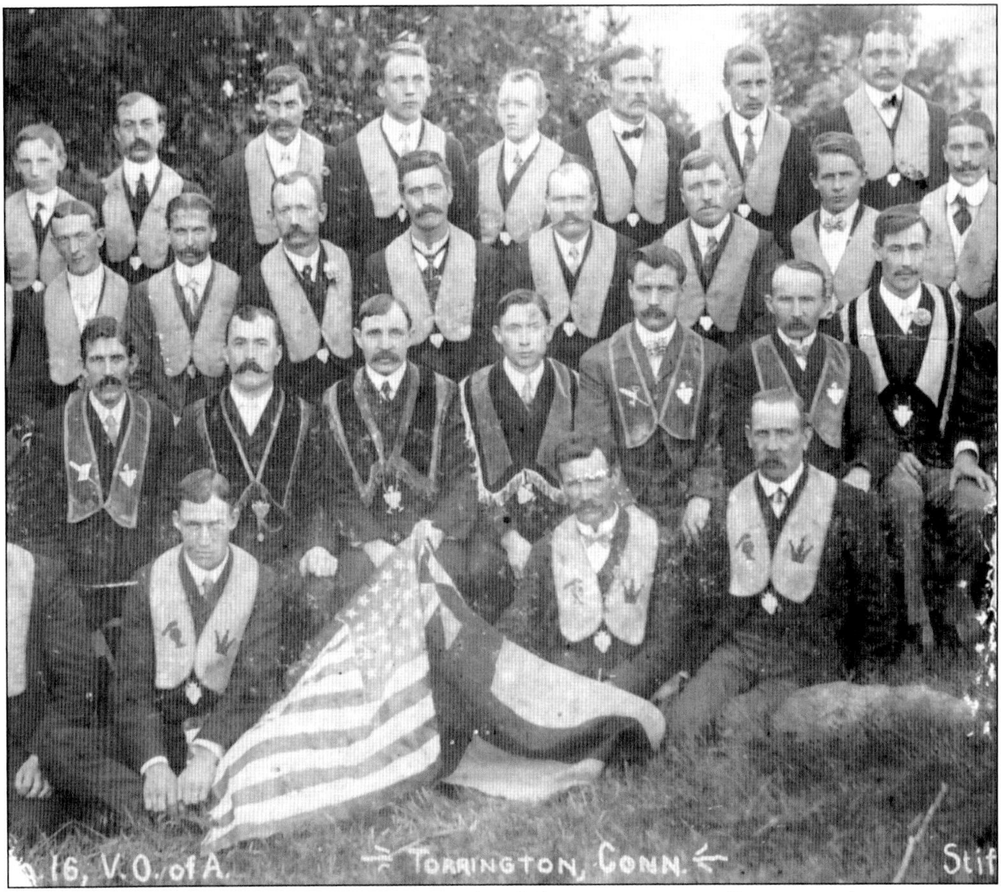

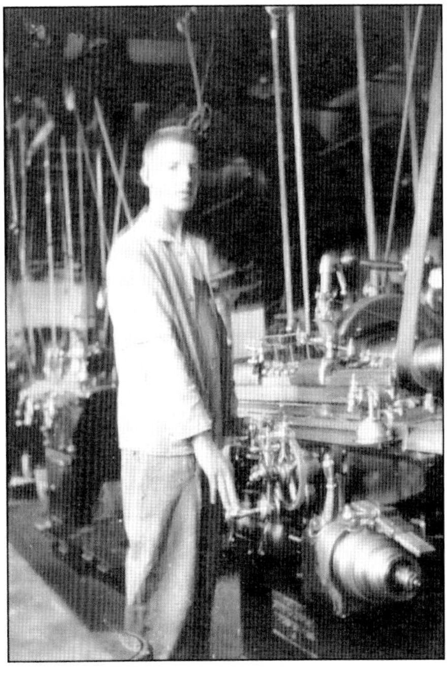

Swedish immigration to Torrington began around 1880 and peaked between 1890 and 1900. In 1898, local Swedes formed a mutual benefit society called the Klippan Society, shown in this 1902 photograph. Unfortunately, none of the men are identified, but some of the group's charter members were Severin and Hugo Aronson, John Soderberg, and Eric Westberg.

This photograph shows Engnar "Eugene" Aronson, a popular amateur boxer, on the job at the Hendey Machine Company. Eugene was the son of Severin Aronson, an early Swedish immigrant and one of the founders of Torrington's Swedish Lutheran Church. Severin worked for 35 years at Hendey, where Eugene later became head of the local CIO labor union.

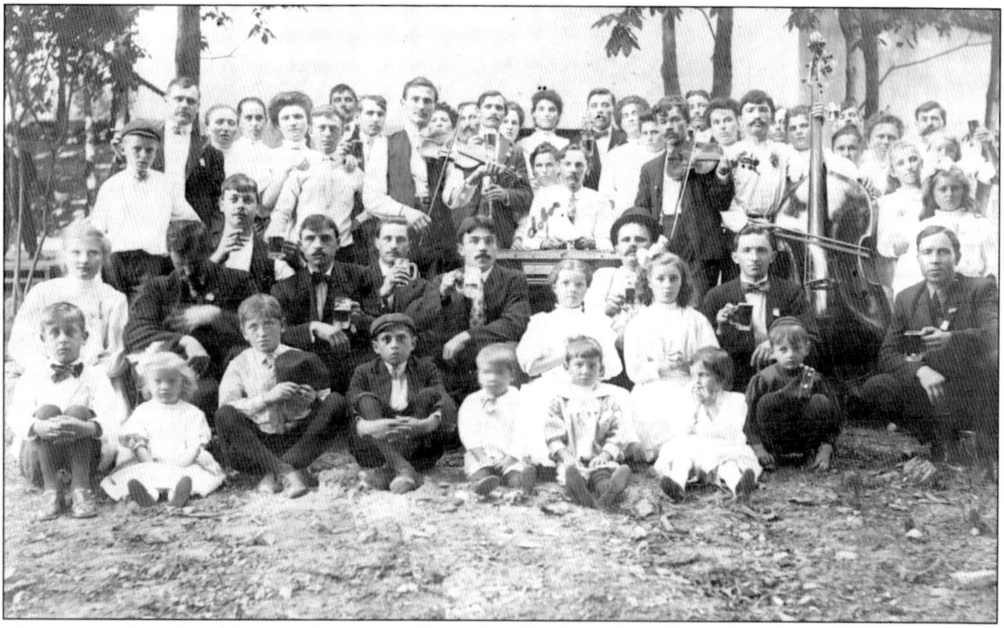

Hungarians Stephen Nagy on bass and "Dobos" on keyboard are the only people identified in this photograph labeled (in Hungarian) "St. Stephen's Catholic Church Society Fund in Full Swing." Hungarian immigrants began arriving in Torrington in the late 1800s. By 1910, there were about 500 Hungarians living here, many of whom worked at the American Brass Company.

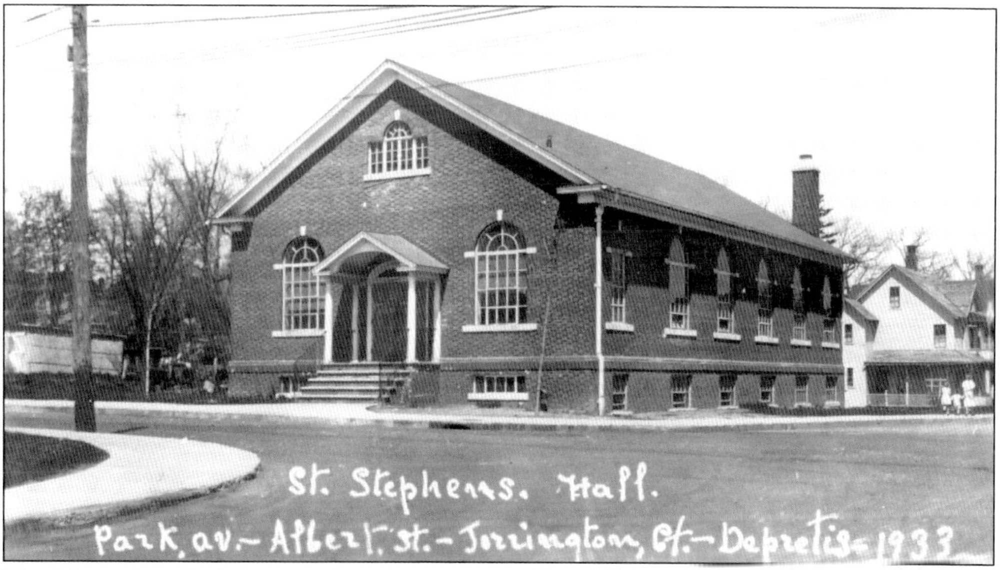

The Hungarian Catholics purchased property on East Albert and Park Streets with the hope of constructing their own church. Instead, this large brick community center was built in 1927. Various Hungarian organizations—including the Hungarian Citizens Club, the Hungarian Benefit Society, and Radoczi—hosted dances, plays, and parties here. The building is no longer owned by the Hungarians but is still in use today.

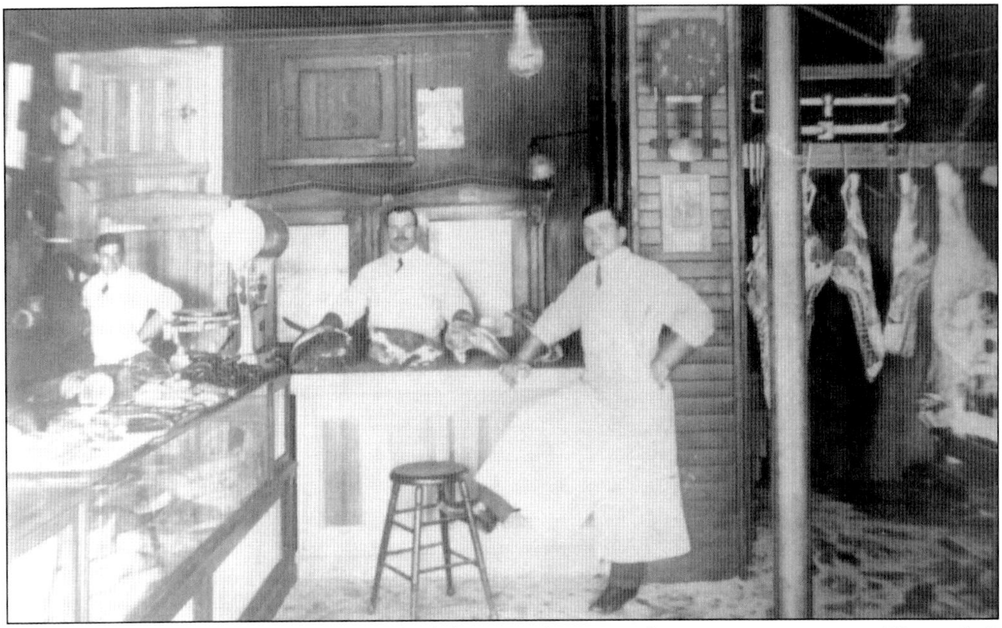

Brothers Marcus (center) and Andrew (right) Horansky are ready to serve customers at Horansky's Market in this c. 1910 photograph. Marcus, a Slovak immigrant, came to the United States in 1896 and to Torrington in 1904. He got his start through his brother-in-law, Nicholas Ostrofsky, a successful businessman who ran the Standard Market on East Main Street. Marcus Horansky operated his own meat market on East Pearl Street until 1942. (Michael Horansky.)

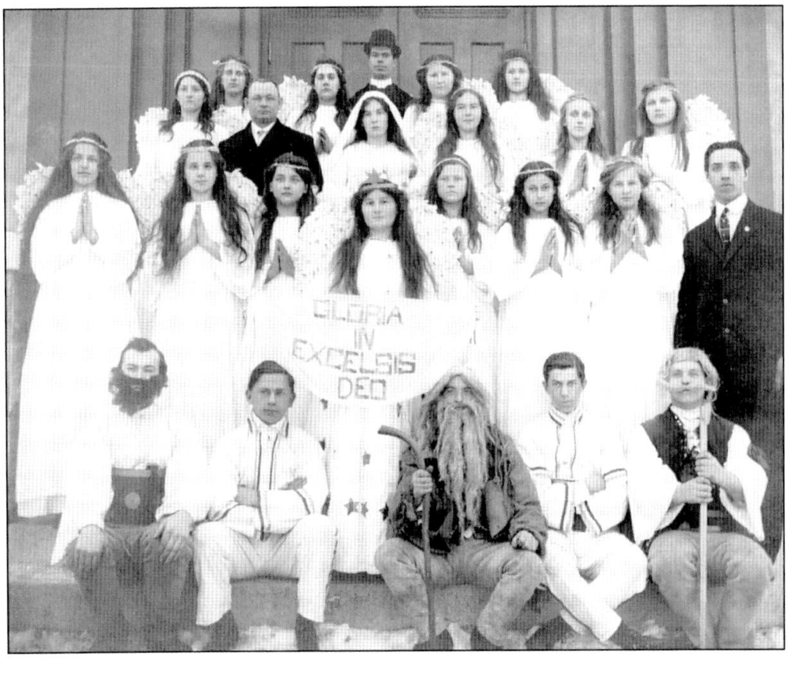

Dressed for a dramatic performance, a group of Slovak children pose in front of Sacred Heart Church, probably to celebrate its dedication in 1912. Fr. Gaspar Panik stands in the center of the back row, while his brother, John Panik, stands at far right in a suit. Thomas Kubina (first row, second from right) died in World War I.

Mary Samok strikes a pose in this 1928 photograph, probably taken somewhere near the family home off Red Mountain Avenue. Many Polish immigrants settled on or near Red Mountain Avenue within walking distance of St. Mary's Church, Torrington's Polish parish. (Roberta Janco.)

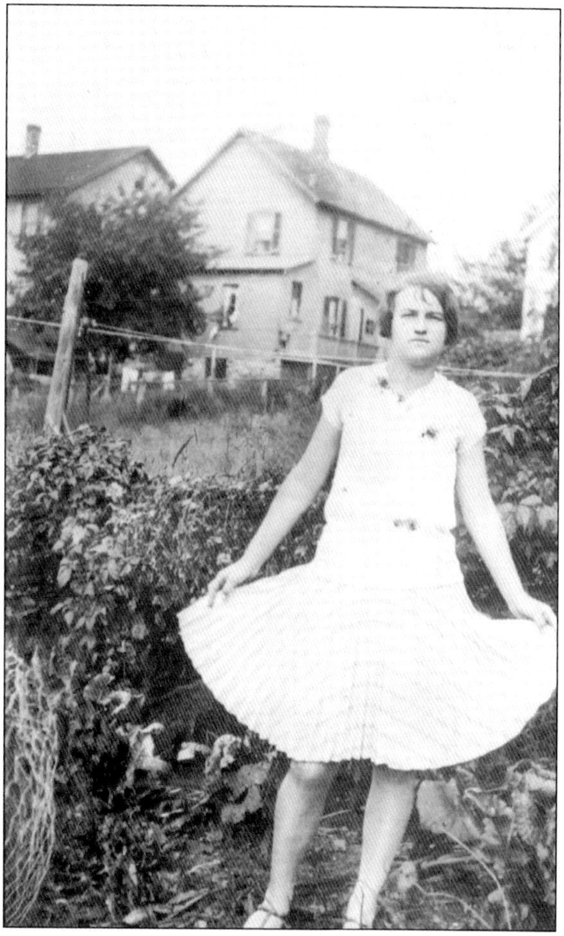

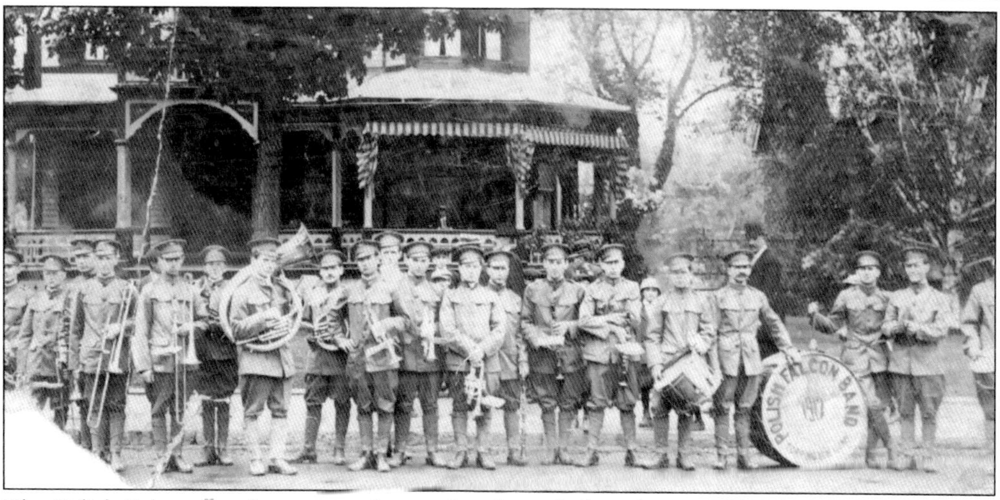

The Polish Falcon Band was one of many bands, including drum and bugle corps, that formed in Torrington in the late 19th and early 20th centuries. During the World War I era, when this photograph was taken, these bands expressed both ethnic pride and patriotism. They marched in parades and escorted their compatriots to the train station as they headed off to war.

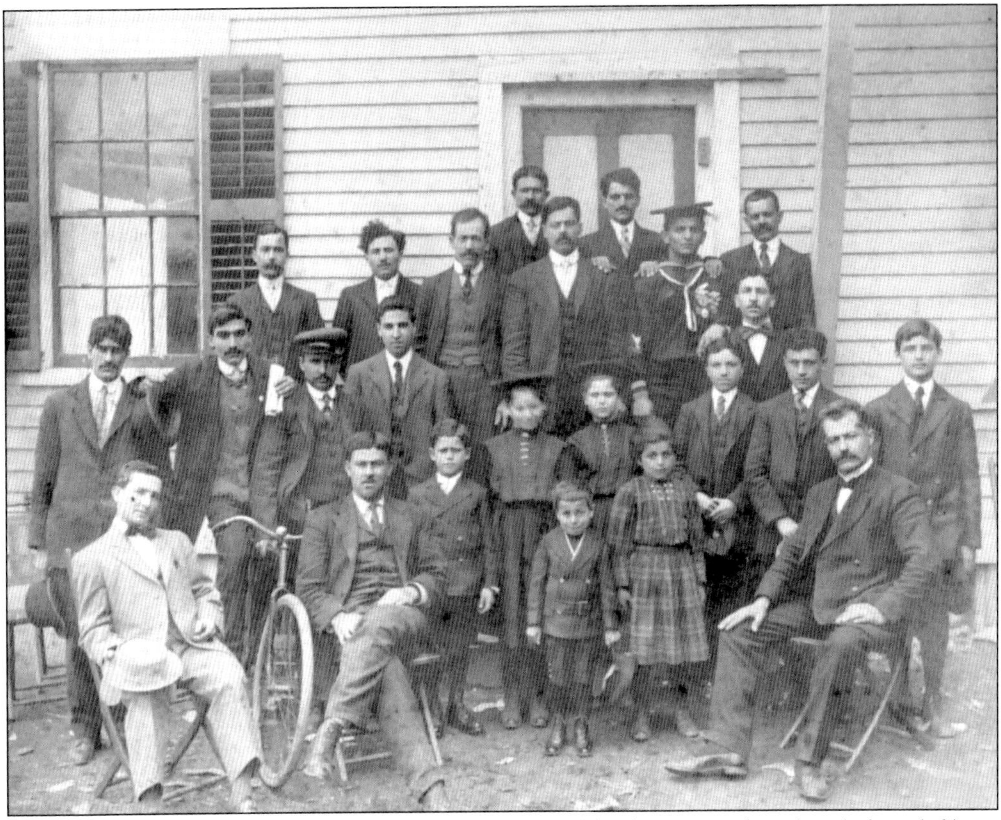

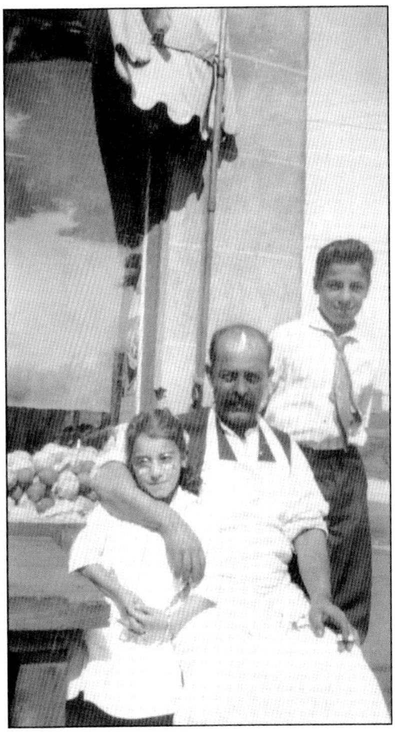

Farris Haddad (third row, standing fourth from left) is sometimes credited with being the first Lebanese immigrant in Torrington. He arrived around 1896, established himself in the North End, and gradually enlarged his own home to accommodate new arrivals. Haddad also set up his countrymen with stock from his dry goods store, which they peddled as far away as Collinsville and Thomaston. (Gary V. Smith.)

By 1920, about 180 Lebanese—or Syrians, as they were known at the time—lived in Torrington. Many worked in the factories, but a sizable number opened small stores. David Haddad, brother of Farris (pictured in the previous image), poses with two of his children, Josephine and Chickery, in front of the family's fruit store at Litchfield Street and Turner Avenue. Chickery later opened Chick's Package Store next to Stormont's Little Book Store on East Main Street. (Gary V. Smith.)

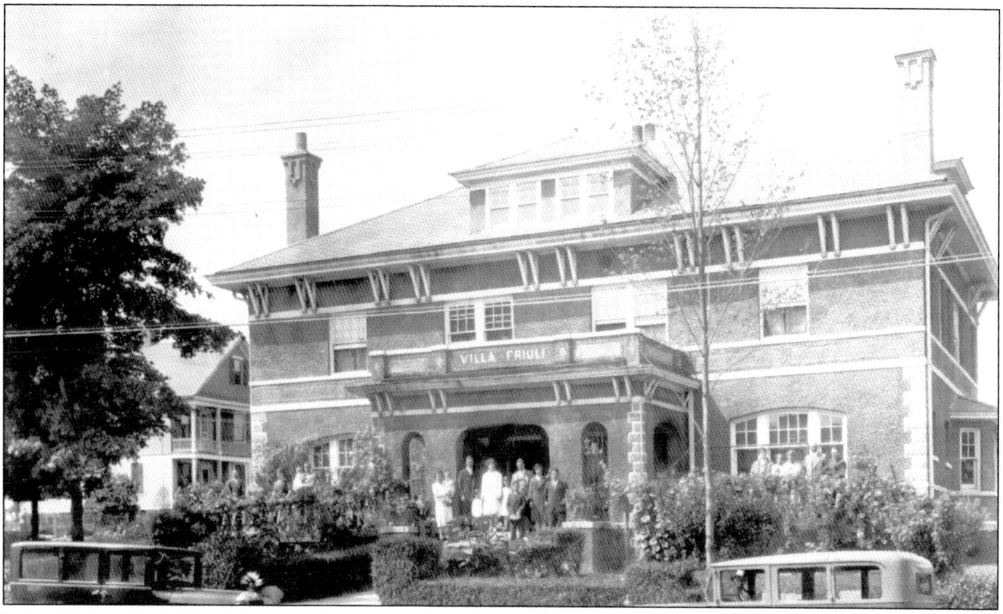

John DeMichiel (far left, standing with family) and his brother Matthew ran a successful road construction business for 40 years. The brothers, who were trained stonecutters, came to Torrington in 1899 and built hundreds of miles of local roads. They married two sisters, Maria and Antunetta Cesca, and lived side by side in Villa Friuli on High Street. The Italian Renaissance design of the 1915 home—reflected in the stucco exterior and carved stone porch balustrade—earned it a listing in the National Register of Historic Places. (Joseph A. Cravanzola.)

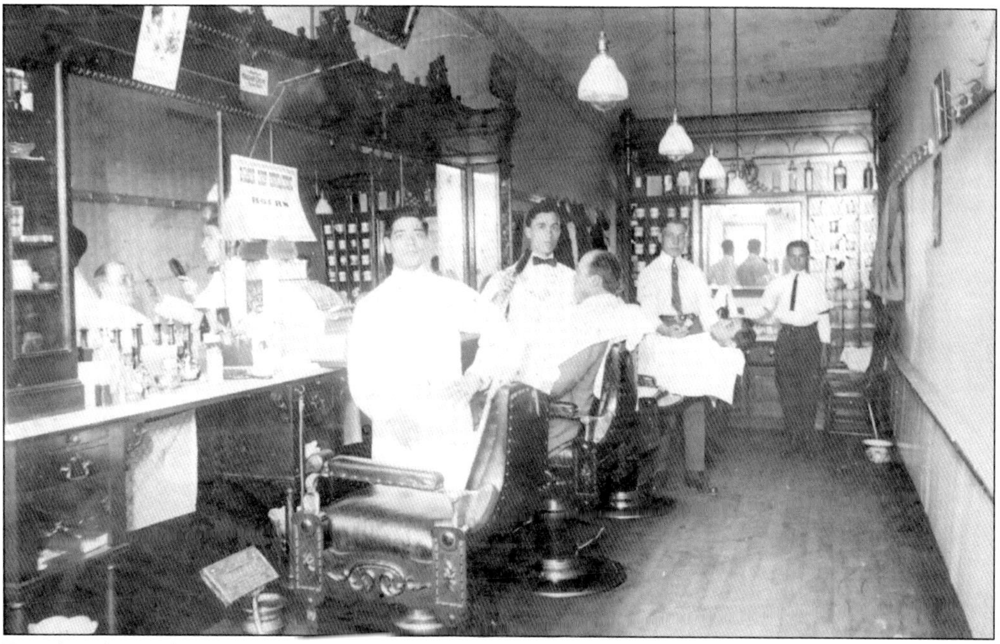

For a brief period around 1915, Joseph Schifini and Carmen Russo barbered together at 235 Water Street. In 1925, Schifini, who is credited with bringing the first permanent wave machine to Torrington, took the bold step of opening a beauty parlor for women and children on East Main Street. He was also instrumental in establishing Torrington's first full-time radio station, WTOR.

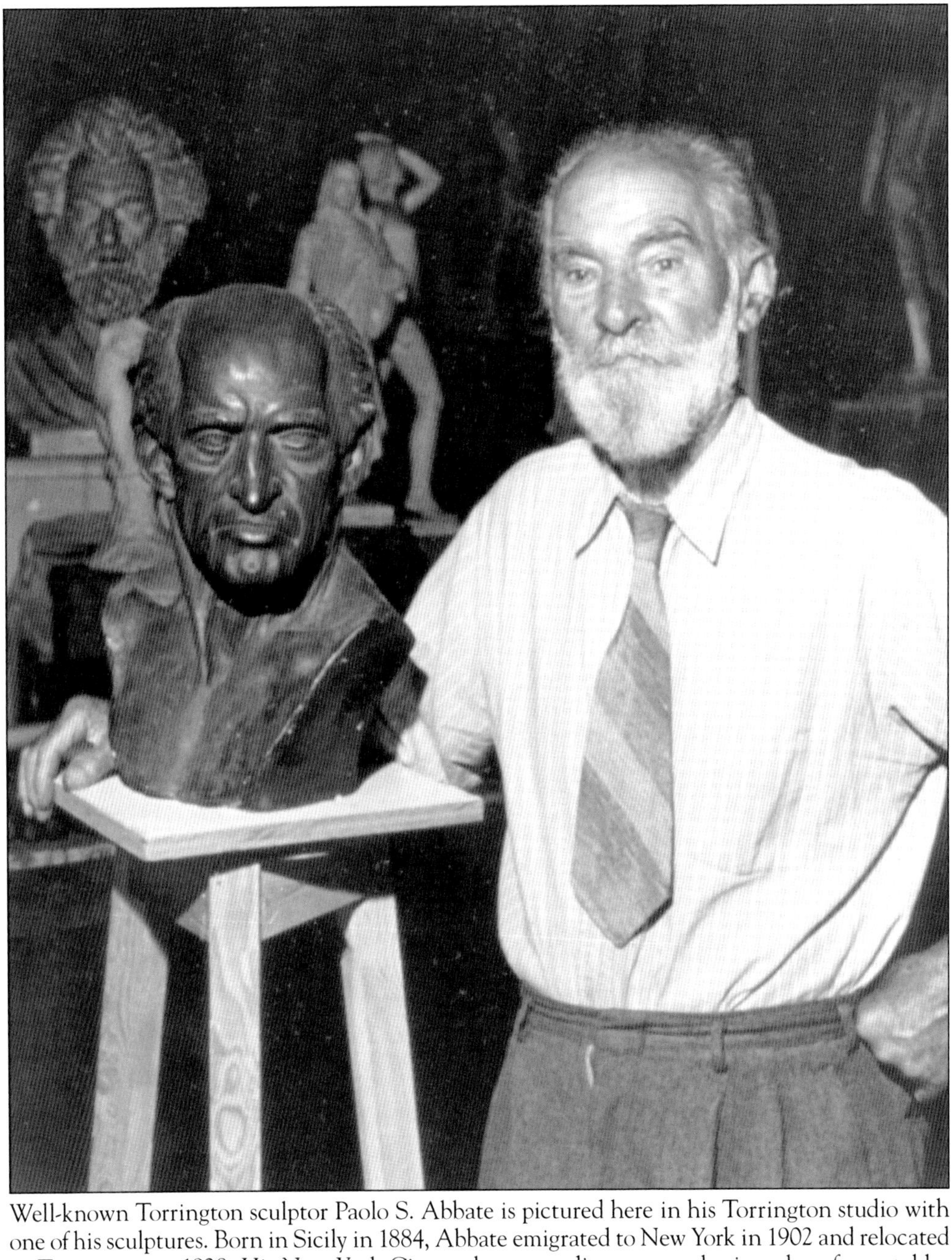

Well-known Torrington sculptor Paolo S. Abbate is pictured here in his Torrington studio with one of his sculptures. Born in Sicily in 1884, Abbate emigrated to New York in 1902 and relocated to Torrington in 1928. His New York City sculpture studio was a gathering place for notables like Enrico Caruso and Joyce Kilmer, both of whom he sculpted. Abbate died in 1973 after a long career as artist and educator. Abbate lived in Torrington's oldest home—the Fowler House, which was built about 1750 and located on top of Highland Avenue. His studio was in the post and beam barn next to the house. Today, many pieces of his work are in the collections of the William Benton Museum (University of Connecticut) and the Torrington Historical Society. In his later years, Abbate sought to create a peace center where the arts, with their meaningful beauty, could inspire and help educate the people in the way of world peace.

Two

Places of Worship

The stately buildings in these photographs tell only a small part of the story of Torrington's religious institutions. When Torrington's first church (later named First Congregational) was founded in 1741 in West Torrington, it only had 17 members, no denominational name, and no house of worship. Members met in each other's homes until a small meetinghouse was built in 1750. This was typical for many local churches in the New England colonies. A handful of people with shared beliefs would meet; then, the group would formally organize and choose a pastor. Finally, a church would be built and dedicated.

In the 18th and 19th centuries, these religious gatherings—where congregants would read Scripture or listen to sermons, sometimes from itinerant preachers—were a testament to people's dedication and perseverance. Roads were bad, buildings were drafty or unheated, and members often sat on rough log benches for hours or met outdoors. Even into the 20th century, some groups simply created a serviceable structure out of an excavated basement, where they would worship until enough funds could be raised to complete a building—a process that often took many years.

For a time, the Universalists offered their three-story brick Academy building on South Main Street as a meeting space. Episcopalians, Methodists, and Catholics, among others, gathered there, with each group hoping someday to have a church of its own. This happened gradually, and then rapidly. Center Congregational was organized in 1832, the Methodist and Episcopal churches followed in the 1840s, and St. Francis Catholic Church was built in 1860. Four more Catholic churches and several other Protestant churches were constructed in the late 19th and early 20th centuries. In 1906, the Sons of Jacob Synagogue was established.

Despite (or perhaps because of) their humble and difficult beginnings, religious congregations formed the backbone of Torrington's development as a civil society. Beloved spiritual leaders often served for decades, providing congregants with safe harbor while fostering ties to the larger community. And in every crisis that Torrington has faced, including wars and epidemics, religious groups have been on the front line taking care of their own and also helping others in need.

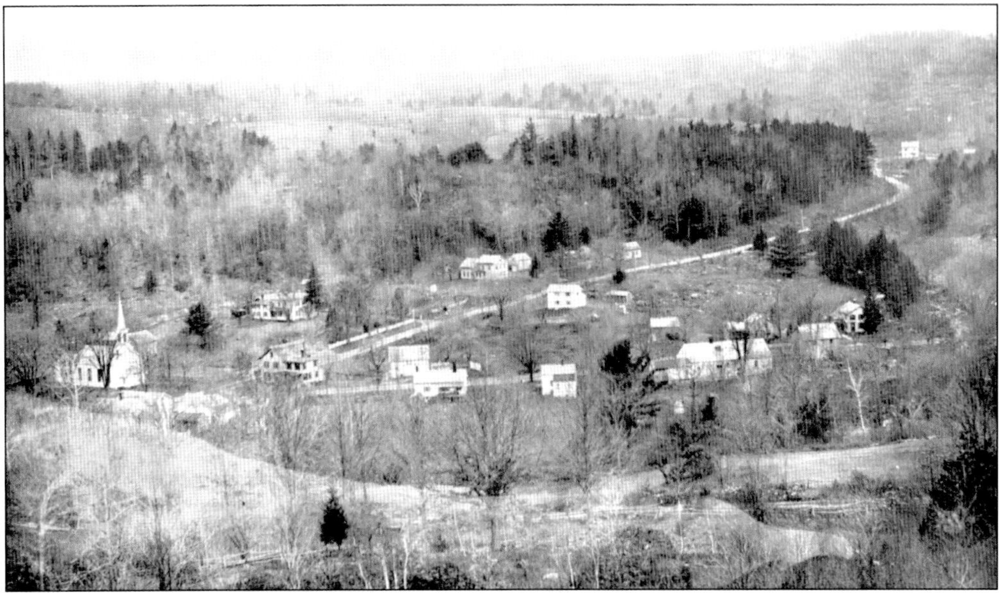

This 1890s photograph gives an excellent bird's-eye view of the First Congregational Church after its relocation to the corner of Riverside Avenue and Goshen Road in 1871–1872. Established in 1741, Torrington's first church initially stood on what is now Klug Hill Road. It was later moved to Hodges Hill, then to its present location in West Torrington when the population shifted to the river valley.

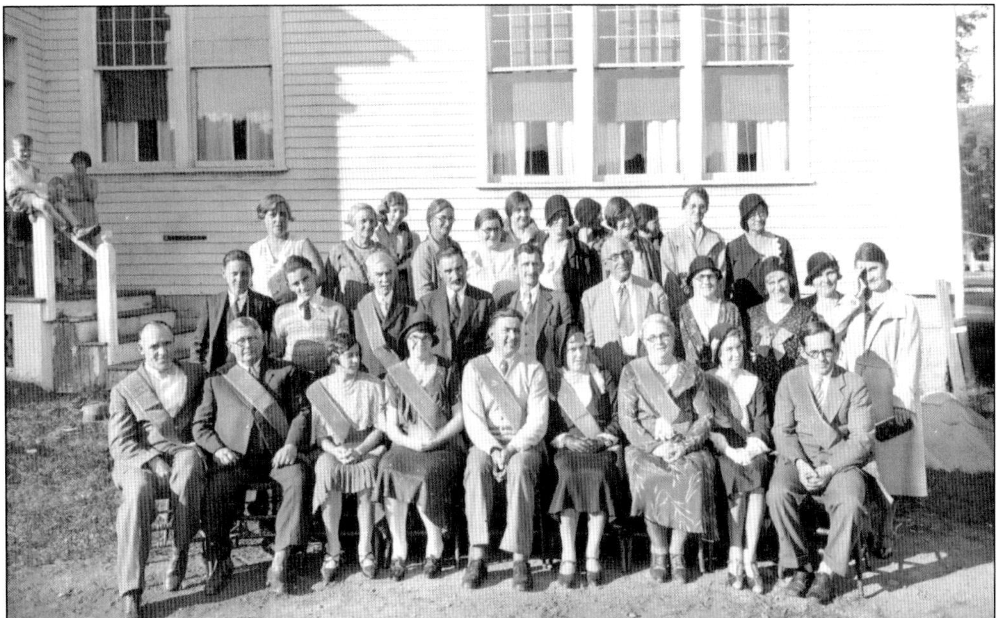

Rev. Enoch Hale Burt (second row, third from left) stands with members of the First Congregational Church on Grange Sunday in 1931. Located on the western, more rural edge of town, the church has historically counted several farming families among its members, including the Deming and Weigold families. Hope Grange was organized in April 1876 in the church's conference room with 12 men and 8 women.

Methodists in Newfield began to meet in the late 1700s, but Torrington's First Methodist Episcopal Church, headed by Pastor George Taylor, was not built until 1843. In 1866, the congregants completed a larger brick church (pictured at right) a block away on Main Street in downtown Torrington, and their smaller wooden church became Torrington's first town hall. The 1885 photograph below shows the original church decorated to commemorate the death of Pres. Ulysses S. Grant. A corner of the new church is visible below. The original wooden St. Francis Church is barely visible at far left, with the Coe residence next to it. The Methodists' brick church was enlarged and renovated over time, but in the 1960s, it was decided that a new building was required. The last worship service in the Main Street church was held in February 1965, and the First United Methodist Church is now located on Fern Drive.

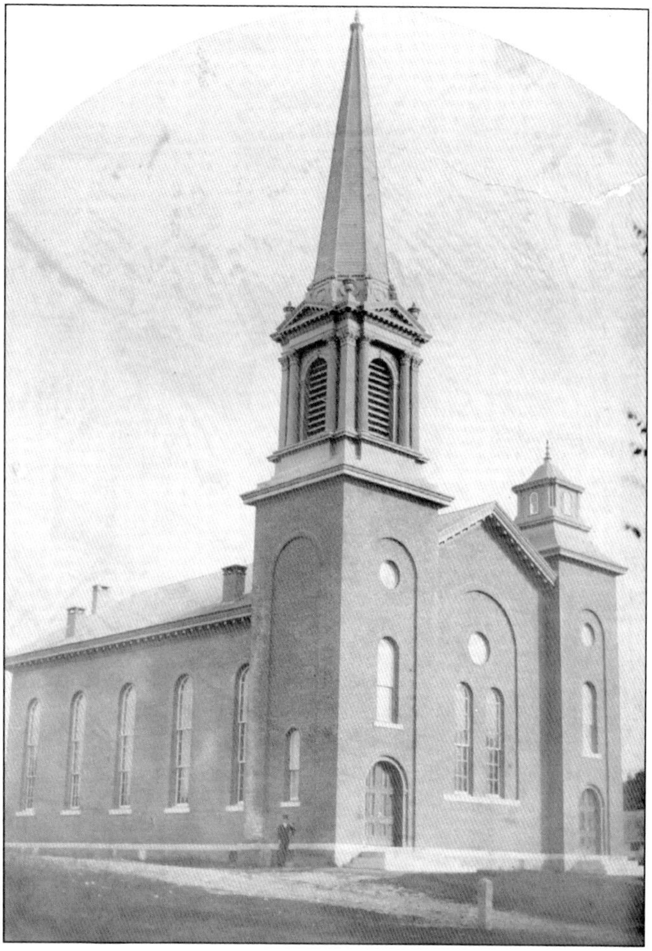

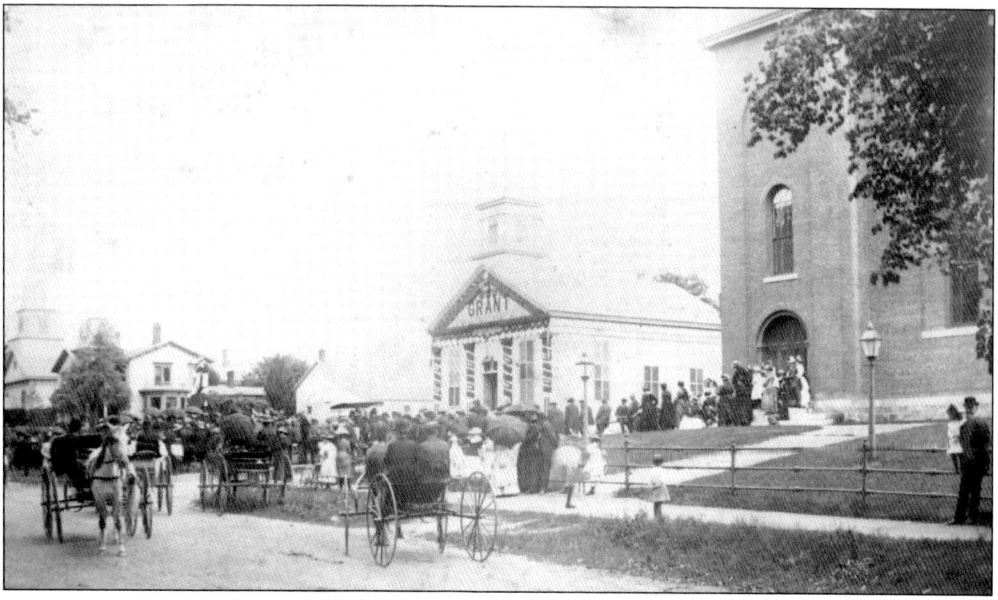

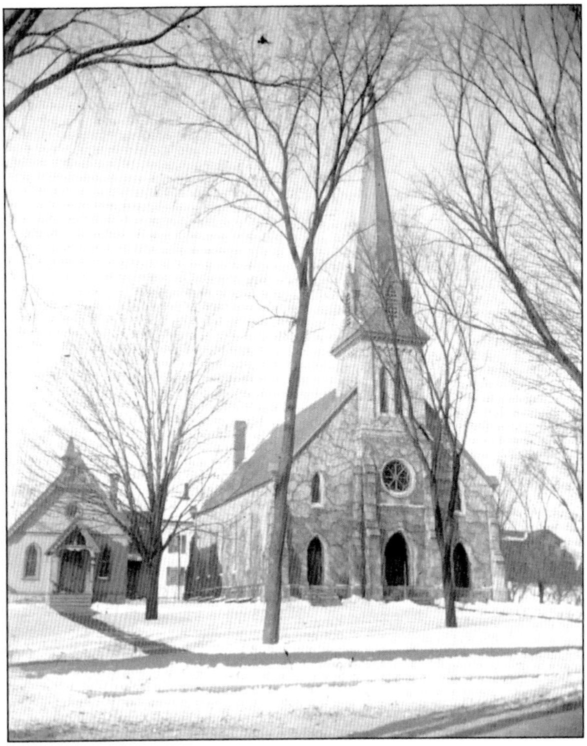

Center Congregational Church was organized in downtown Torrington in 1832. The wooden meetinghouse donated by Uri Taylor is barely visible in the background of this photograph. In 1864, the wooden building was moved to make room for the larger granite structure. In 1979, a fire almost destroyed the building, but its thick stone walls survived, and the church was rebuilt.

Center Congregational Church ministered to Torrington's German, Swedish, French, Hungarian, Syrian, and Italian immigrants. Rev. Gennaro Giordano started the church's Italian Mission in 1907. Here, the "Orchestra of the Italian Congregational Mission" poses in front of the church in 1911. Rev. Adam Tangerone, appointed in 1923, led the Italian Mission until its closure in 1948. (Center Congregational Church.)

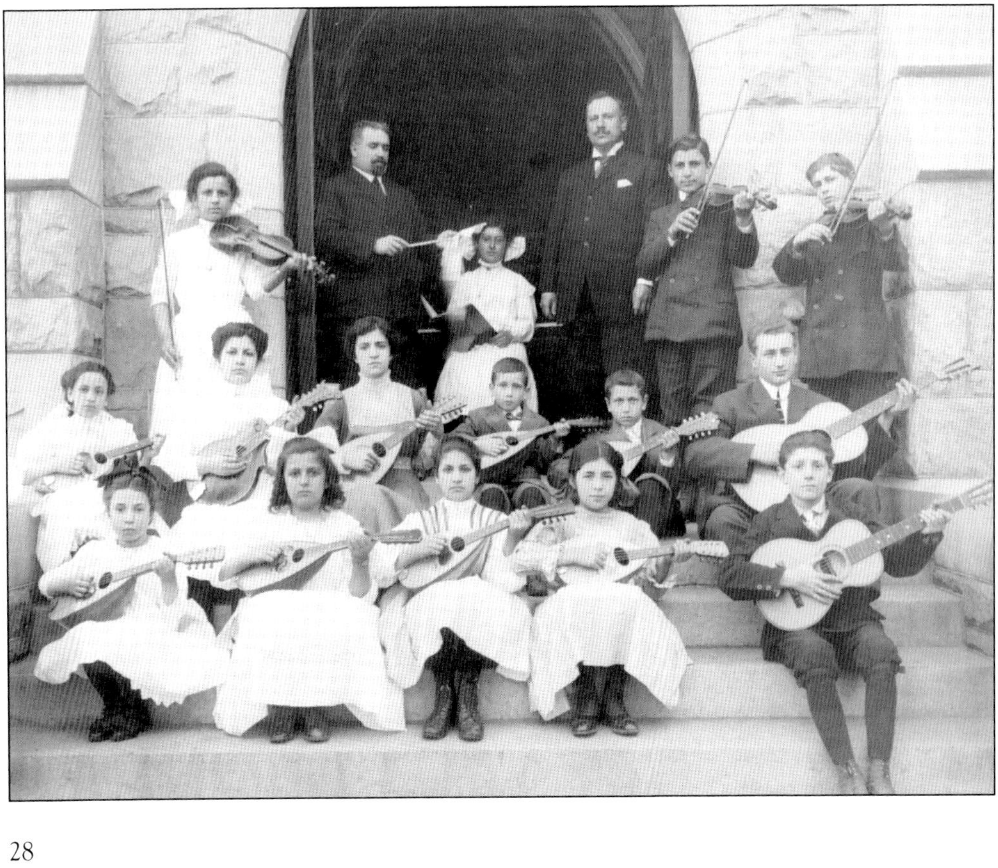

In 1842, only a handful of Catholic families lived in Torrington. By 1860, there were enough Catholics to build the first St. Francis Church, a wooden structure on Main Street that was later enlarged and then replaced by the impressive brick building pictured at right, which was dedicated in 1887. A rectory (right), convent (left), and school soon followed. Irish-born Rev. Patrick Duggan, who served as pastor from 1879 until 1911, spearheaded the construction. Most of Connecticut's early Catholics came from Ireland, and by 1875, seventy-five percent of Connecticut's immigrants were Irish. Named after St. Francis of Assisi, the church welcomed all Catholics but was known as Torrington's Irish parish. Below is a photograph of the interior of the church before its extensive renovation in the 1960s.

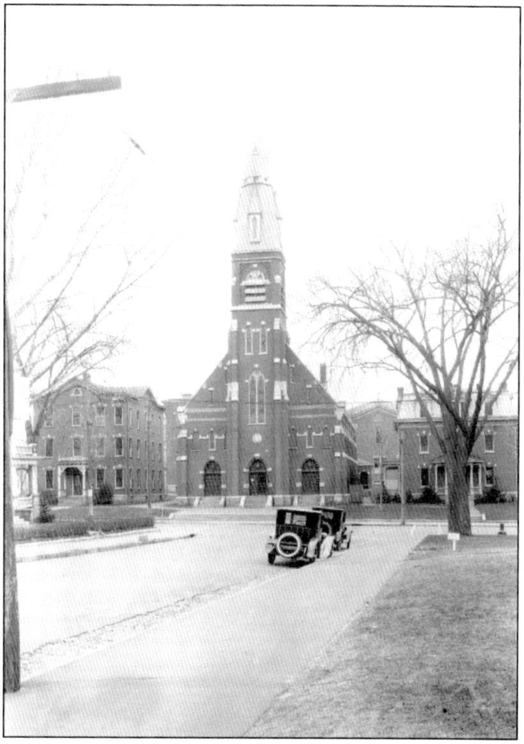

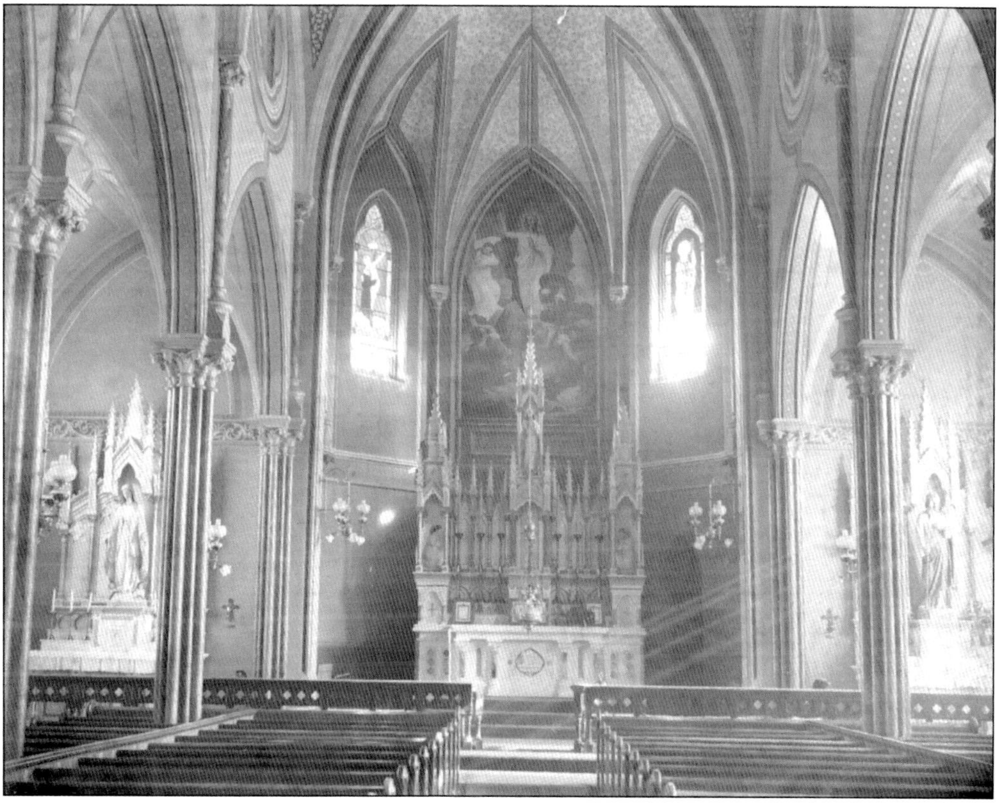

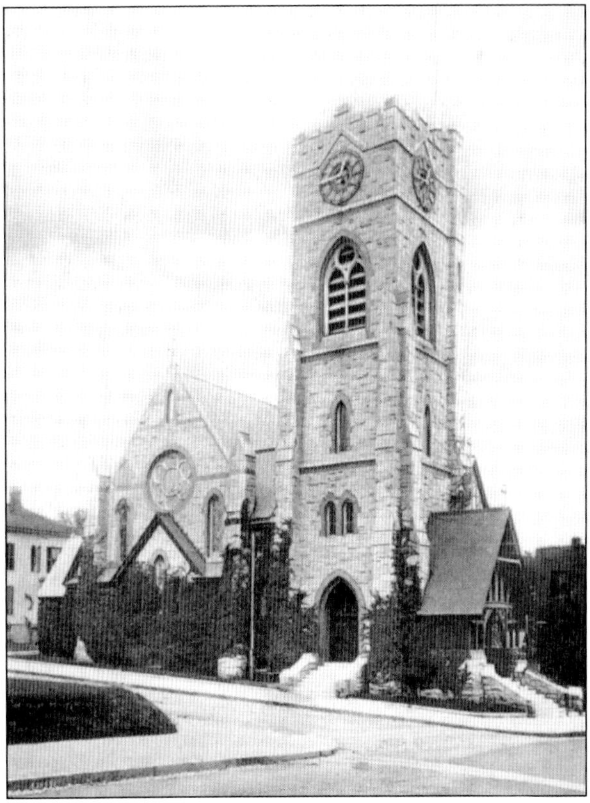

Between December 1843 and December 1844, Trinity Episcopal Church's small group of committed families raised $2,000, bought a plot of land at the corner of Water and Prospect Streets, and built a wooden church—the "finest in the town," according to a historical sketch of the church. By the start of the 20th century, there were almost 400 members, and the present church (shown here at the same location) was dedicated in 1898. The 92-foot granite clock tower housing a bronze bell (cast in 1846) is one of the church's defining features.

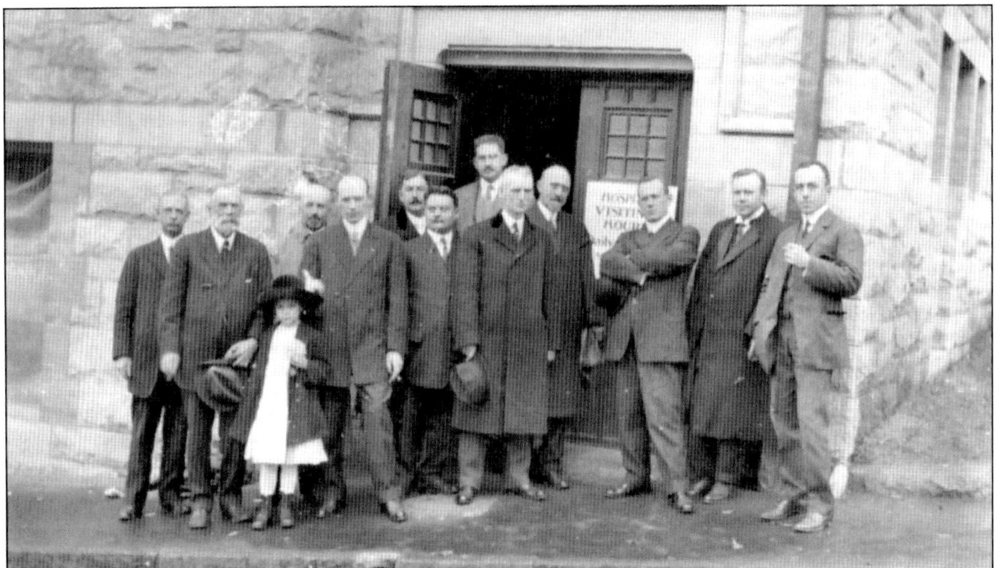

Community leaders gather in front of the Trinity Episcopal Parish House during the 1911 typhoid epidemic. Torrington had no hospital at the time, and Trinity's parish house served as a temporary clinic for four months, saving dozens of lives. Warden William Dayton (second from left) lost his wife to typhoid in 1876 and his daughter, Katherine, in the 1911 epidemic. Katherine's daughter, Betty Hammond, stands next to her grandfather.

In 1884, fifty-six German Lutherans founded the Evangelical Lutheran St. Paulus Gemeinde Church. Ten years later, they dedicated their new church building (pictured) on South Main Street and renamed it St. Paul's Lutheran Church. C.D. Janssen, a prominent local German architect and contractor, designed and built the church with its beautiful exterior finish work. The light salmon exterior was painted by J.F. Baldauf.

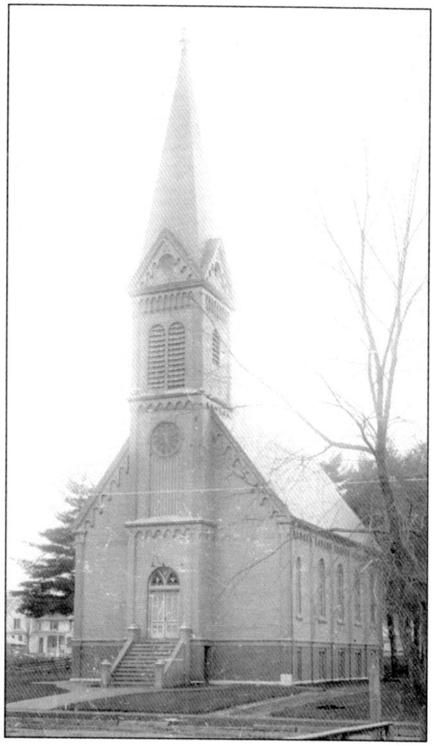

The pastor of St. Paul's Lutheran Church, Rev. Otto Seidenstuecker, stands in the front row next to Mayor Ernest Novey (second from right). During Seidenstuecker's tenure (from 1900 until 1938), the church installed a bell and central heating, founded a brass choir, enlarged the interior of the building, and built a new porch. Beloved by all, Reverend Seidenstuecker was presented with an automobile in appreciation of his service in 1926, which may have been the occasion of this photograph.

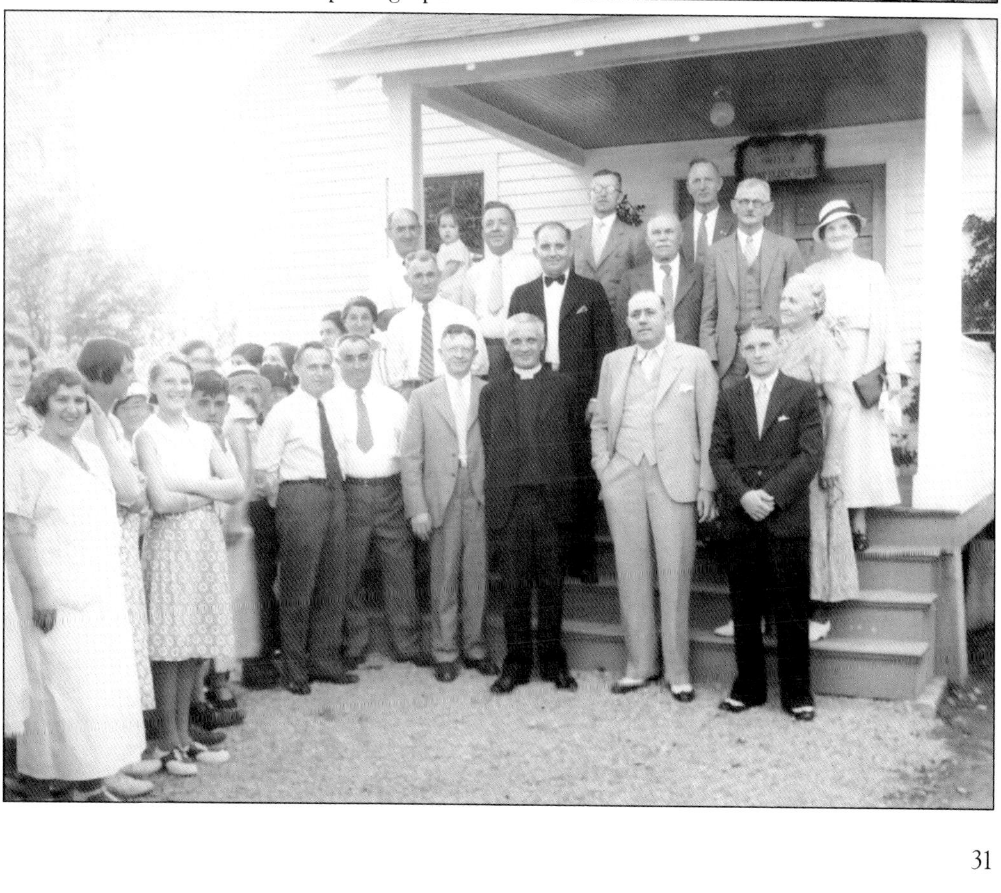

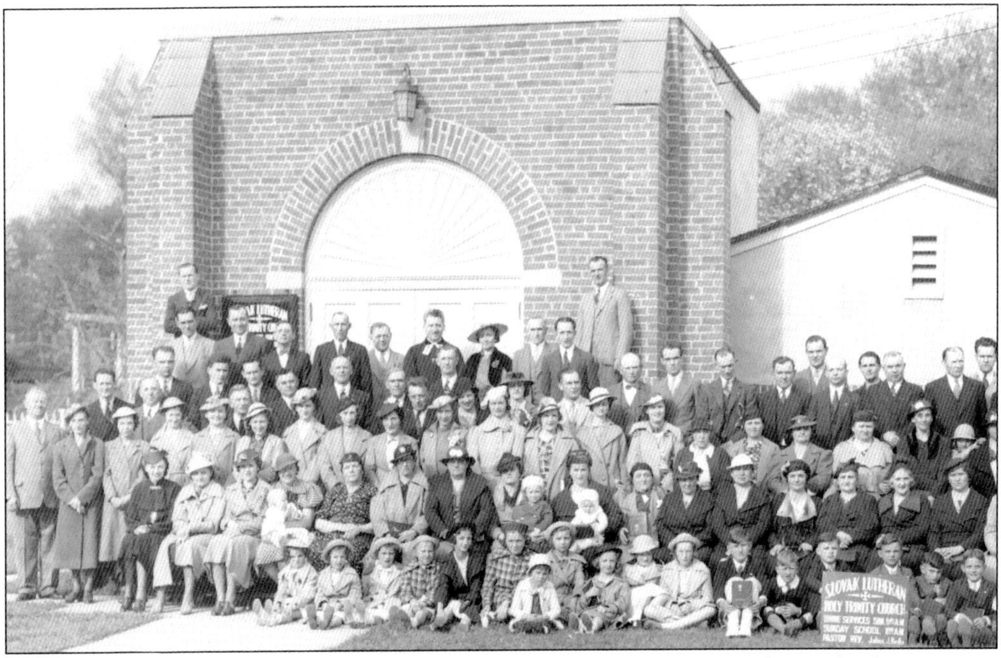

Holy Trinity Slovak Lutheran Church was founded in 1912 with 33 members. The first services were lay-conducted in people's homes or at other local churches, but in 1934, the Slovak Lutherans dedicated this church on Berry Street. In 1964, the Slovaks merged with Torrington's Swedish Lutherans. A small congregation still worships on Berry Street.

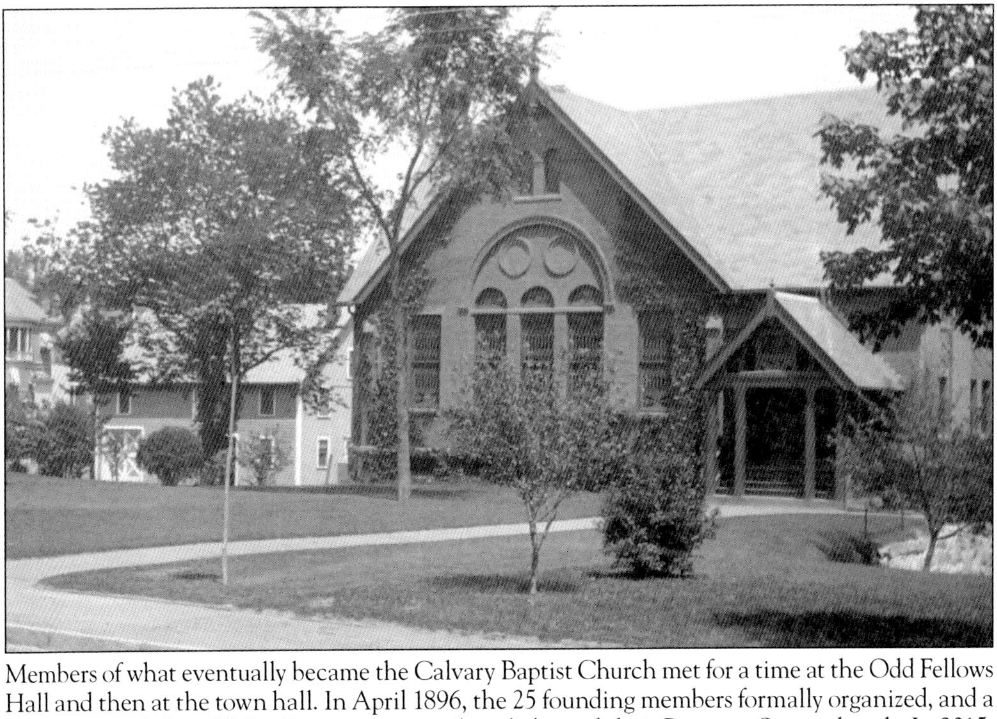

Members of what eventually became the Calvary Baptist Church met for a time at the Odd Fellows Hall and then at the town hall. In April 1896, the 25 founding members formally organized, and a year later, with Rev. Philip Evans as pastor, they dedicated their Prospect Street church. In 2015, Calvary Baptist merged with Northwest Hills Community Church.

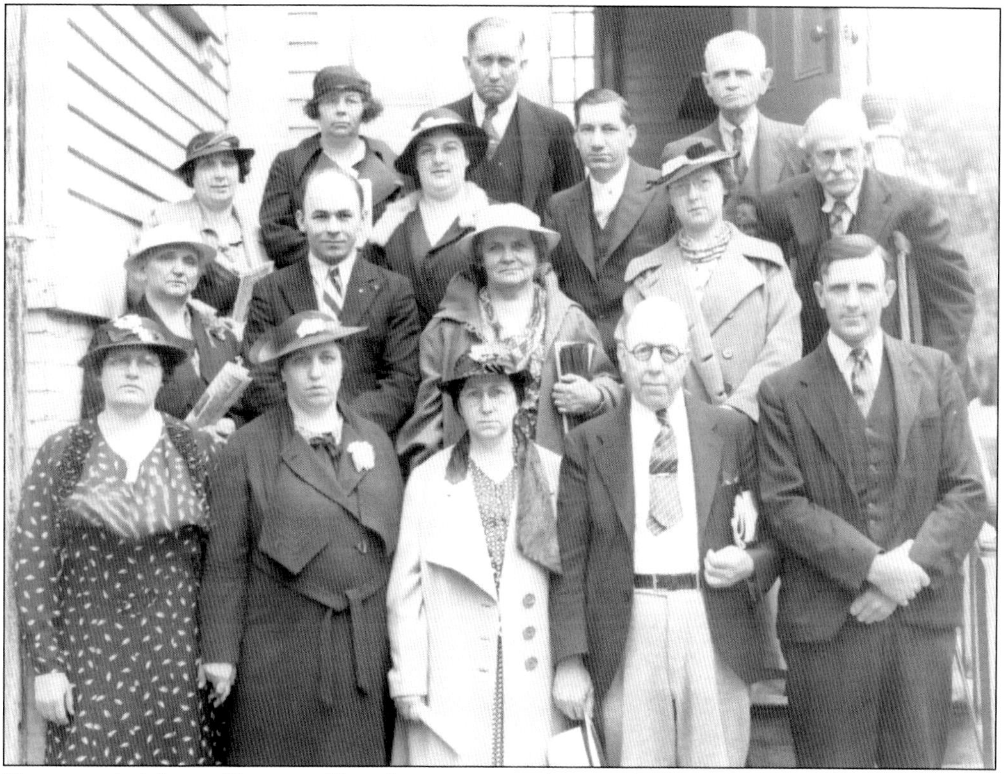

Torrington's Advent Christian Church was organized in April 1886. Church construction, which started in 1888, was delayed when a rainstorm washed out the new foundation. Local carpenters Edwin Delano and Ephraim Allen stepped in to help, offering to do two weeks of work in exchange for one week's pay. The men later joined the church. Church member Louis Benedict made the pews. Pictured below, the original frame building on Barber Street (now a private residence) is one of two historic wood-frame churches still standing in Torrington. The undated photograph above shows members gathered in front of the original church. Edna Richard stands at farthest left in the first row. Elder Walter Wells is in the light slacks in the first row. In 1969, the congregation relocated to a larger structure on New Harwinton Road. Much of the labor involved in building the new church was also done by the men of the congregation.

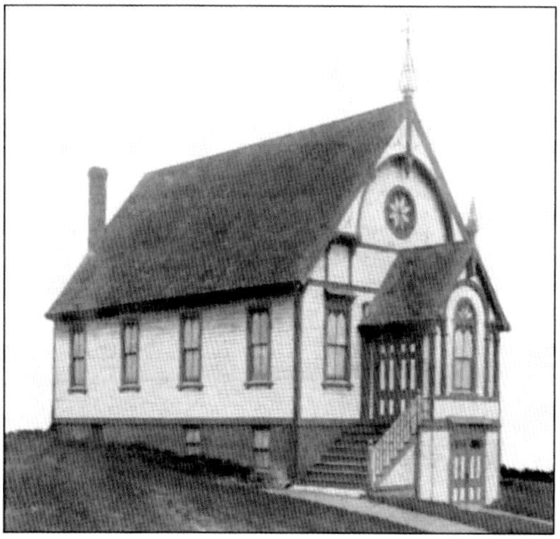

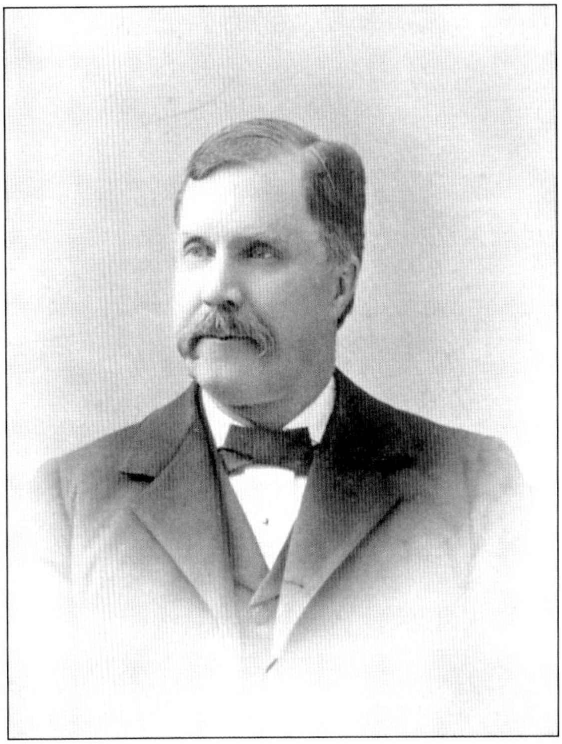

In 1895, a Baptist missionary was invited by Torrington's small African American community to establish an "all-colored" mission. A few years later, Rev. W.B. Caines, from the African Methodist Episcopal (A.M.E.) Zion Church, became resident minister, but without funds to build, the congregation worshiped at various locations. Rufus Johnson approached his employer, George Workman (left), president of the Warrenton Woolen Mill, for financial help, and Workman agreed to pay for the church if the congregants purchased the land. They raised $375 and bought a lot on Brightwood Avenue. The church building (below) cost $7,000 and was dedicated in 1905. In 1920, the church was renamed the Workman Memorial A.M.E. Zion Church in honor of George Workman. His sister, Anna, purchased a house for the church parsonage and also set up a trust fund to help with church expenses.

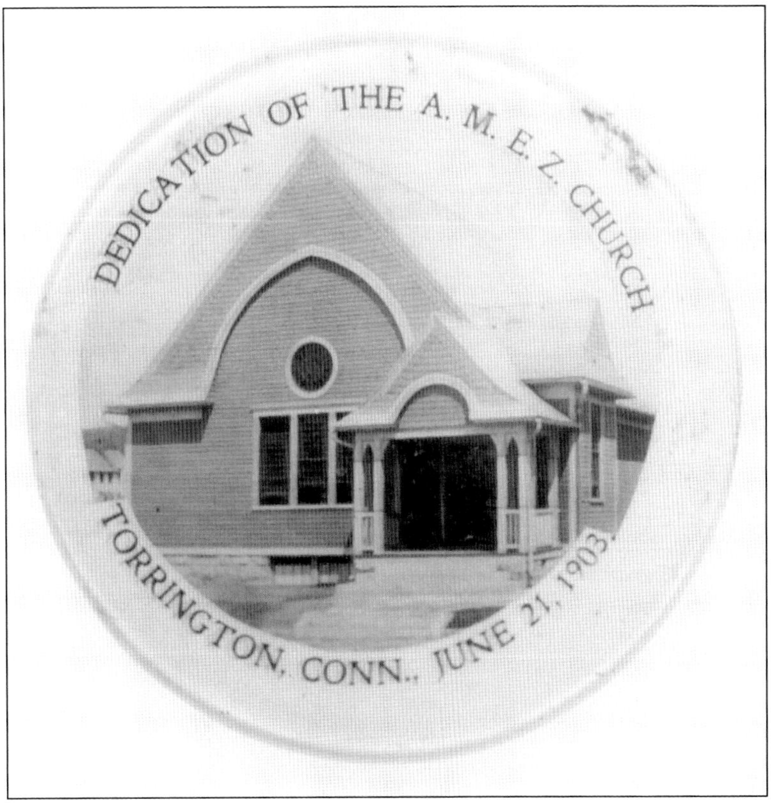

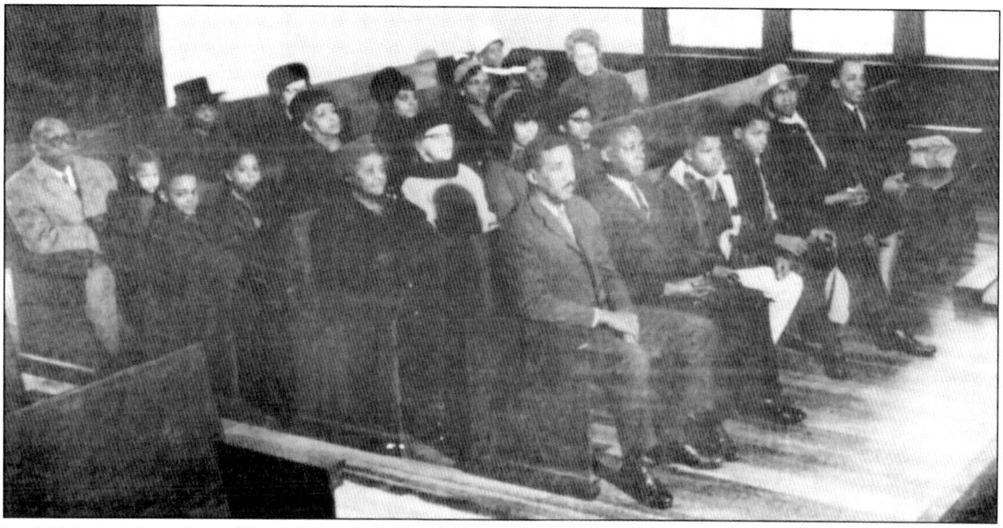

In 1916, A.M.E. Zion Church was damaged by a fire and later restored. This 1950s photograph of the church interior was included in a commemorative booklet. Elder Charles Gunn sits at farthest left in the front row. Members of the Powell, Ormsby, Jones, and Durante families also appear here. (Workman A.M.E. Zion Church/Shirley Durante.)

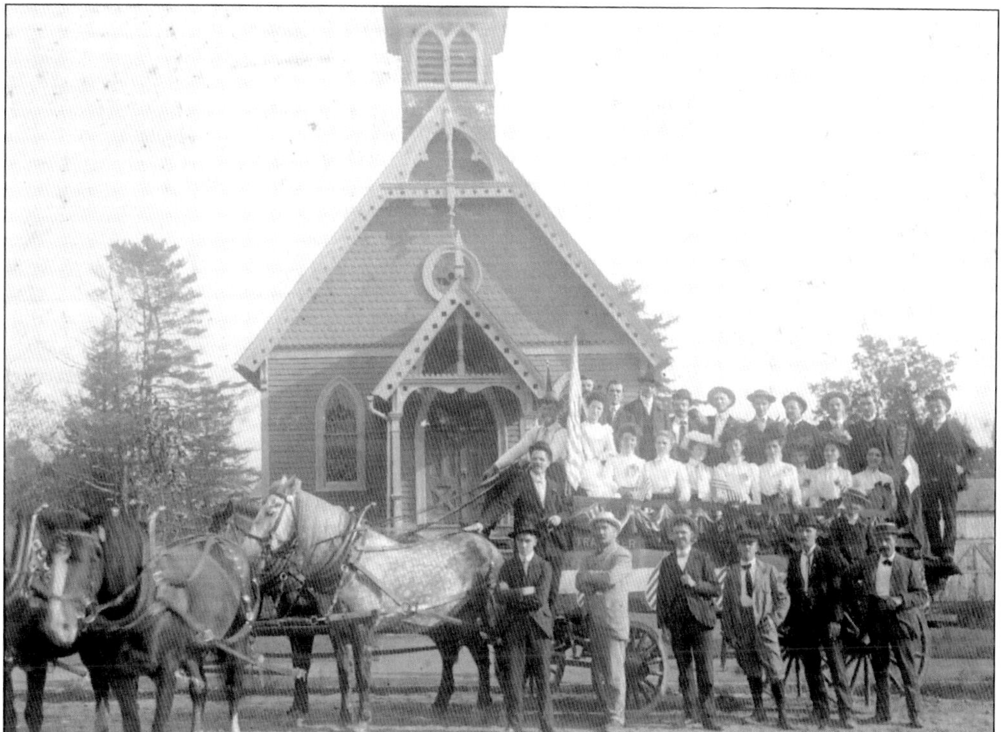

The French Congregational Church shown here was originally the chapel of Torrington's Center Congregational Church. In 1899, Center Congregational donated the chapel to its French-speaking Swiss congregants, who moved the building to its current site on East Pearl Street. This photograph may feature a July 1900 picnic excursion to Edmond Perrageux-Dielf's farm in Goshen. (The return trip via Litchfield took four hours!) The church is now a private residence.

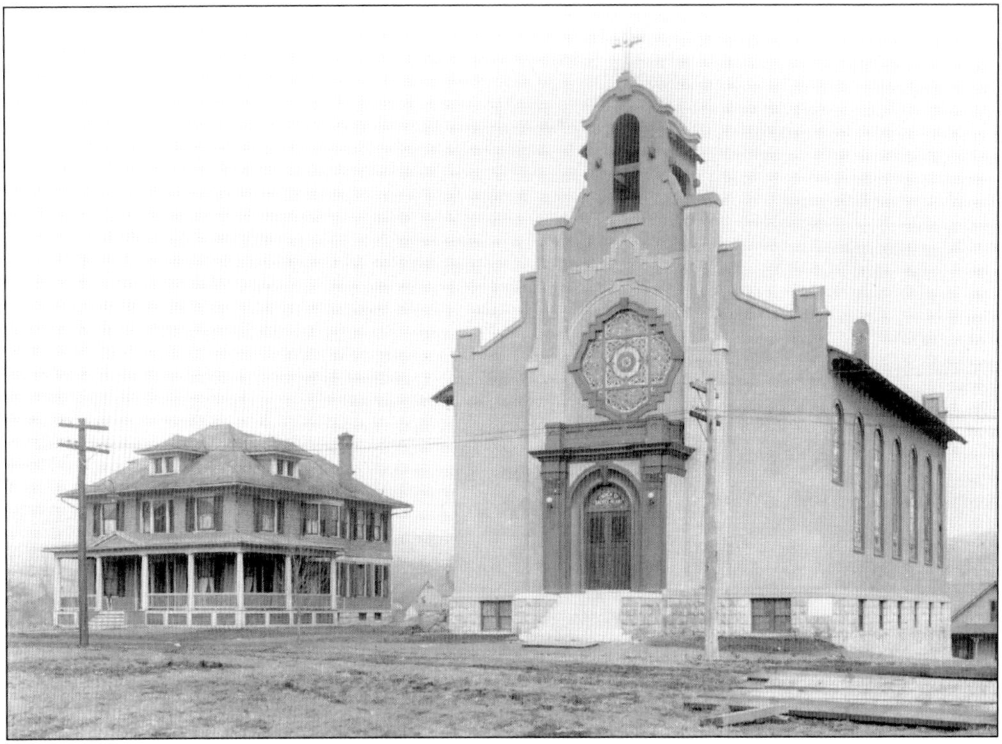

In 1893, 12 Slovak and Hungarian immigrants founded the St. Joseph Society, a mutual aid society that became the nucleus of Sacred Heart Parish. The group purchased land on Grove Street in 1905, but it was not until Fr. Gaspar Panik arrived in 1910 that fundraising began in earnest. The Slovaks' Sacred Heart Church was built in the Spanish Mission style and seated 600 people. Below, members of the St. Joseph Society have gathered on the church steps, probably at the church's 1912 dedication. In the upper right, John Amrich, one of the church's founding members, stands next to his young son John. Father Panik is seated in the center of the first row.

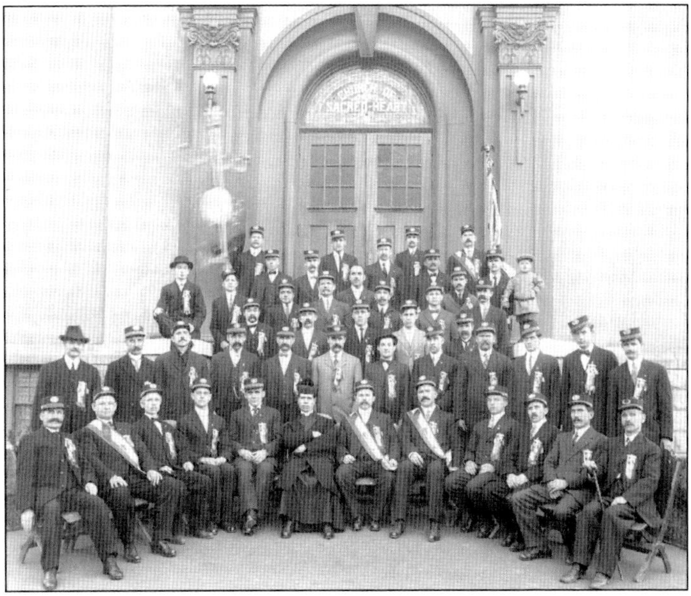

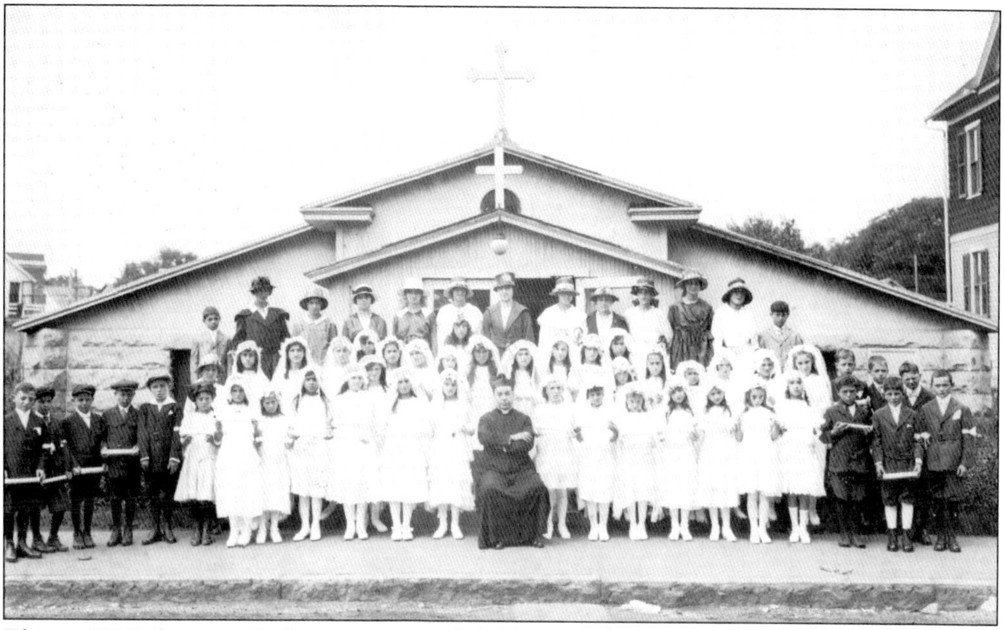

This c. 1920 photograph shows a group of children, perhaps First Communicants, posing in front of the original St. Peter Church on Center Street. Torrington's Italian Catholics purchased the property in 1908, and over 5,000 people attended the laying of the cornerstone that year. Contractors Charles and Louis Longhi excavated the cellar, installed roofing, and made the structure useable.

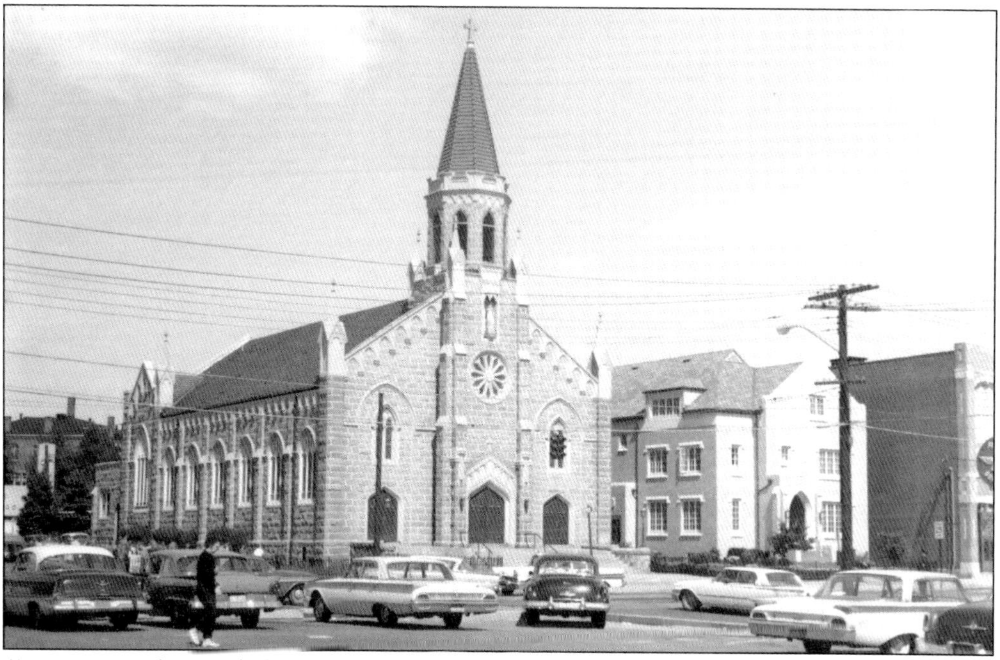

Torrington's Italian Catholics eventually selected a more prominent site on East Main Street for their stately new St. Peter Church. Charles Longhi and Son was awarded the building contract with a bid of $83,100. The firm used local granite provided by John DeMichiel and completed the structure in 1928. Italian-born Fr. Salvatore Bonforti was pastor when the church was dedicated.

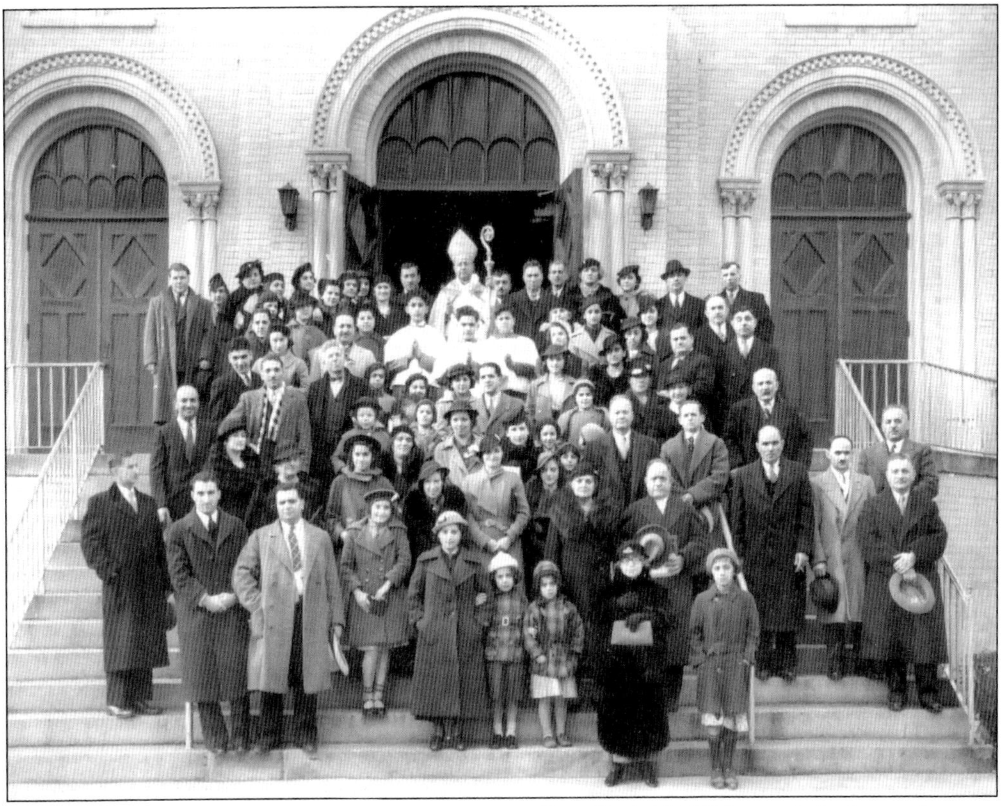

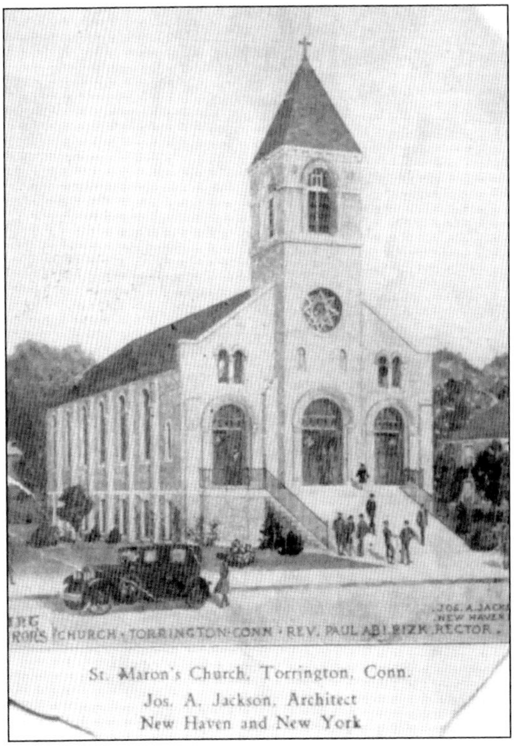

Rev. Paul Abi-Rizk stands in front of St. Maron Church with some of his parishioners, including Barbara and Emily Jacob (in plaid jackets in the front row). This Catholic church founded by Lebanese immigrants is located in Torrington's North End and follows the Maronite (Eastern) Rite. Soon after their first meeting in 1911, members of the Syrian Union (later the Lebanese-American Society) petitioned the bishop of Hartford to build an Eastern Rite church. In 1916, Pastor Semaan Acle, with a parish of about 200 families, dedicated the one-story St. Maron Church on north Main Street. The building shown at left was not completed until 1929. Today, a century after its founding, St. Maron Church remains a strong neighborhood presence. (St. Maron Maronite Catholic Church/Helene Haddad.)

In 1909, Torrington's Catholic Polish immigrants held raffles and dances and canvassed as far away as Collinsville until they raised $1,500 to purchase their church property on Union Street (later renamed Pulaski Street). In 1920, Fr. John P. Kowalski arrived, and the building of St. Mary of Czestohova Church (known as St. Mary's) began. The first Polish Mass was celebrated on Christmas Day 1921. The main church (pictured) was completed in May 1927. (Stanley Levicki.)

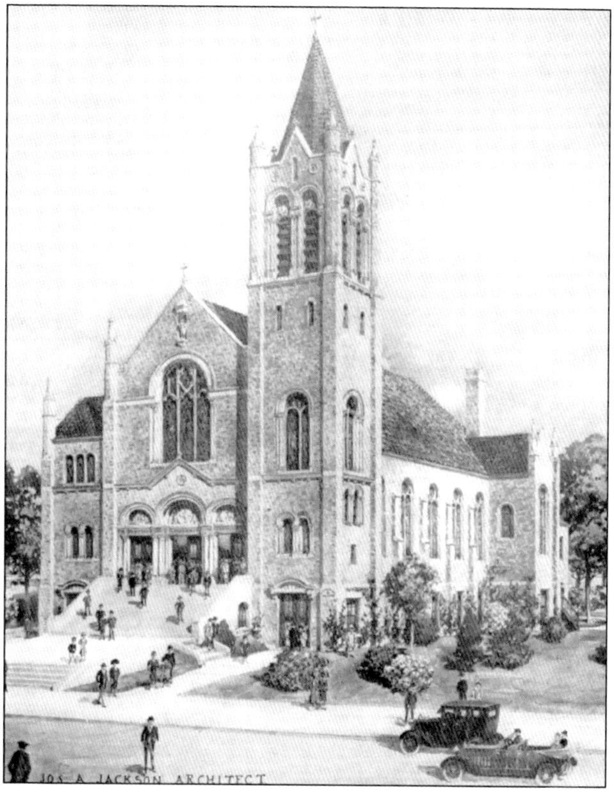

In this 1934 photograph, Fr. John P. Kowalski poses with a First Communion class in front of St. Mary's Church. Father Kowalski died in 1954 after having served as pastor for 35 years. The church census counted 282 Polish families as members in 1920. By 1943, there were more than 400 families at St. Mary's. (Joanna Arnista.)

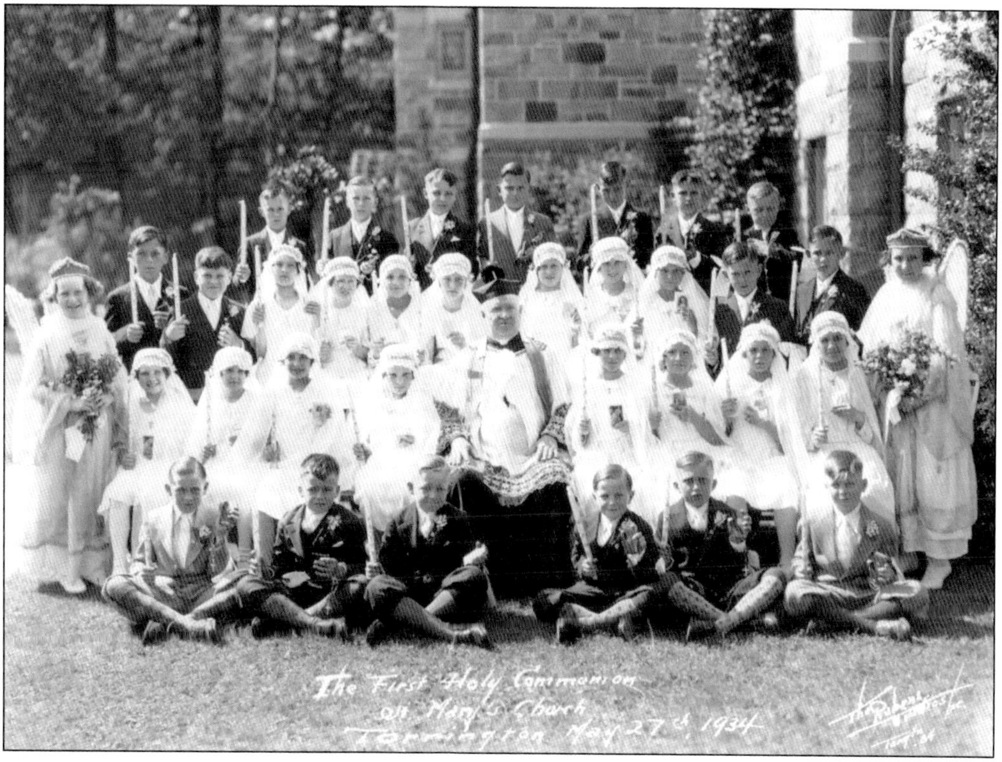

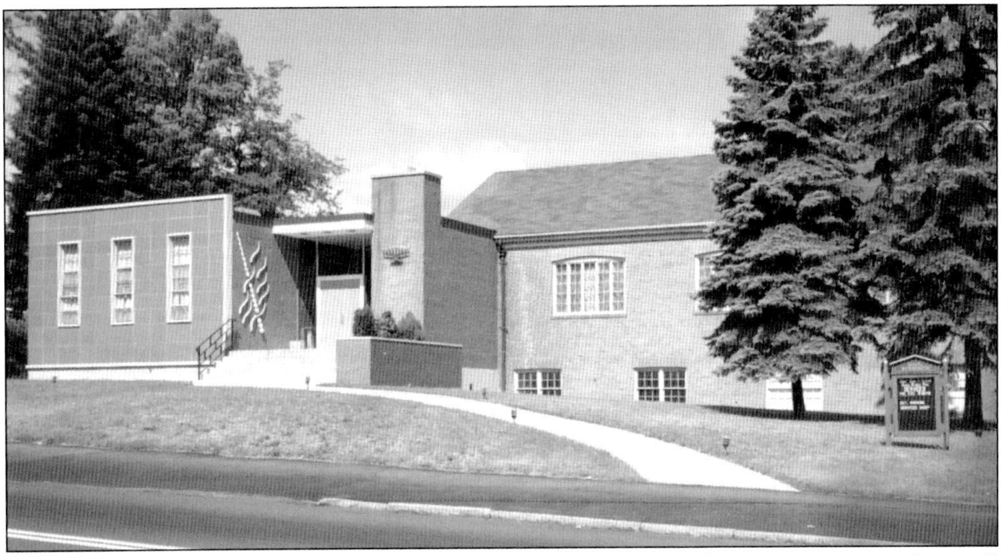

Jewish farmers and shopkeepers began arriving in Torrington in the late 1800s. In 1900, the small Jewish community bought land on the Winsted Road for a burial ground, and in 1906, the Sons of Jacob Synagogue was formed. Several years later, the group purchased the Swedish church on Spear Street to use for services. In 1929, the 70 members split into two congregations, but in 1947 they rejoined and formed Beth El Synagogue. A successful fundraising campaign enabled them to build a new synagogue, seen above, that was completed in September 1950. In the 1931 photograph below, young people from Beth El Synagogue gather for a party. Edythe (Temkin) Garbus (second row, far left, wearing a kerchief) and Gertrude (Silverman) Brenner (seated in front of Garbus) were still Beth El members 60 years later in 1990. The synagogue closed in 2017.

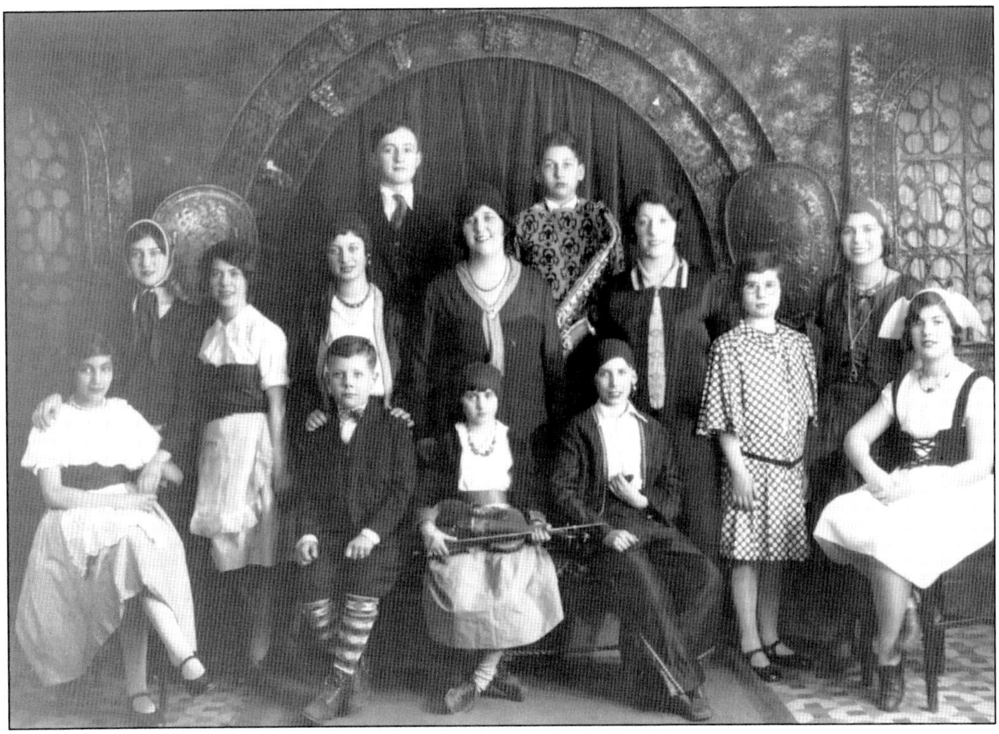

Three

Farms, Factories, and Floods

The Naugatuck River, which is 40 miles long and flows almost due south through western Connecticut, helped make Torrington an industrial powerhouse in the 19th and 20th centuries. Between 1800 and 1870, many small manufacturers set up shop on the two branches of the Naugatuck that flowed through the town. In 1813, a woolen mill (later Warrenton Woolen Mill) opened on Water Street. In 1834, the Coe Brass Company got its start. Between 1863 and 1870, four more major companies were founded in the area—Turner & Seymour (originally Waterbury Hook and Eye), Union Hardware, Excelsior Needle, and Hendey Machine Company.

These and other factories provided thousands of good jobs, although working conditions were hard. Buildings were cold in winter, hot in summer, and poorly ventilated. In the early 1900s, workers generally toiled 11 hours a day and 6 days a week with no paid vacations, sick days, or holidays. Serious injuries were common. Nevertheless, work was steady and friendships were strong. Men and women took pride in their work and often remained with the same company for decades. Over time, job actions, competition for workers, and especially the formation of labor unions led to substantially improved working conditions and a shorter workweek.

The river that powered Torrington's early industries could also unleash devastating floods, including the great floods of 1938 and 1955, which resulted in both loss of life and extensive damage to homes and businesses. Eventually, new energy sources and improved flood control measures reduced the Naugatuck River's role—for better and worse—in the local economy.

Torrington also has a rich agricultural history. From its earliest days, the rural areas surrounding the current town center were filled with farms ranging from West Torrington in the west to Newfield in the north and Torringford in the east. The 1948 *Torrington Directory* lists more than 150 farmers, most of whom ran small dairy farms. For decades, these small farmers were a familiar sight in Torrington's neighborhoods, offering locals the freshest produce, eggs, and milk.

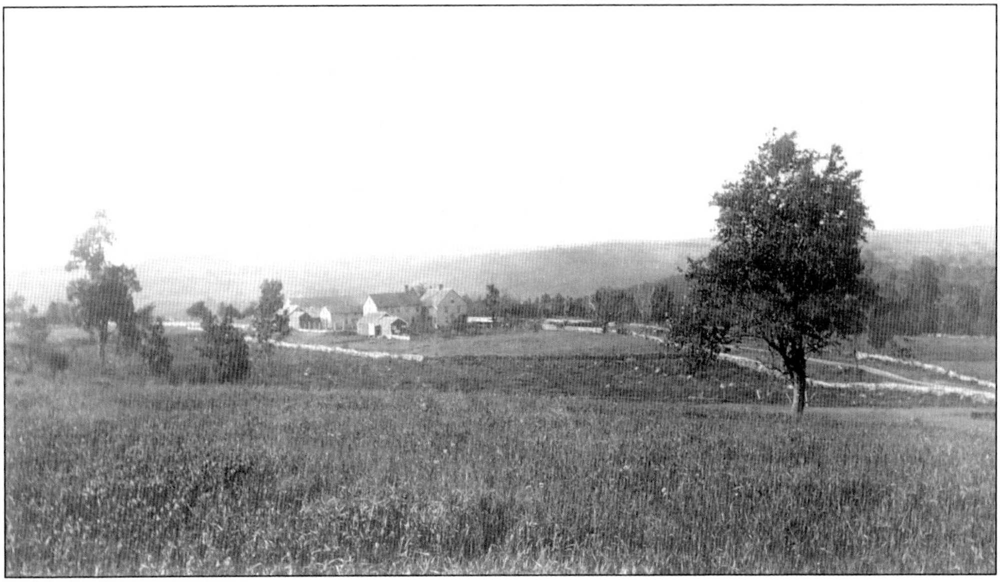

Torrington supported its own town farm on a 91-acre plot in the Brandy Hill area. It served about 15 residents—men, women, and children who were infirm or destitute and who had no family to take them in. A caregiver and his family lived in separate quarters on the farm site. The town farm closed in 1951, and the buildings were later razed to make way for the Torrington branch of the University of Connecticut.

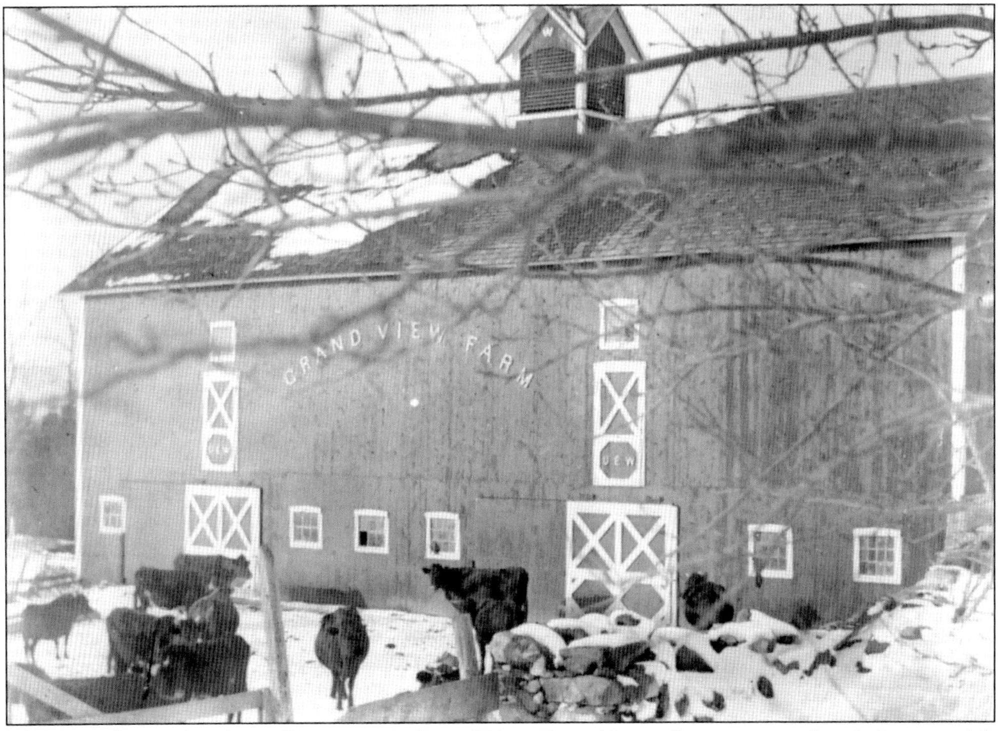

The Uri Whiting family ran Torrington's Grand View Farm (shown here in an undated photograph). Grand View was located on the New Harwinton Road on the eastern edge of town, an area popular with early farmers because of its superior soil. The original farmhouse is still standing.

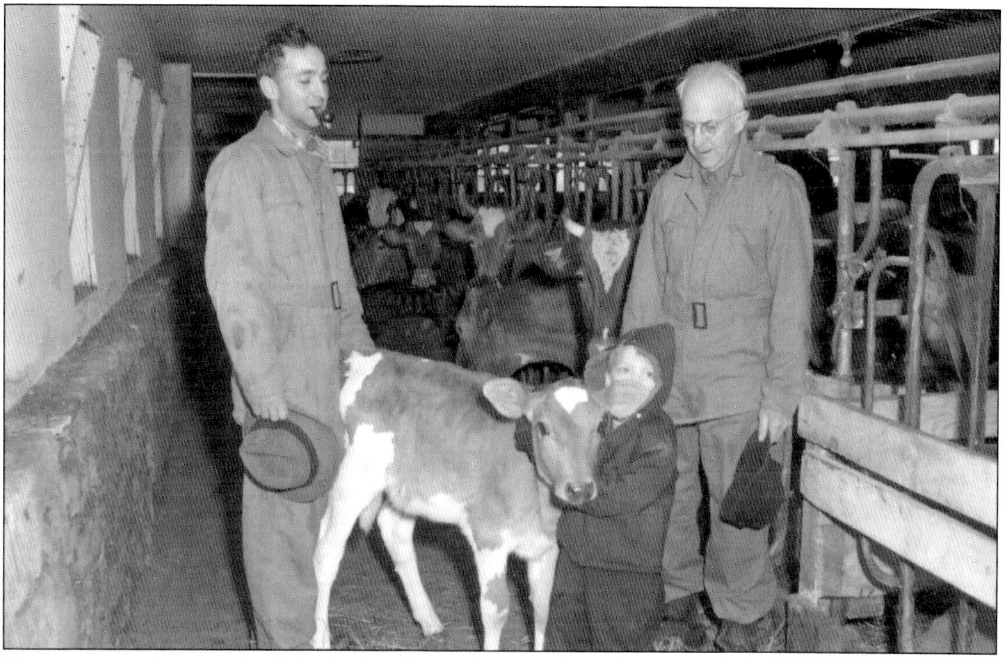

Three generations of the Wright family—John Joseph (left), grandfather John W. (right), and grandson John Jay—pose with their dairy cows. John W. and family relocated to Torrington from Barkhamsted Hollow in 1936. They purchased the Weed farm on Goshen Road and, for the next 20 years, ran Wright's dairy farm with a herd of Guernsey cows. In the 1960s, the repurposed barn became a popular dance club for teenagers. (Wright family.)

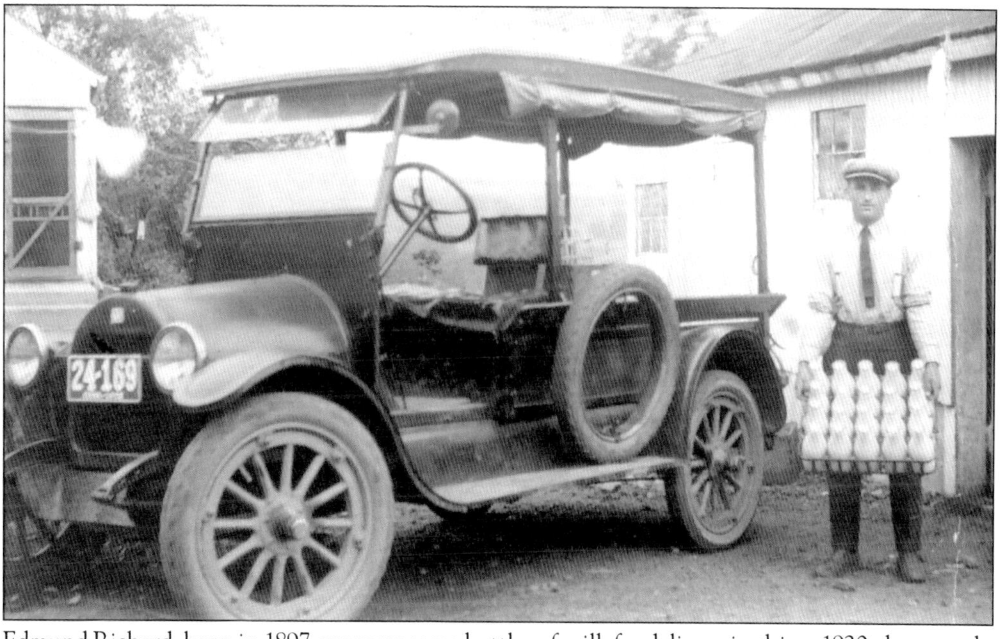

Edmund Richard, born in 1897, prepares some bottles of milk for delivery in this c. 1920 photograph. He was the son of Gad and Berthe Richard, Swiss immigrants who established the Walnut Hill Farm on Richard Road. At the time when this photograph was taken, fresh milk delivery was the norm. (Richard family.)

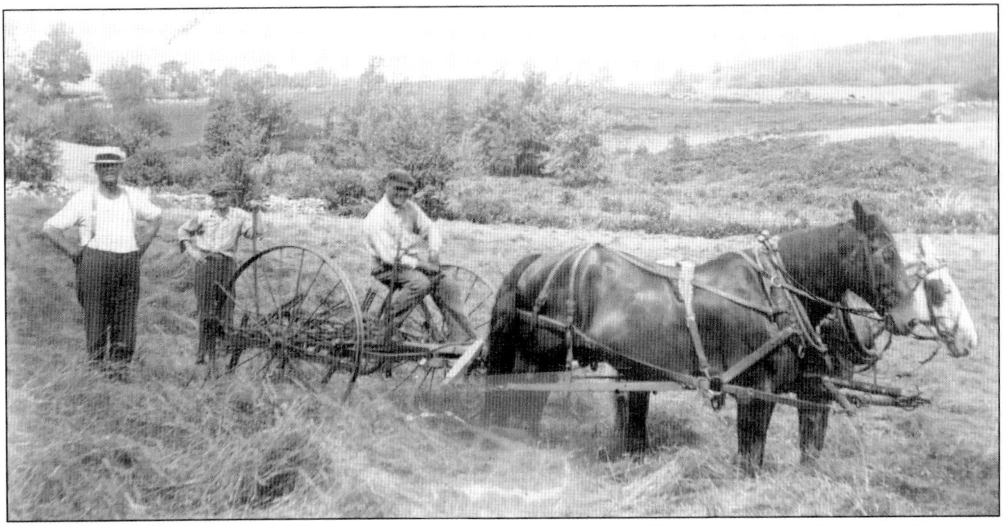

Walnut Hill Farm's Gad Richard and his sons Ray (left) and George (right) take a break in one of their fields in a 1922 photograph. At 18, Gad traveled to Connecticut from Switzerland with his friend William Besse. Gad married his childhood sweetheart, Berthe Perrit, and after a stint at the brass mill, he began farming on land close to what is now the Litchfield/Torrington border. (Richard family.)

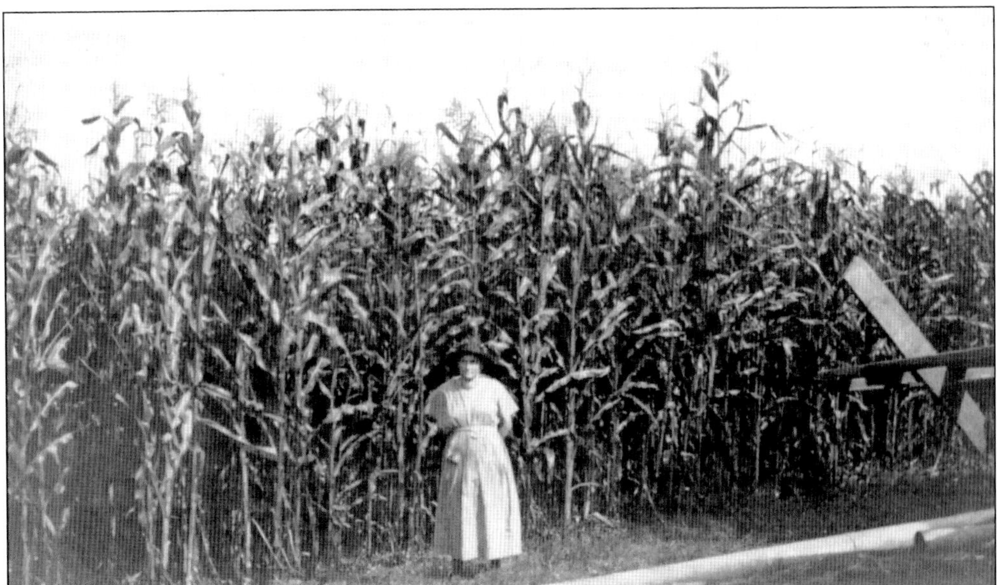

Berthe Richard is dwarfed by 15-foot-tall Eureka corn in this 1911 photograph. Corn—along with beans, peas, rye, English wheat, and pumpkins—was one of the first crops planted by Connecticut farmers. In the earliest years of settlement, the yields were poor, just at subsistence level, and this bumper crop certainly would have astonished and gratified colonial farmers. (Richard family.)

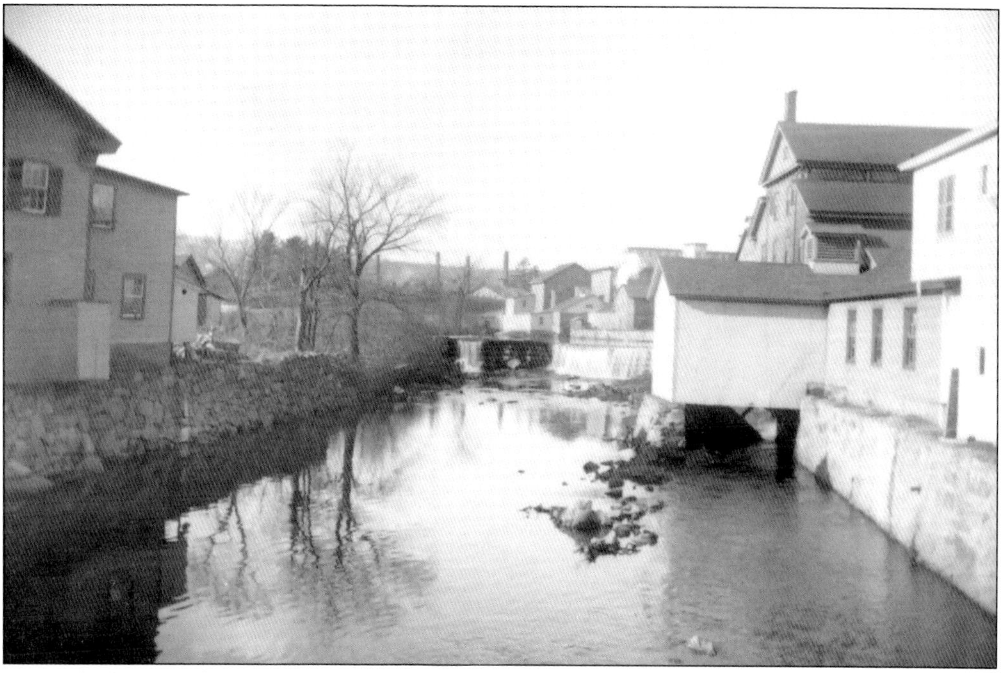

A view looking up the West Branch of the Naugatuck River from Center Bridge around 1890 shows the Turner & Seymour Manufacturing Company on the right (below the dam) and the woolen mill (above the dam). The tall building with the gabled roof was built in 1844 as a cotton mill, and the dam supplied its waterpower. The chimneys of the brass mill are visible in the distance.

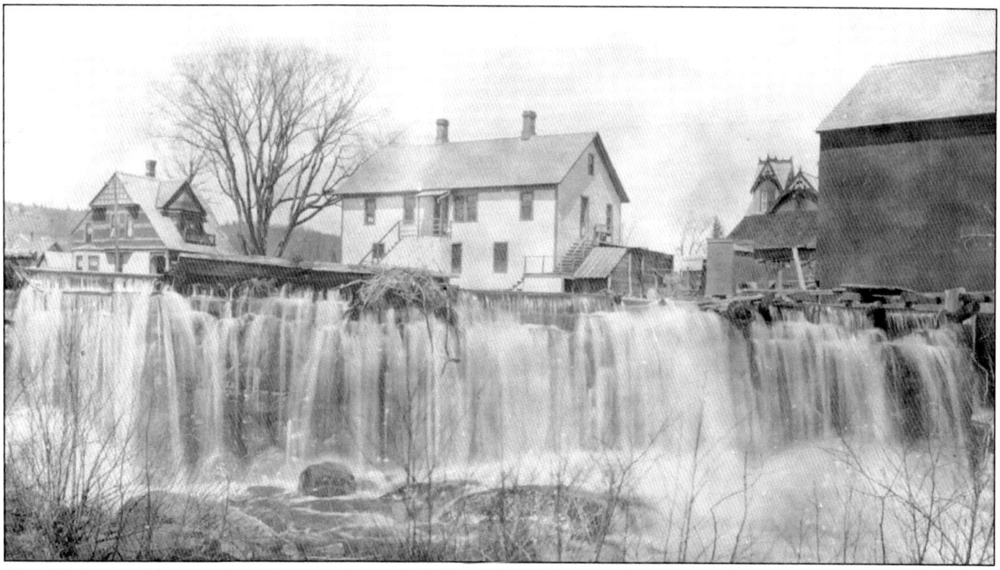

Cook's Dam (shown here) was about 100 feet downstream from Cook's Bridge on Main Street and Prospect Place in Torrington's North End on the East Branch of the Naugatuck River. This photograph gives some idea of the power of the river. Lewis Cook relied on it to run his saw- and cider mills, as did the Dayton Organ Factory and the Ashborn Guitar Factory farther upstream. Circus elephants not convinced of the bridge's sturdiness sometimes opted to wade or swim across the river.

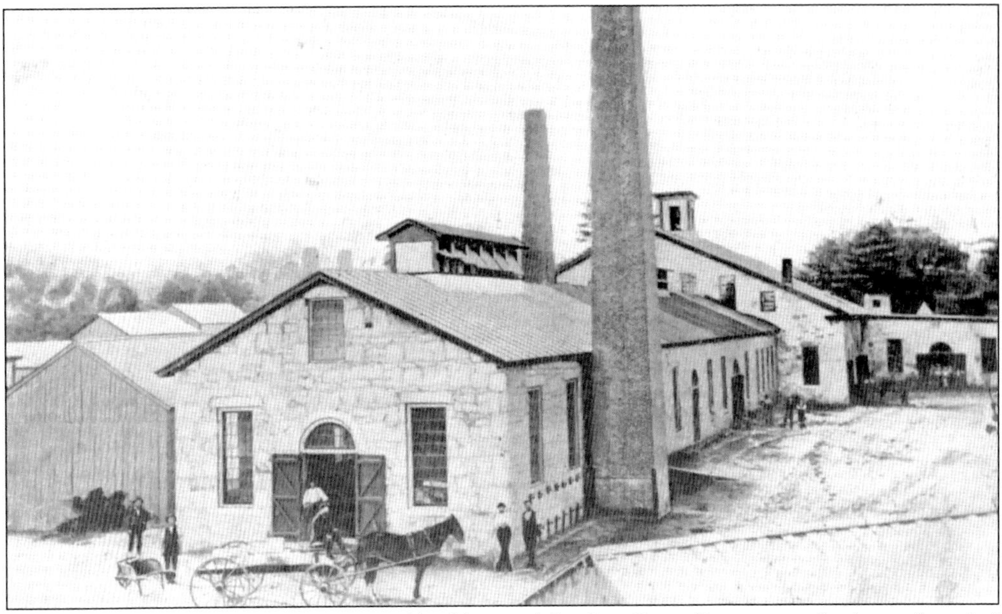

These stone structures were the original buildings of the Coe Brass Company, which was founded in 1834 by Israel Coe, John Hungerford, and Anson Phelps. Lyman Coe acquired the brass mill in 1863 and turned it into Torrington's largest industry. The brass mill later merged with the American Brass Company, and then with Anaconda Brass and Copper. The mill closed in 1964.

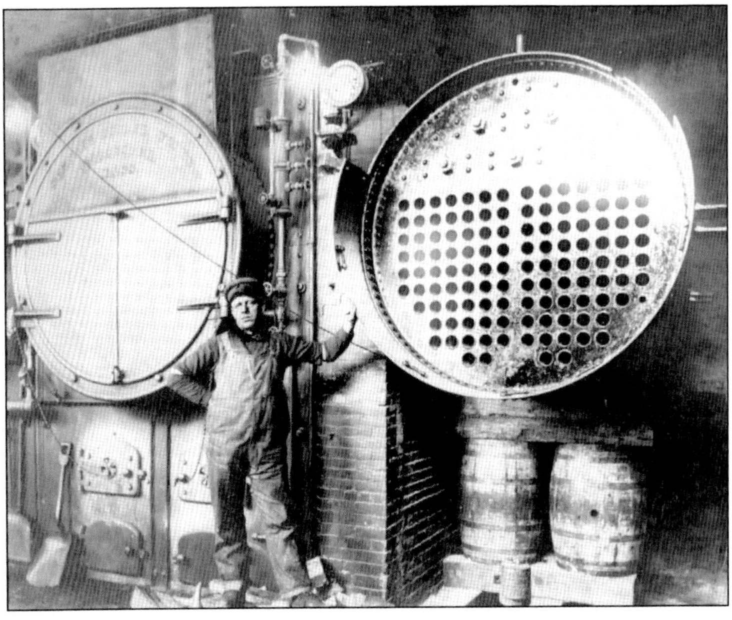

John Palmer, who later served as chief of Torrington's Fire Department, stands in front of the coal-fired boilers at the American Brass Company during World War I. The mill required a tremendous amount of power to produce brass and then shape it into sheets, rods, tubes, and wires. The mill originally used wood fires and waterpower until the railroad began supplying it with coal after 1849.

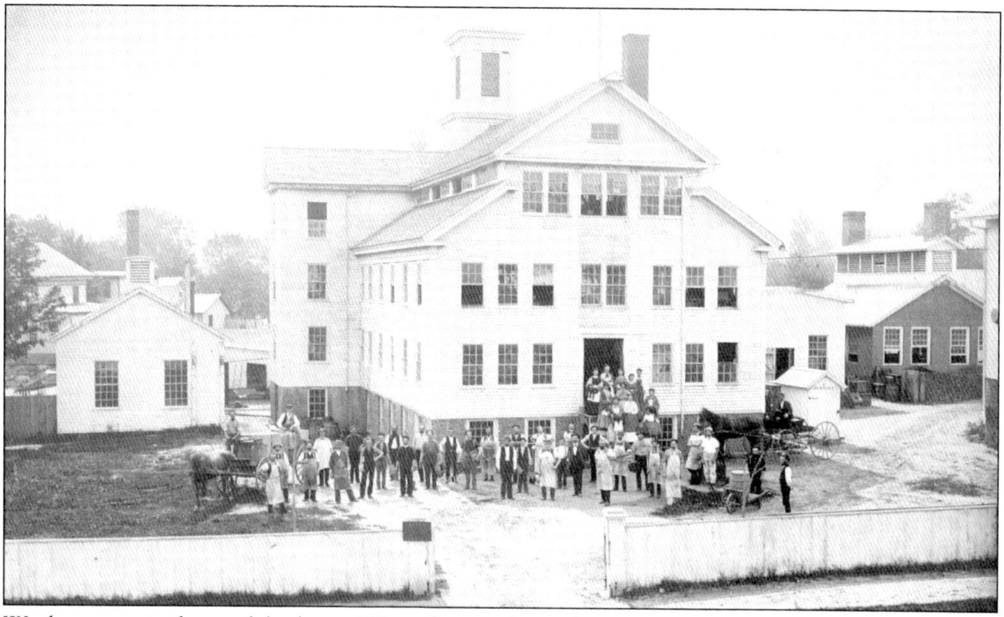

Workers pose in front of the lower Water Street plant of Turner, Seymour, & Judd, known locally as the Hook and Eye Shop. John O'Meara and his horse, Old Dick (at left), had helped move the company from Waterbury to Torrington. In the 1860s, the company manufactured a variety of items, including curtain and window hardware, picture nails and hooks, drawer pulls, cupboard latches, and hat hooks.

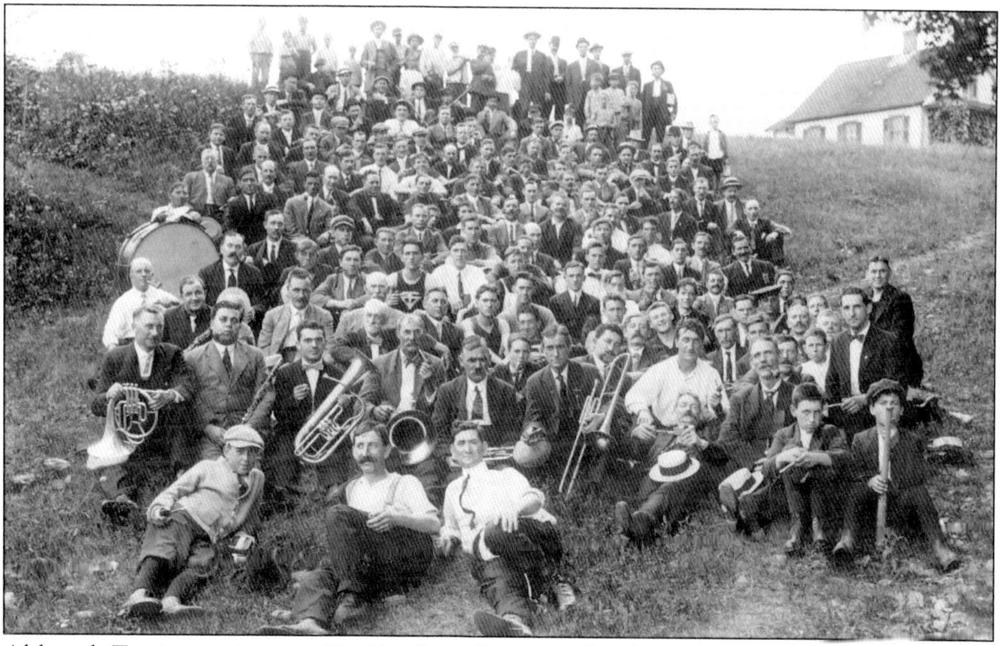

Although Torrington is some 40 miles from the coast, the clambake, complete with track-and-field events, was an annual tradition for local factories. In this August 1912 photograph, 200 Turner & Seymour employees holding company-provided Missouri Meerschaum corncob pipes gathered for music, littleneck clams, lobster, and beer. A foundry-versus-factory baseball game closed out the day.

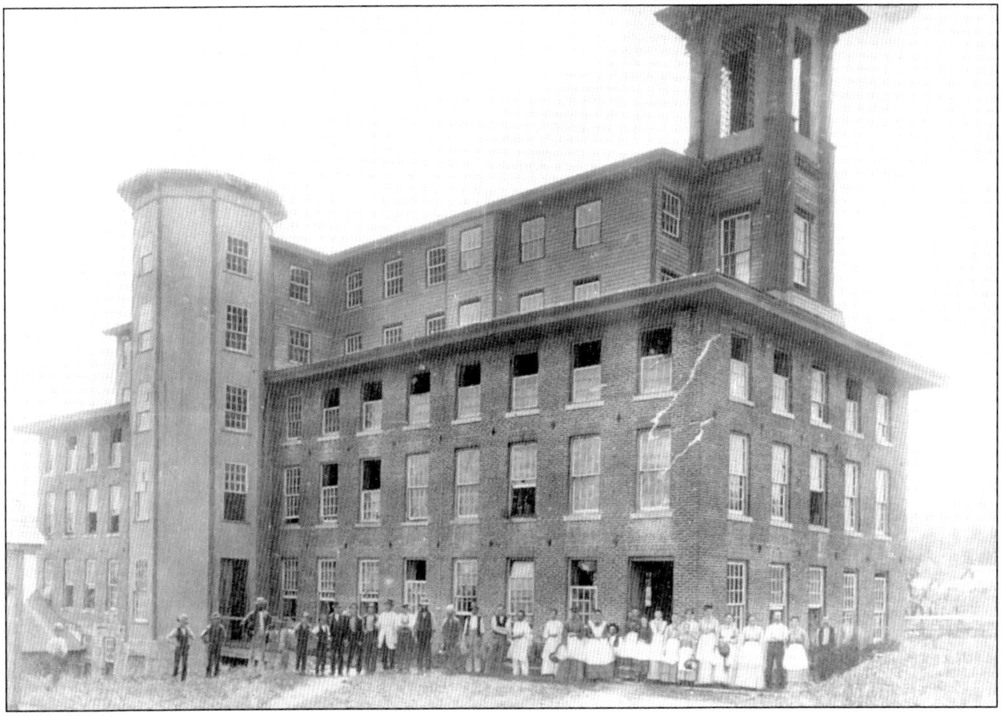

This c. 1875 photograph shows some of the men, women, and boys who worked at the Union Manufacturing Company on upper Water Street. Renamed Warrenton Woolen Mill in 1894, the company did its own "cleaning, sorting, dyeing, spinning, weaving, and finishing" on-site.

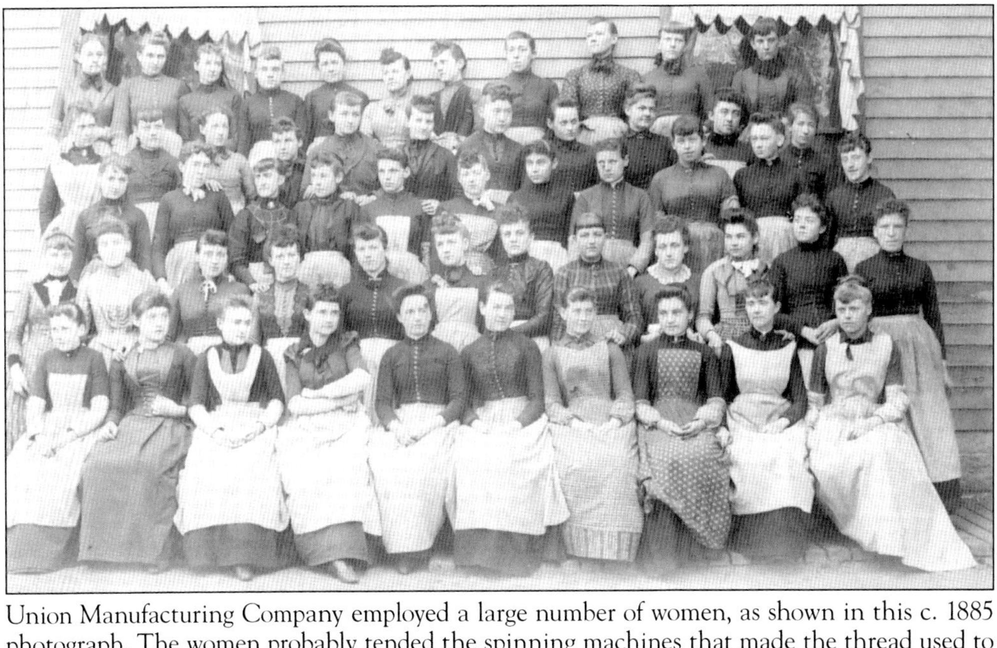

Union Manufacturing Company employed a large number of women, as shown in this c. 1885 photograph. The women probably tended the spinning machines that made the thread used to weave woolen cloth. Many of these women lived in the company's boardinghouses on Water Street, which was known as Boarding House Hill. In 1879, the mill employed 75 people making about 500 yards of cloth per day.

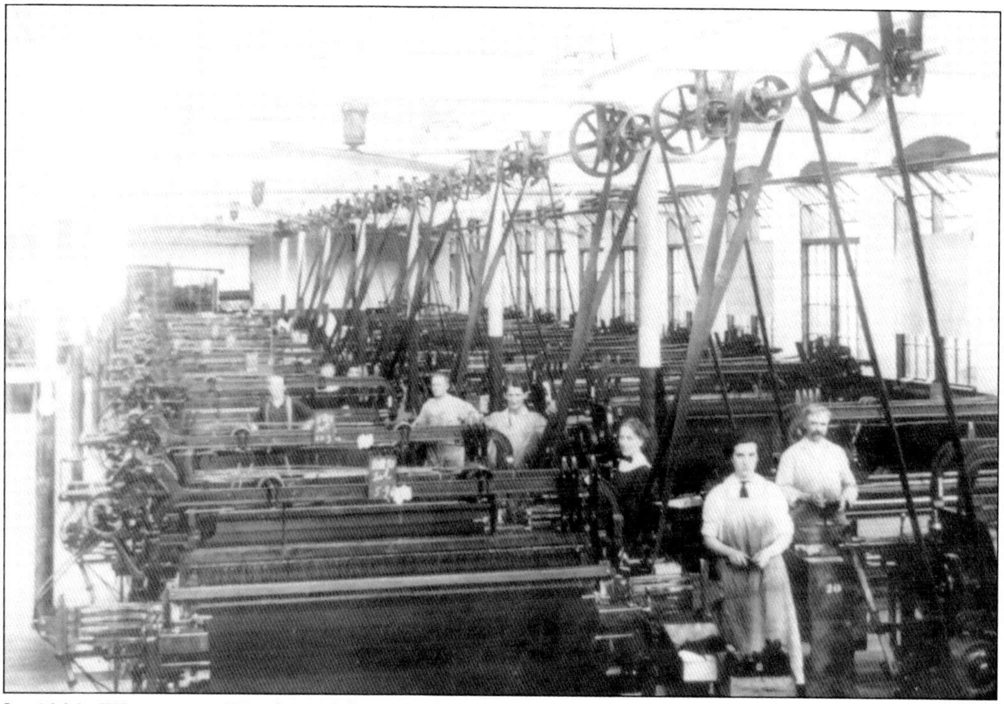

In 1908, Warrenton Woolen Mill moved north to 839 Main Street. The factory, designed by Charles T. Main, consisted of two large buildings, each more than 250 feet in length, and several smaller outbuildings. This undated photograph captures some workers amid the machinery. The factory was closed in 1984 and converted to condominiums. In 1987, it was listed in the National Register of Historic Places.

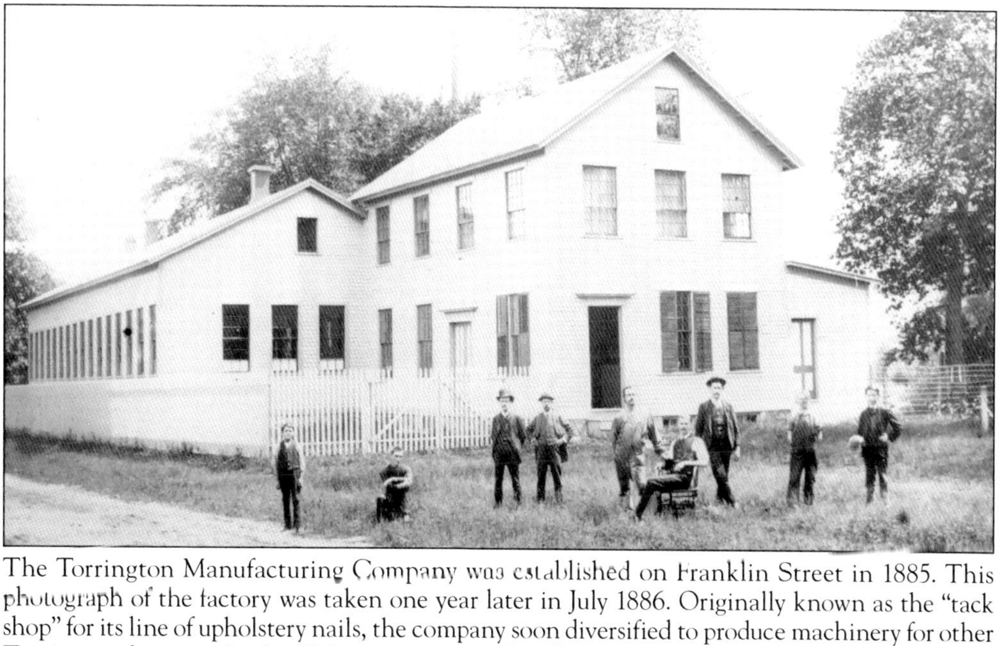

The Torrington Manufacturing Company was established on Franklin Street in 1885. This photograph of the factory was taken one year later in July 1886. Originally known as the "tack shop" for its line of upholstery nails, the company soon diversified to produce machinery for other Torrington factories. In the 20th century, it produced a wide variety of spring coiling machines and fans.

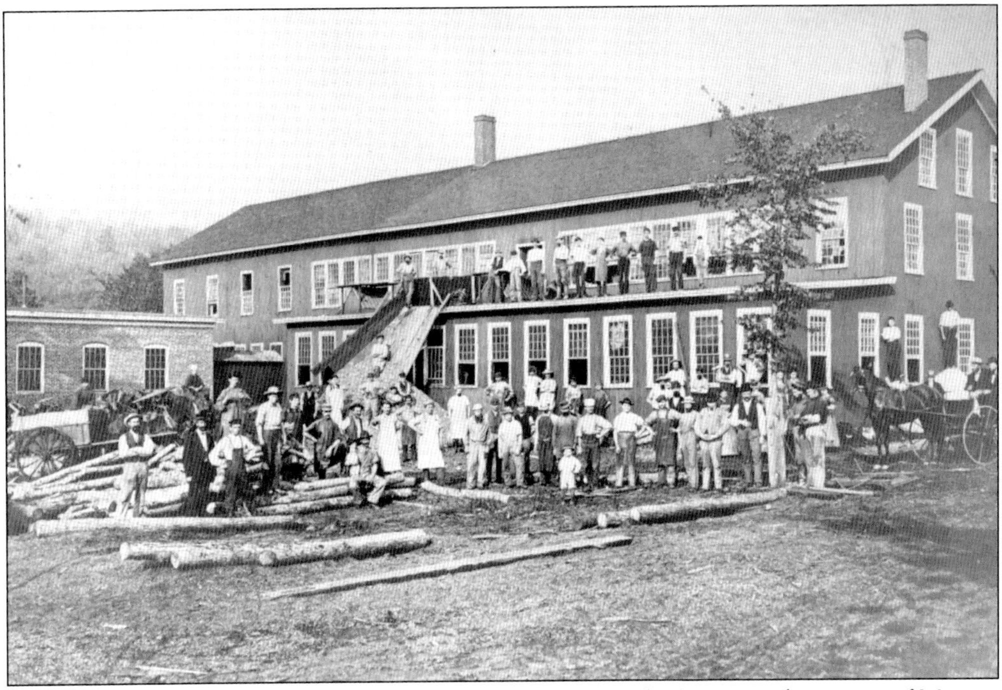

Incorporated in 1864, the Union Hardware Company secured 15 acres at the corner of Migeon Avenue and Goshen Road in 1865. The company, known locally as "the skate shop," eventually became the largest manufacturer of ice and roller skates in the world, although its product line included other sporting goods, hand tools, and police equipment like handcuffs and whistles.

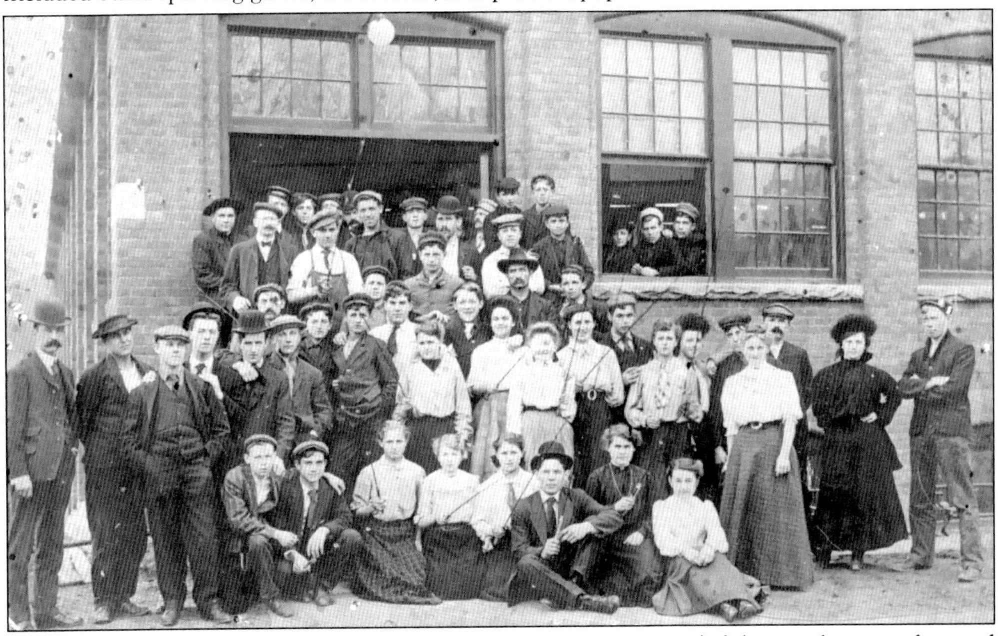

This early photograph shows Union Hardware employees posing with fishing poles manufactured at the plant. The shop made bamboo fishing rods from start to finish—splitting the cane, making the hardware, and completing the finish work. In later decades, the plant produced steel fishing poles.

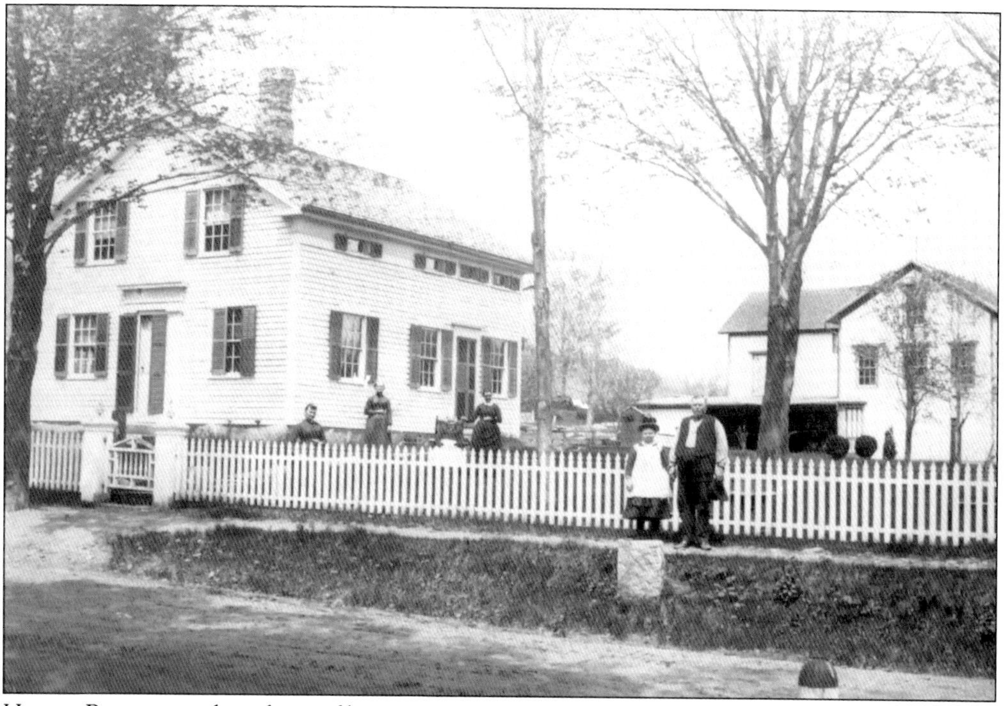

Harvey Barnes stands in front of his Migeon Avenue home in this undated photograph. Barnes, a sawyer at Union Hardware, at one time supplied all the wood for the company's skates. Barnes was also a skilled dowser. Using a small apple branch, he located the springs that supplied Union Hardware's drinking water for several years. He retired in 1893 after 19 years as foreman of the wood room. During Barnes's 30 years at the company, the workforce grew from 15 to 250. Below, an undated photograph shows the interior of the Union Hardware skate shop.

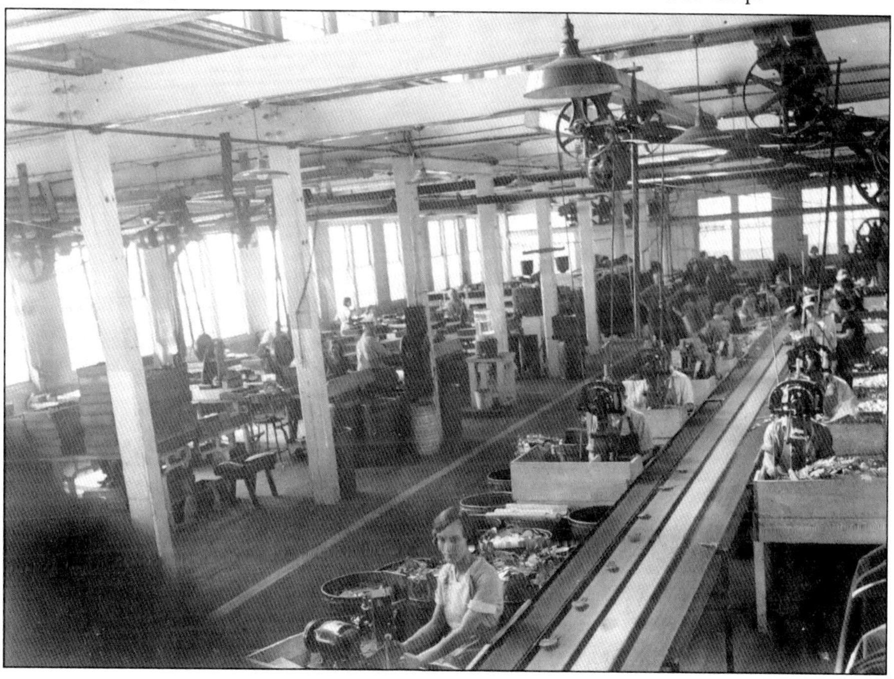

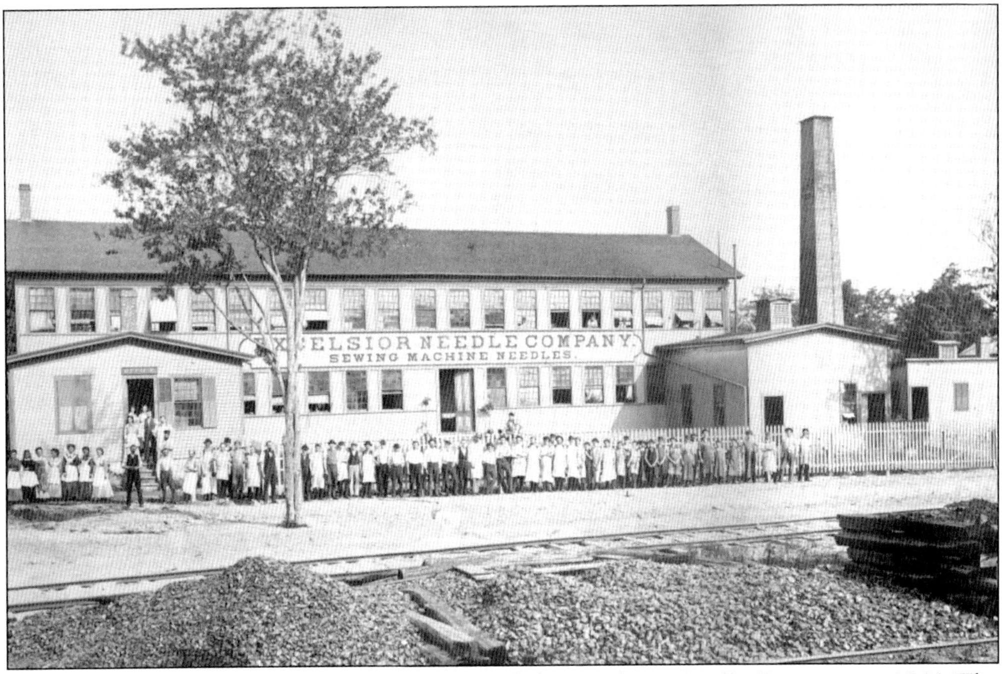

Achille F. Migeon and Charles Alvord organized the Excelsior Needle Company in 1866. The company's first factory was on Newfield Road, but by 1870, it had constructed this new facility on Church Street near the railroad crossing. Around the time of this 1875 photograph, workers were producing 30,000 sewing needles each day, six days per week.

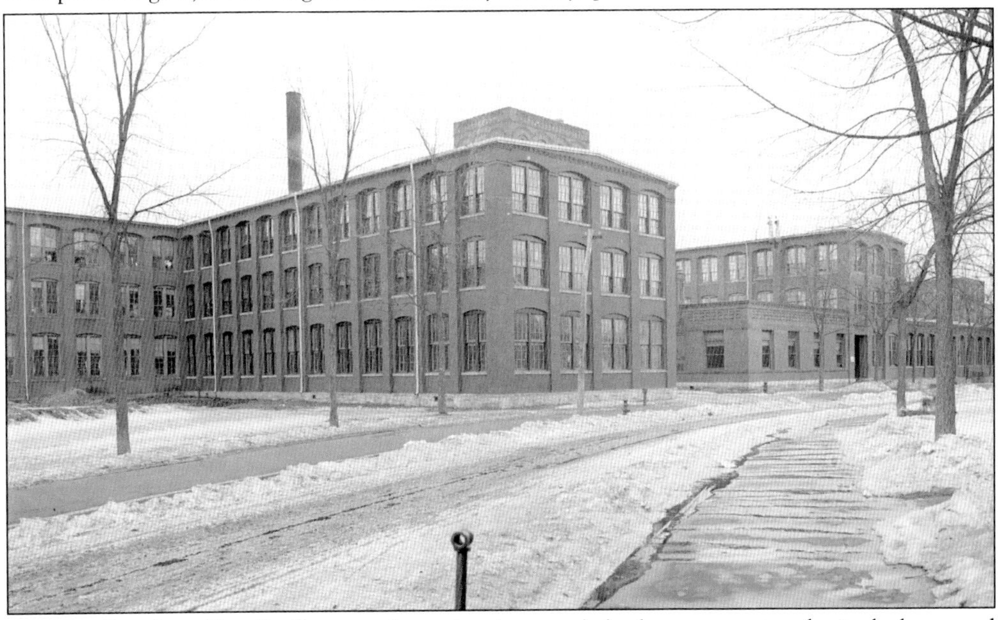

By 1890, Excelsior Needle Company's production needs had outgrown its physical plant, and this much larger brick facility was constructed on Field Street. Field Street remained home to the corporate headquarters of the ever-expanding manufacturer, which reincorporated as the Torrington Company in 1898. By the 1960s, the company had eight domestic plants as well as facilities in Europe, Canada, and Japan.

Excelsior Needle Company became a division of the newly incorporated Torrington Company in 1898. The company owed its success in needle-making to its development of the cold swaging machine (shown here), which shaped metal wire or metal rods between revolving dies. With the swaging machine, the Torrington Company could make a wide variety of products, including bicycle and automobile spokes, which became the mainstay of its Standard Spoke and Nipple Division.

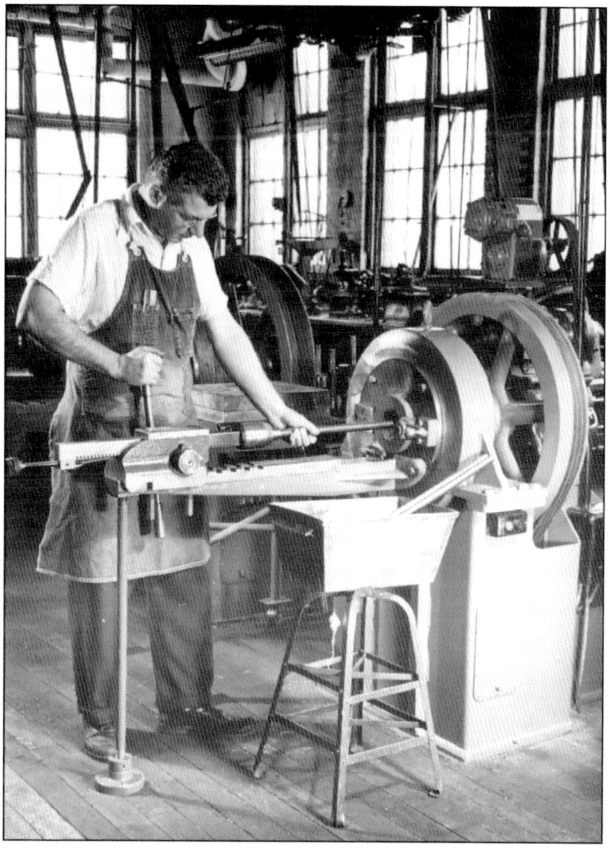

The Torrington Company diversified its product line to include latch and hook needles, surgical needles, and eventually ball bearings and needle roller bearings. The building where needles were manufactured continued to be known as "the needle shop." This early undated photograph shows some employees from the "grooving room."

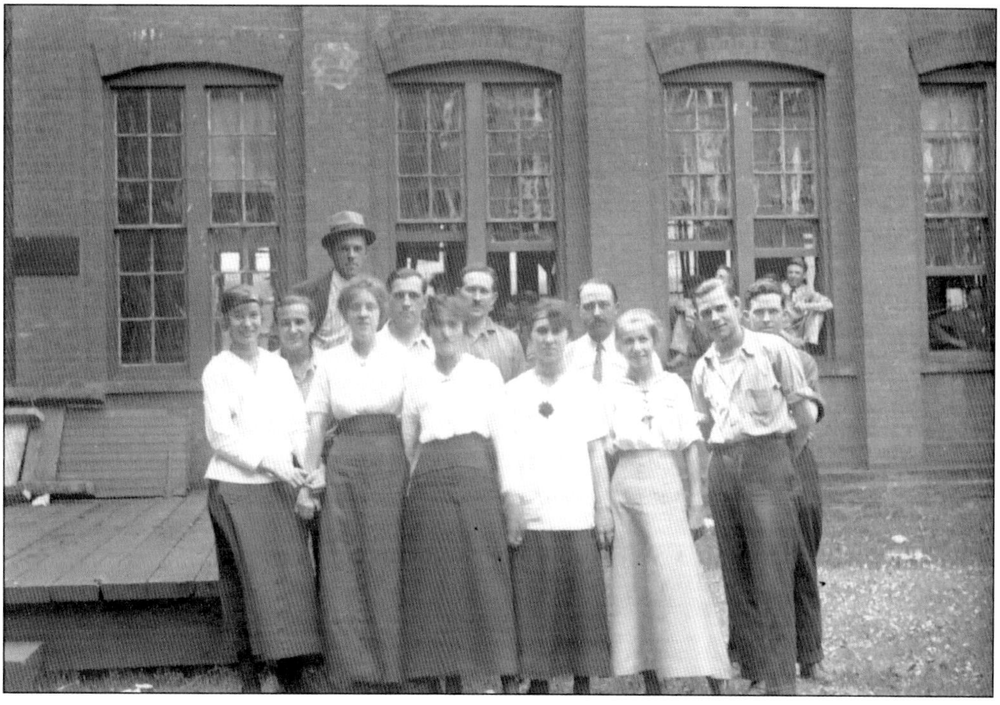

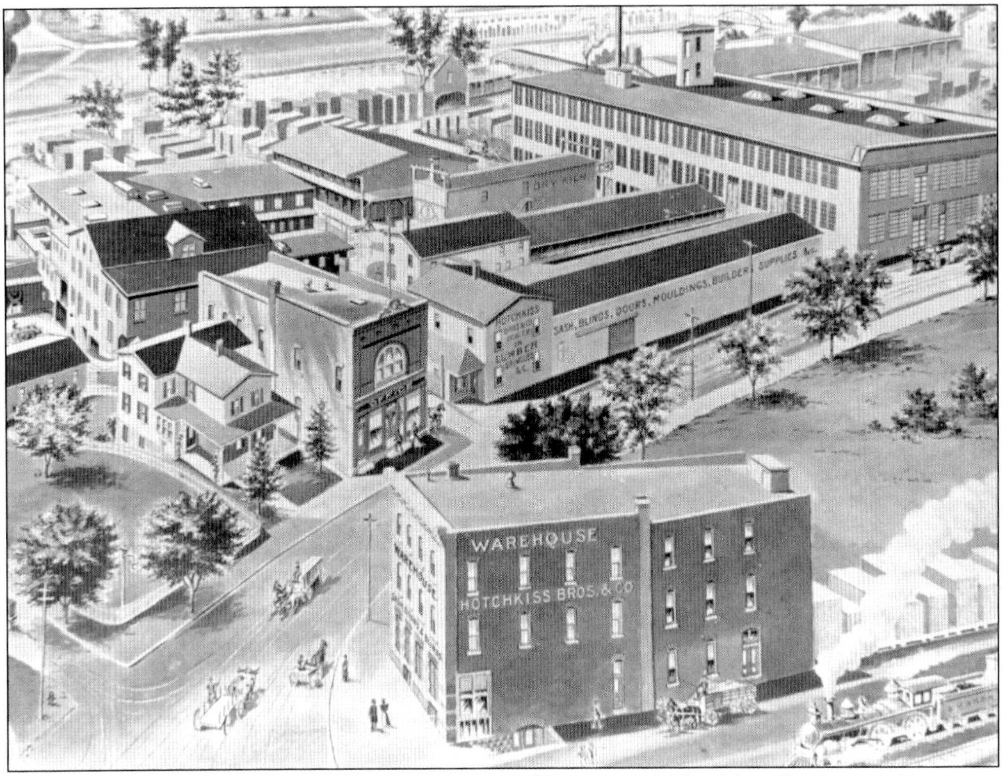

The print shown above captures the expansiveness of Torrington's Hotchkiss Brothers & Company, which, by 1897, covered about four acres on the north side of the Naugatuck River on upper Water Street. The company, which started as a sawmill owned by Charles Hotchkiss, became a millwork and construction business as well as a wholesaler and retailer of lumber and building supplies under his sons, Edward and Henry. Gradually, steam rooms, storage houses, three kilns, a large modern mill, and other smaller mills and outbuildings were added. Hotchkiss Brothers, a complete woodworking establishment, did "scroll, jig, band-sawing, planing, turning, and cabinet making" on premises. Its sashes, moldings, and doors were sold throughout New England and New York. Below, workers stand alongside a shipment.

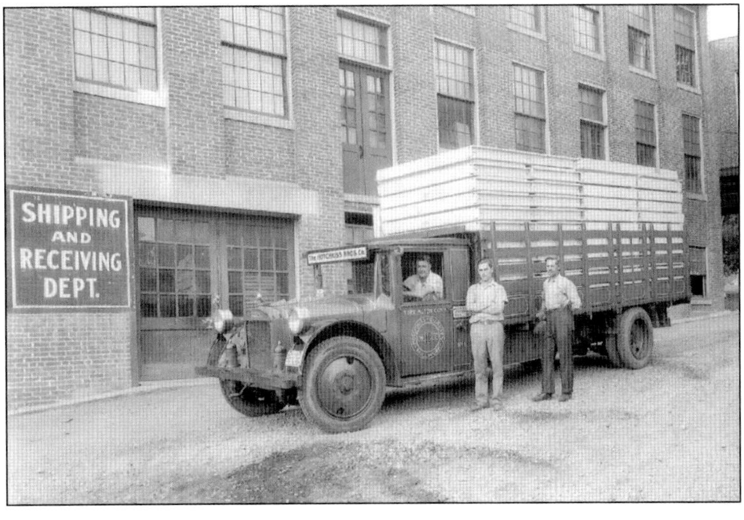

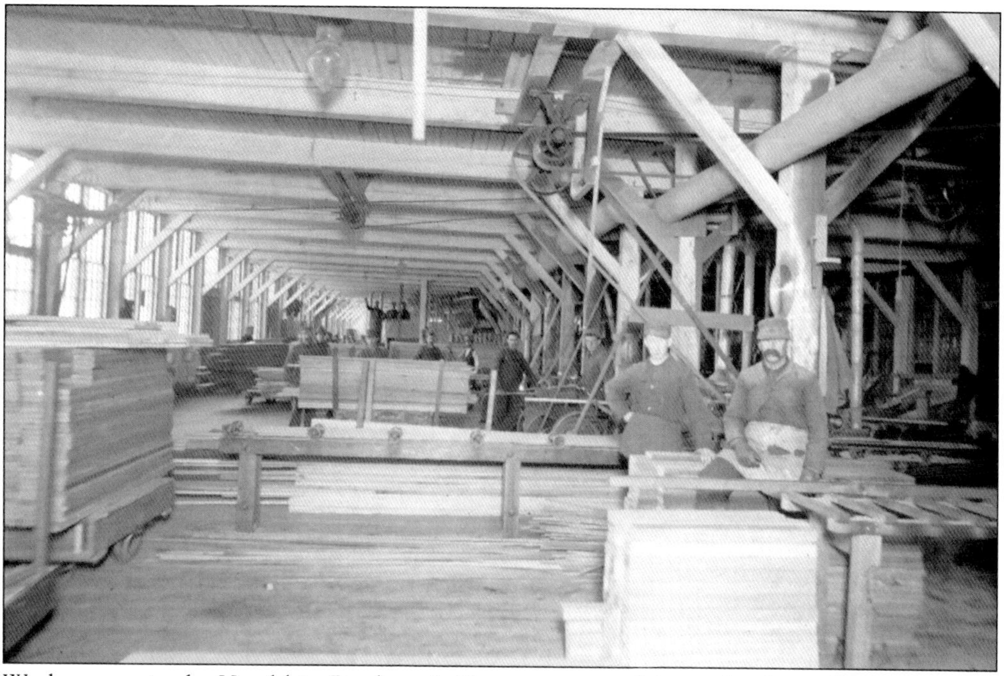

Workers pose in the Hotchkiss Brothers & Company state-of-the-art lumber mill in an undated photograph. The three-story mill was designed to provide workers with excellent natural lighting via floor-to-ceiling windows. Electric lights—powered by the company's own plant—were also installed.

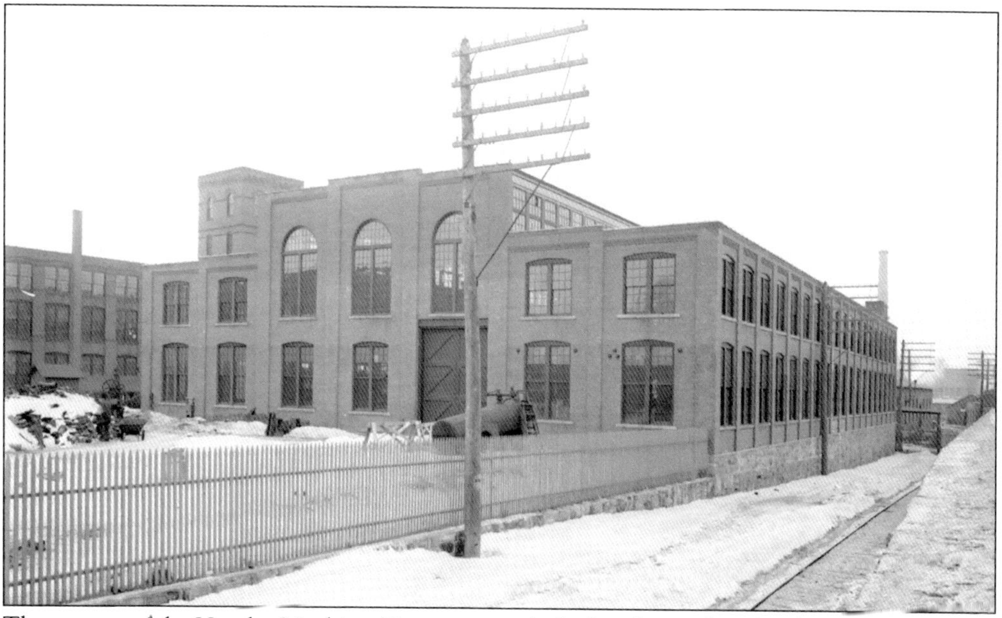

The success of the Hendey Machine Company was linked to the quality, durability, and precision of its line of machine tools. The company was established in 1870 and rapidly grew to become an industrial giant where generations of workers produced machines, some of which are still in use today. This photograph shows one of Hendey's newly constructed factory buildings shortly after completion in 1907 along the railroad tracks.

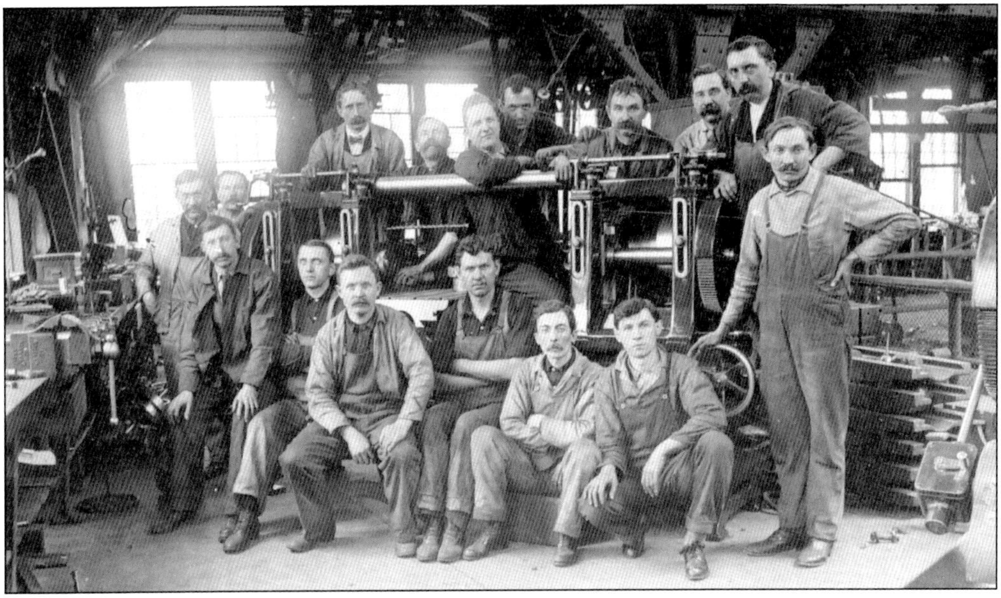

Many German immigrants were skilled craftsmen and worked as machinists in local factories. In this 1910 photograph of the Hendey Machine Company machine room, at least 10 of the workers have German surnames, including foreman Max Tieman (seated, third from the left in the first row) and assistant foreman Sidney Tieman (second seated man from right).

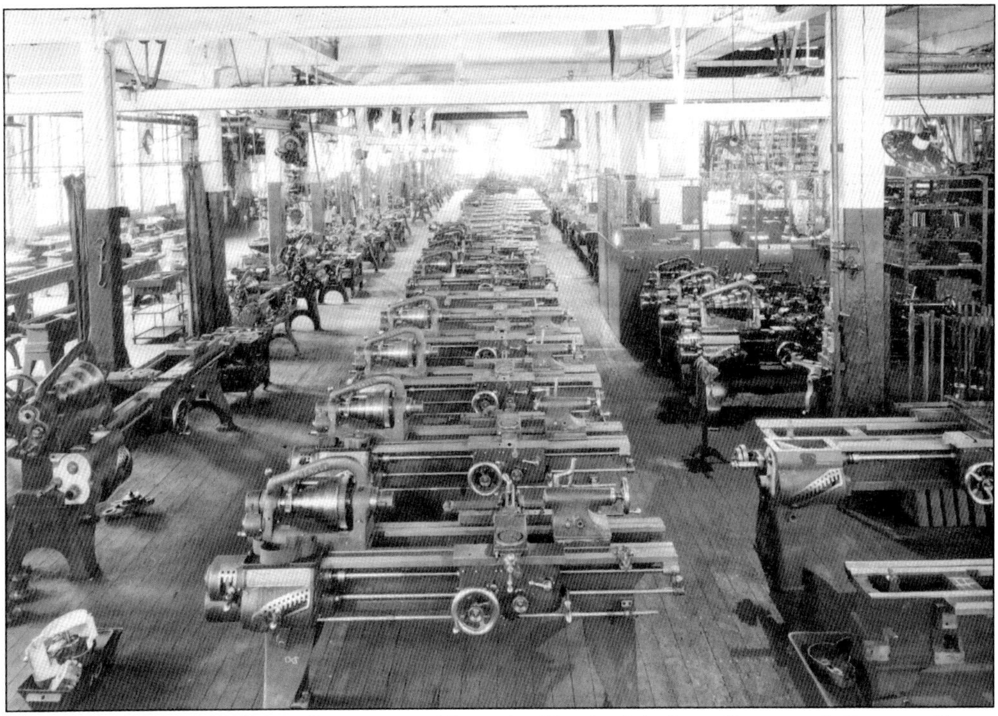

A long row of lathes is shown during assembly in the Hendey Machine Company's Summer Street factory. The metalworking engine lathe was Hendey's most famous product, and it was shipped all over the world. The popularity of Hendey's lathe was largely due to its quick-change gearbox, which was invented here by factory superintendent Wendell P. Norton.

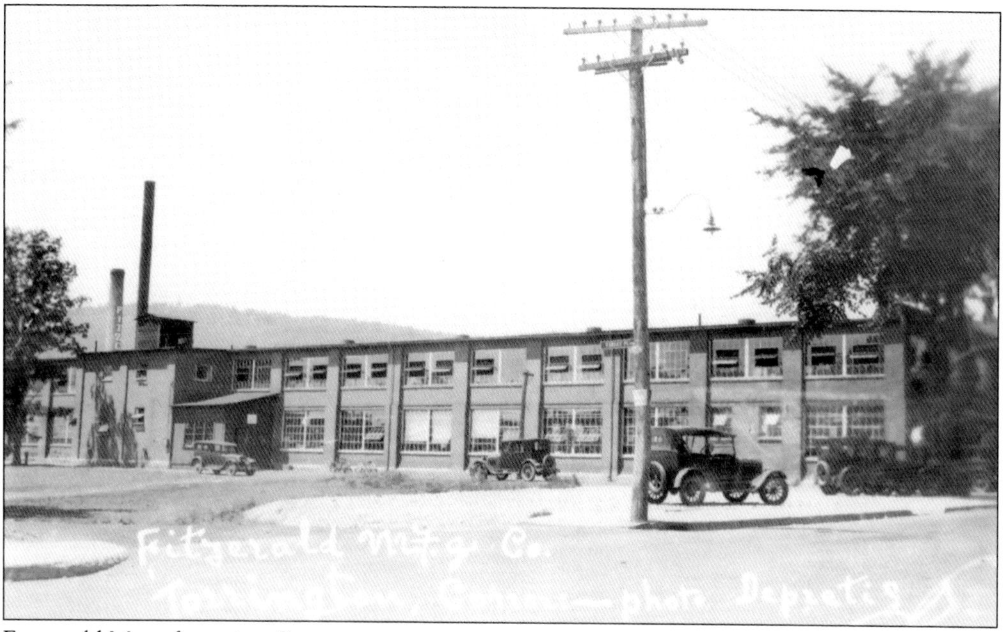

Fitzgerald Manufacturing Company was founded in 1906 by P.J. and M.F. Fitzgerald in a small shed in the rear of the Fitzgerald home. The company, which specialized in gaskets and seals for combustion engines, expanded rapidly. After a fire destroyed its Winsted plant, Fitzgerald rebuilt in Torrington on the northwest corner of Farley Place and Main Street. It continued manufacturing under the Fitzgerald name until the mid-1970s.

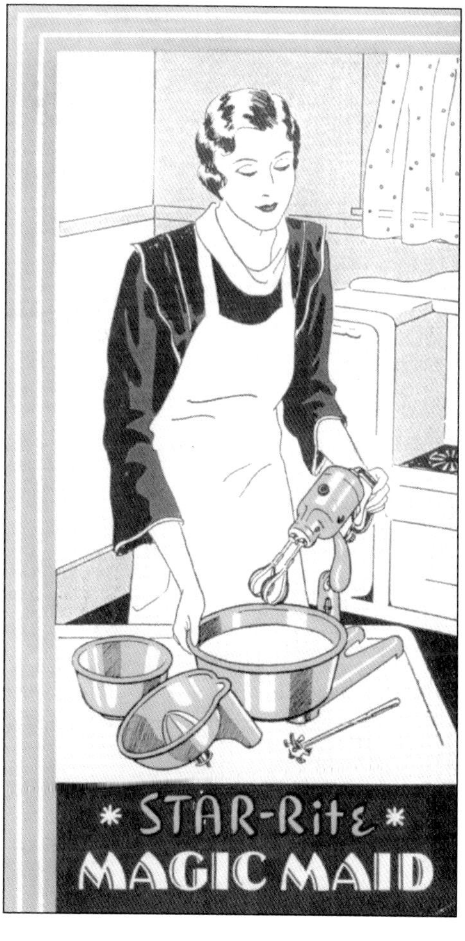

Although its main products were seals and gaskets, Fitzgerald manufactured other items as well, such as spark plugs, horns, and electrical fans. It also produced small household appliances like toasters, waffle irons, and the mixer featured here. Some of Fitzgerald's quirkier products, like the Star-Rite Violet Ray Machine, are now highly sought-after by collectors.

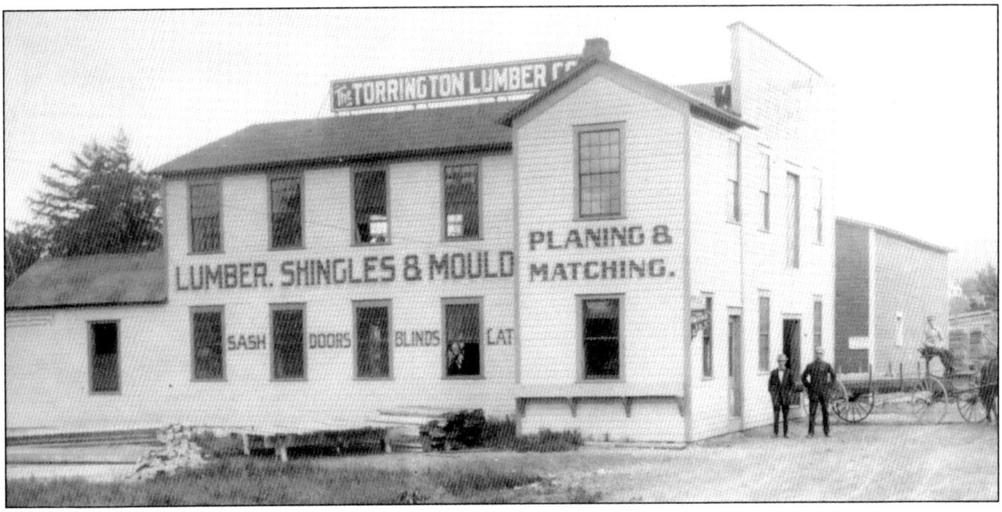

The Torrington Lumber Company was founded in 1875 and incorporated in 1906 by owners James L. and Thomas D. Farley. The firm was a prominent general building contractor that also dealt in lumber and millwork. James's sons, Jim and Steve, known as "the sawdust twins," pose here in a c. 1900 photograph taken at the company's Main Street and Farley Place site.

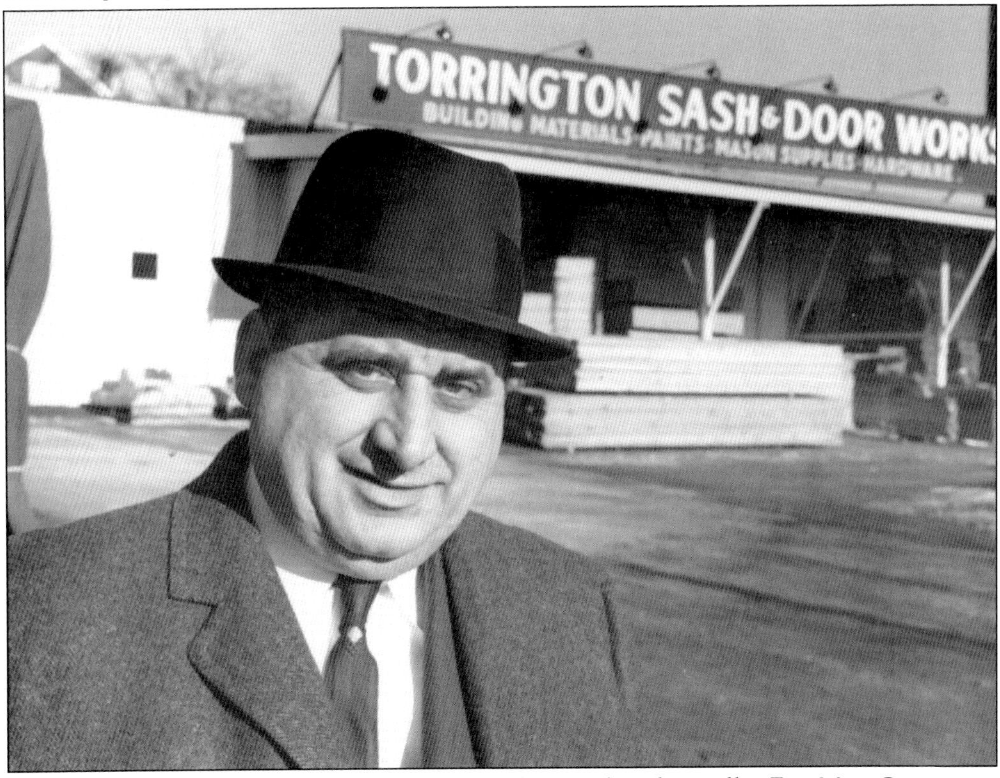

Torrington Sash & Door Works founder Joseph Sabia stands in front of his East Main Street store in this undated photograph. Sabia, who honed his skills at Hotchkiss Brothers, opened his own business in 1939 as a manufacturer of "inside and outside doors." His nephew Ralph Sabia ran the business for many years, and now Joseph's son, Joseph Sabia Jr., continues to operate Torrington Sash & Door at its East Main Street location. (Joseph Sabia Jr.)

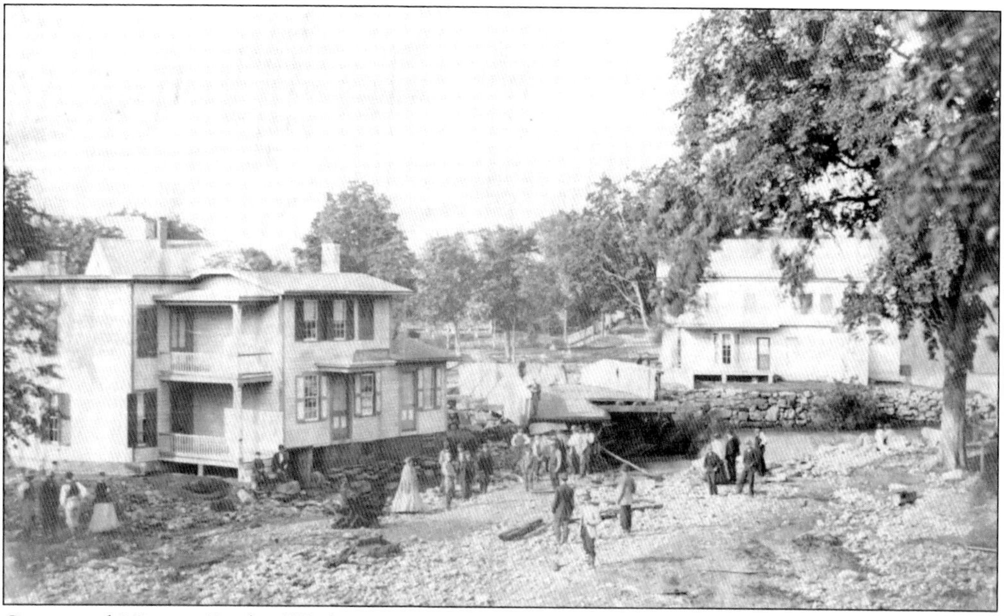

Captioned "Center Bridge Washout June 1869," this photograph with a view looking south was taken on Main Street after heavy rain partially swept away the old Coe Brass dam and torrents of water flooded the downtown area. Train passengers were stranded, and billiard tables in the Allen House Hotel basement floated to the ceiling. The town's 3,000 residents were forced to rely on rowboats until a temporary bridge could be built.

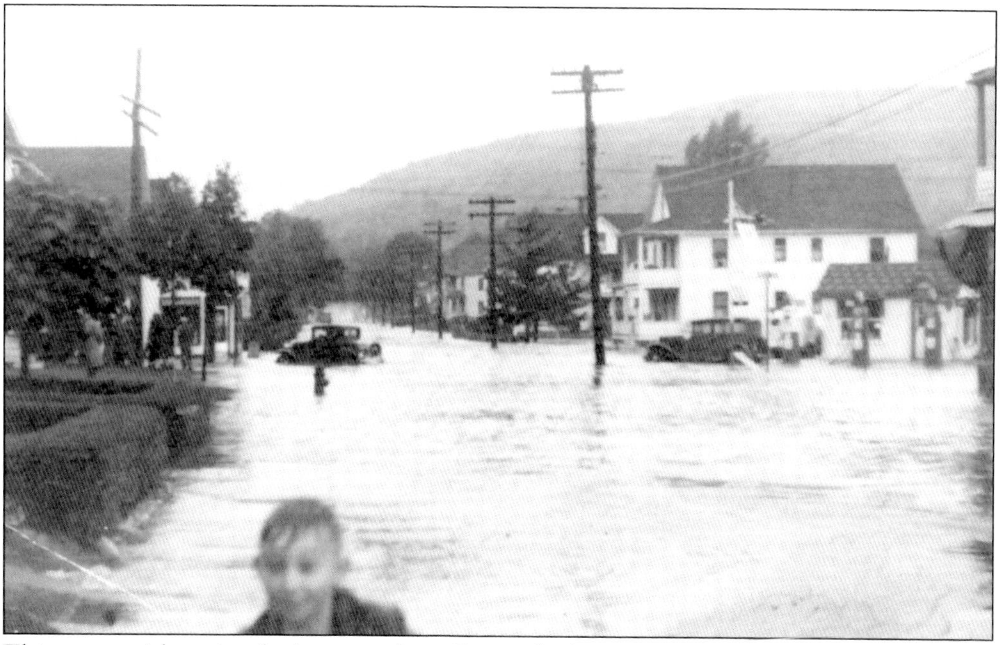

This scene with a view looking north on Riverside Avenue at its intersection with Wolcott Avenue captures the aftermath of the September 21, 1938, hurricane. The 80-mile-per-hour winds and 11.57 inches of rain combined to uproot trees, inundate roads, flood cellars, and carry away small buildings. The nearby Wolcott Avenue Bridge was covered with two feet of water. (Joanna Arnista.)

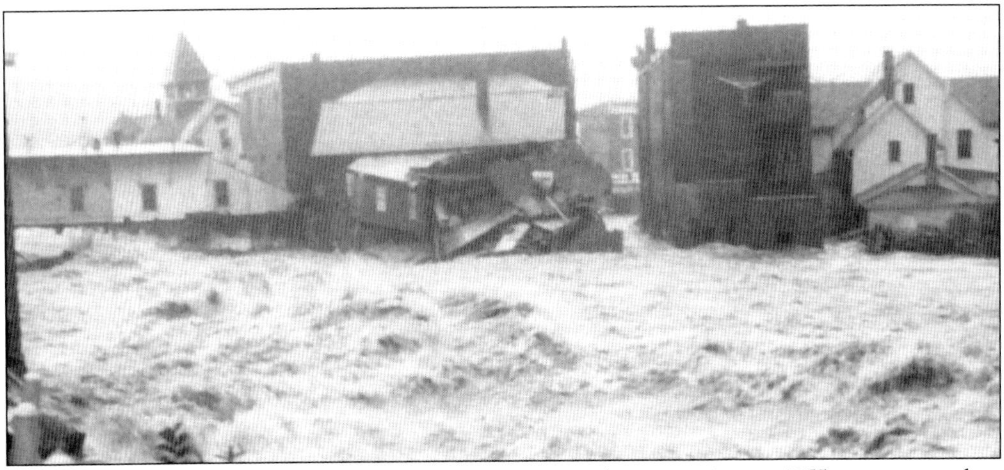

The flooding in Torrington caused by Hurricanes Connie and Diane in August 1955 was catastrophic. The floodwaters destroyed and damaged hundreds of homes, businesses, stores, and factories in one of the worst natural disasters in Connecticut history. This photograph was taken at dawn on August 19, 1955, by James Miller on a riverbank near Prospect and Water Streets.

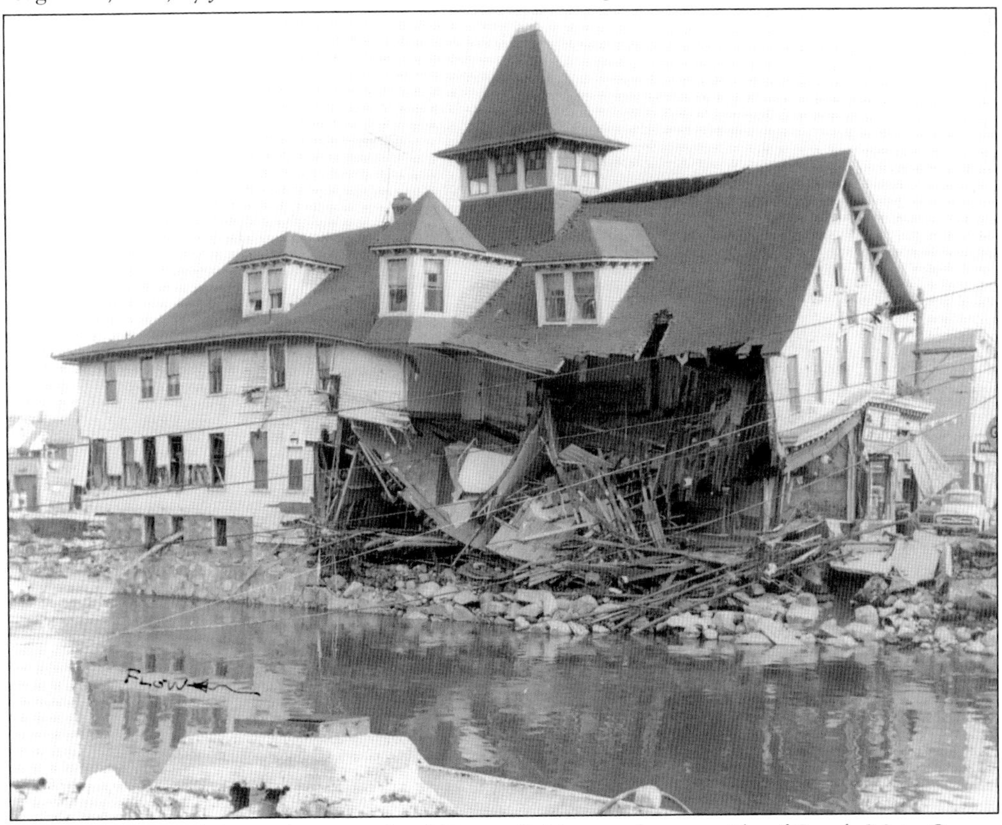

The Central Hotel, located just south of Center Bridge on the east side of South Main Street, is shown partially collapsed as a result of the 1955 flood. The hotel, which began life as the Farnham House in the 1800s, was an impressive downtown landmark but was not rebuilt. All the properties on or near the bridge were wiped out by the floodwaters, and Torrington's downtown streetscape was forever changed.

Four

Schools

Torrington's first non-native settlers established themselves on the outskirts of the area now known as Torrington, some on the western hills, others to the north and east. Accordingly, the first schoolhouses were built not in what is now the town center but rather on Brandy Hill and Lyman Hill (now Klug Hill) to the west, Torringford to the east, and Newfield in the north-central part of town. For a time, Newfield was a populous area with about 100 students attending school there in 1799.

With the coming of industry and the need for waterpower, a steady migration began away from the hillsides and into the river valley. Early schoolhouses were built on Church Street and Litchfield Road. The George Street brick schoolhouse, constructed around 1830, still stands as the oldest remaining school building in downtown Torrington.

In 1859, Lauren Wetmore donated land for a two-story wooden school building on Church Street called the Academy, which later became Center School, a free grade school for children. Eventually, newer grade schools eliminated the need for Center School, and by the late 19th century, it was used solely as a high school. In 1913, the high school burned to the ground and shortly thereafter was replaced by a new brick high school. Today, this building and a later addition house the Vogel-Wetmore Elementary School.

As the immigrant population surged at the turn of the 20th century, more neighborhood elementary schools were quickly constructed—South School, North School, Southwest, East, Migeon Avenue, and others. Torrington's first Catholic elementary school was built by St. Francis Parish in 1893, while the Slovak Catholics opened Sacred Heart School in 1922. Decades later, two more Catholic schools, St. Mary and St. Peter, followed. In 1926, a freestanding State Trade School offering vocational training at the high school level was built on South Main Street.

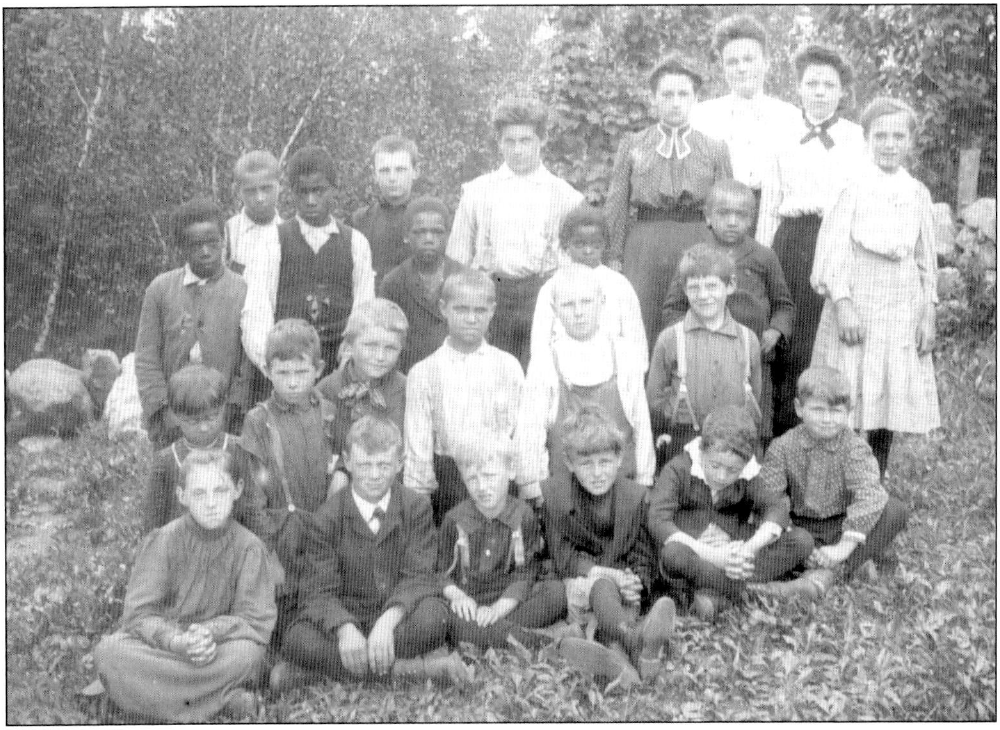

There were two early schoolhouses on Brandy Hill in West Torrington, both built before 1859. This 1904 photograph includes teacher Esther J. Allen and students from some well-known Torrington families, including the Bradley, Fyler, and Perregeaux families. At Christmas, the school's Christmas tree—along with a bushel of popcorn balls supplied by the Kimberly and Wadhams families—was enjoyed by the whole Brandy Hill community.

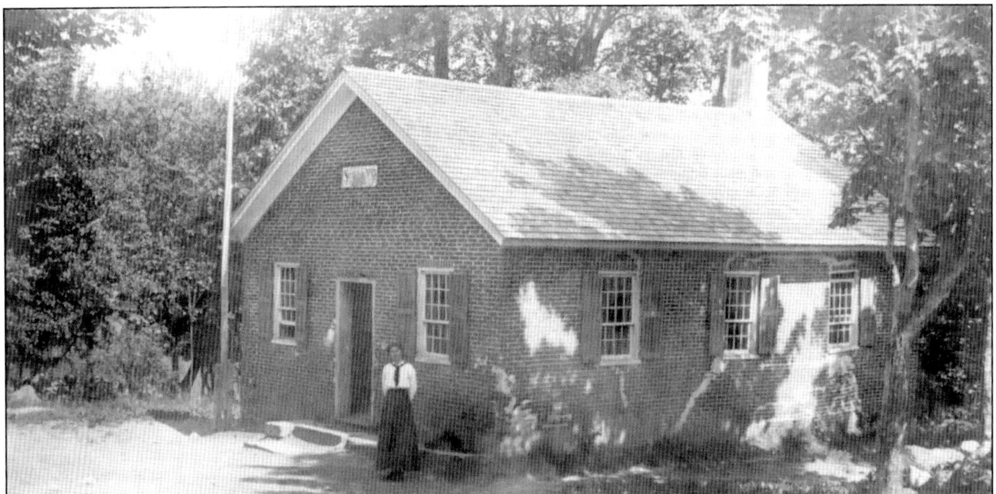

The first Newfield schoolhouse was built in 1790. For a time, the Newfield school district in the north end of Torrington was the most populous, and its large schoolhouse even boasted two fireplaces. The brick schoolhouse in this 1912 photograph was constructed in 1850 on Marshall Lake Road. Teacher Mary Colodney stands in front of the building, which became a private home in 1995.

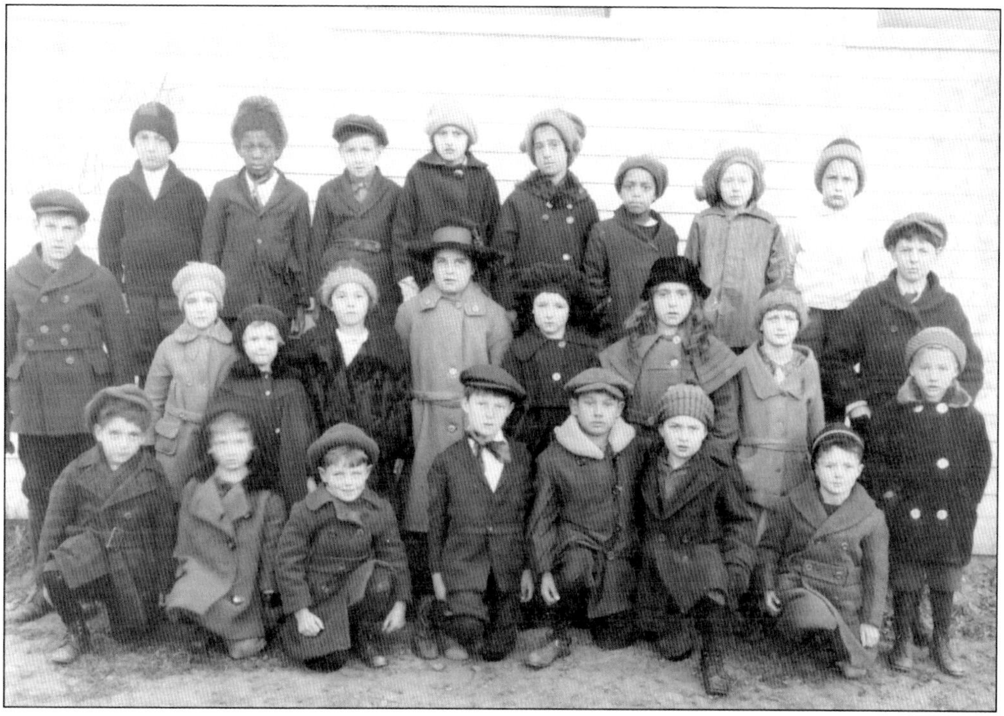

Students of the Burrville School stand outside in their winter jackets in this undated photograph. The schoolhouse, which opened in 1896, was located off Old Route 8 between Torrington and Winsted. It had no central heating or indoor plumbing until 1947, when an extensive remodel added a second classroom. Between 30 and 40 children were enrolled each year. Geraldine Tino and Olive Mignerey were the last teachers at the school, which closed in 1976.

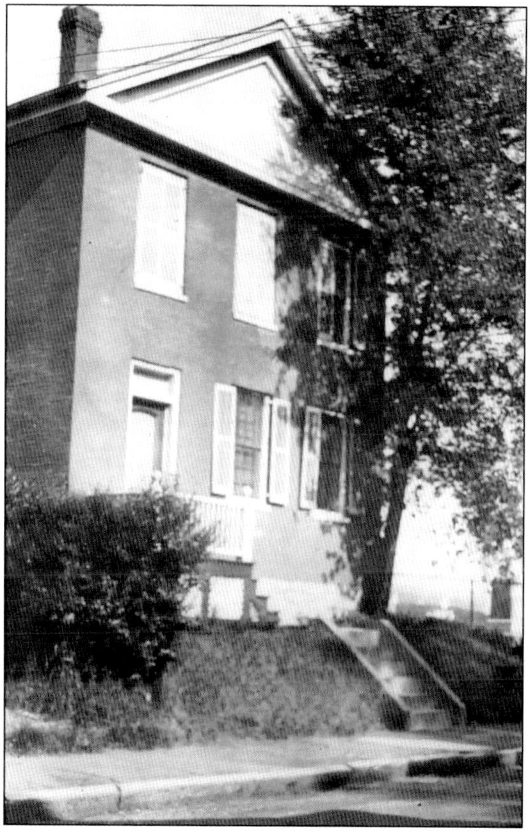

This brick schoolhouse was built in 1830 and is now a private residence at 4 George Street. Built in the Greek Revival style, it is the oldest surviving school building in Torrington.

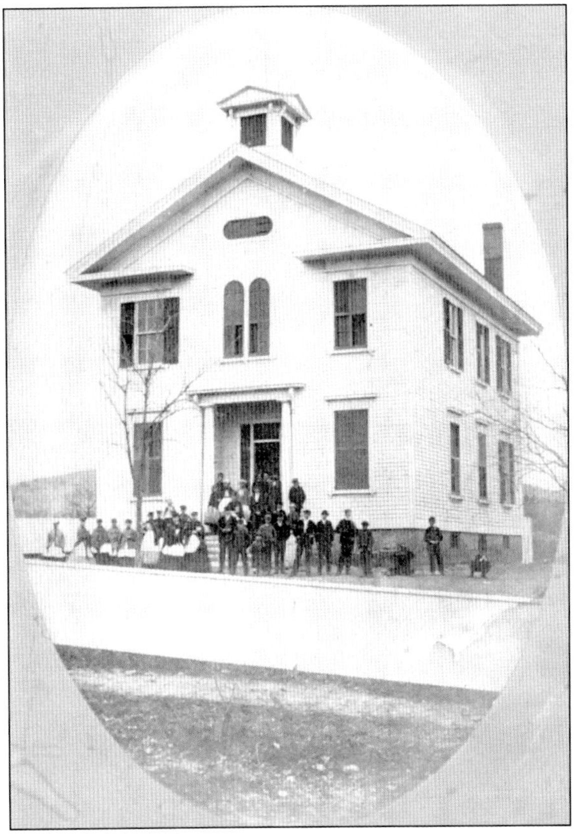

Professor H.M. Morrell stands with his students in front of the Academy, later known as Center School, facing Church Street in this 1864 photograph. Built in 1859, the school was Torrington's largest and stood at the corner of Prospect and Church Streets. At the time, there were only three homes north of the school, and the land to the northwest was brush. Center School served all elementary grades and eventually expanded to include high school students as well.

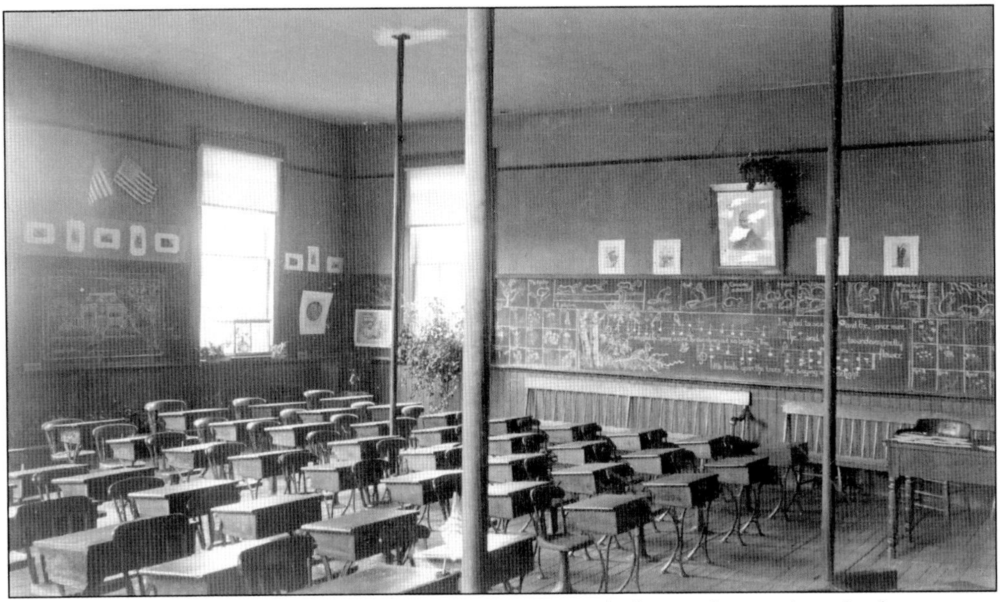

This undated photograph gives a rare glimpse into an early first-and-second-grade classroom at Center School. Mary L. Brooker wrote a detailed description on the back of the photograph, noting, among other things, the frieze of squirrels along the top of the blackboard and the glass case with stuffed birds in the window.

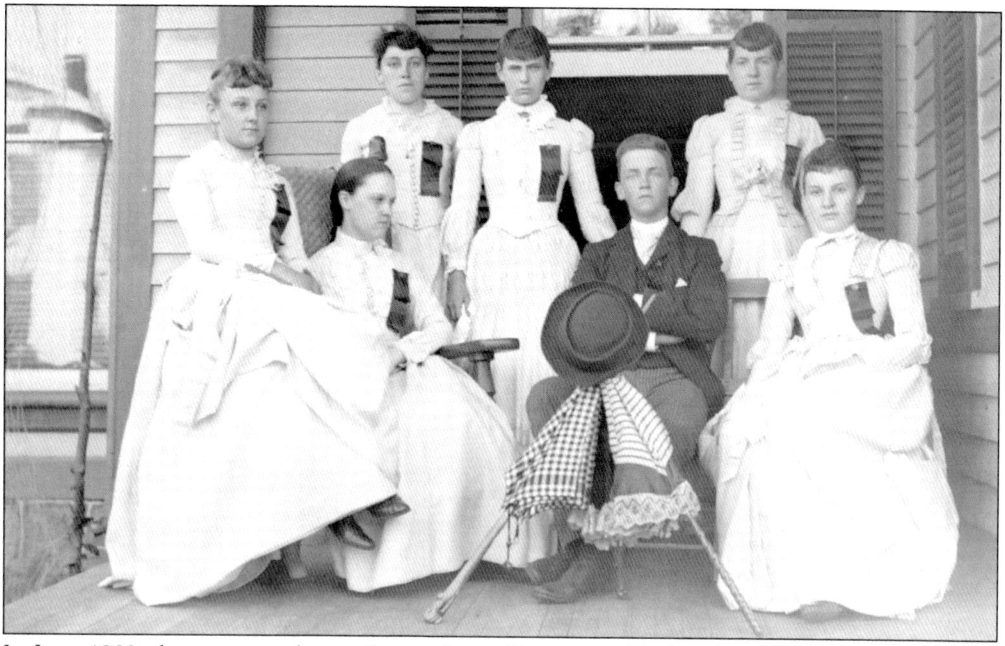

In June 1889, the seven students who made up Torrington High School's first graduating class posed for this photograph. From left to right, they are Emma Andrus, Margaret Sherman, Lucy Miner (salutatorian), Sophronia Coe, George Alvord (valedictorian), Ellen Joy, and Gertrude Hall. Three of the six women went on to attend college. Five became teachers, one of the few reputable jobs available to women at the time. Alvord, who graduated from Yale University, later became president of Progressive Manufacturing in Torrington.

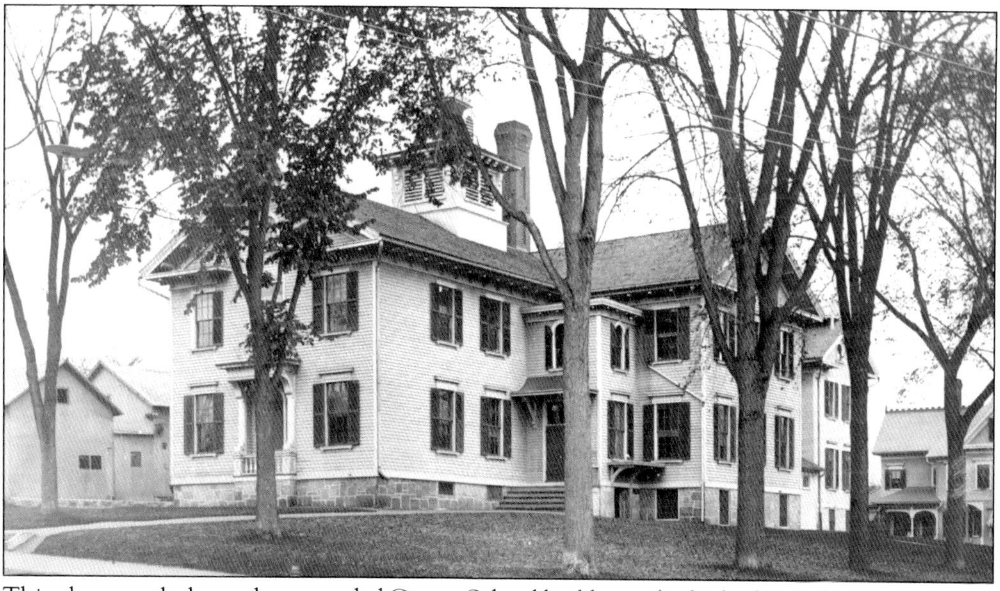

This photograph shows the expanded Center School building, which also housed the high school. Superintendent Edwin Forbes, a Yale graduate who came to Torrington in 1886, standardized the high school curriculum to include college, business, scientific, and English courses. Within a few years, a diploma from Torrington High School was sufficient for admission to many colleges. However, dozens of students never finished high school, opting instead to work or marry.

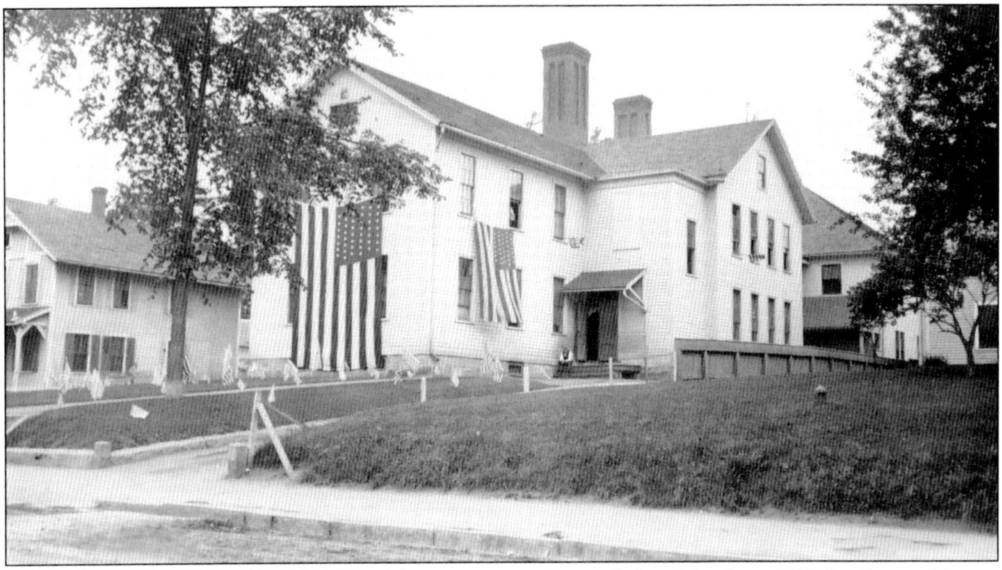

Torrington's early school buildings had few amenities. South School, built in 1878 (with an addition in 1889), had electricity only in the principal's office, where one light hung on a cord. A tin cup attached by a chain to the faucet was used for drinking water. The school was located on South Main Street approximately where the State Trade School was eventually built.

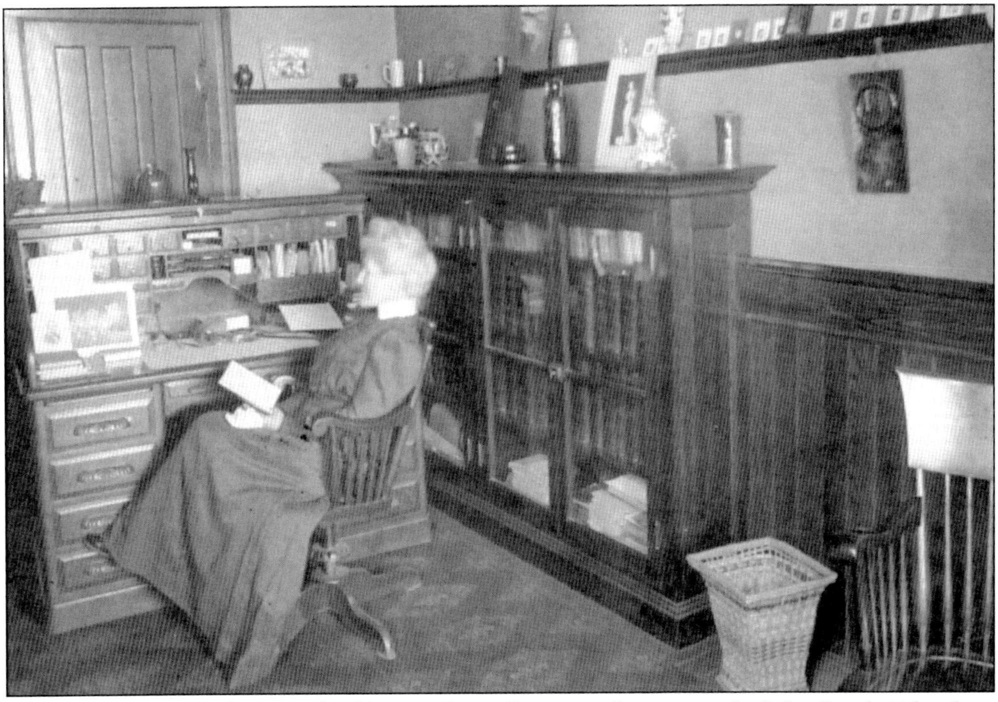

Margaret B. Carter, photographed here in her office, was the principal of the South School on South Main Street for 42 years and supervised the move from the original wooden schoolhouse to a new brick building down the street. Carter began her teaching career at age 15. When she retired in 1930 after 55 years in Torrington, her sister, Maude Wheeler, took over as principal.

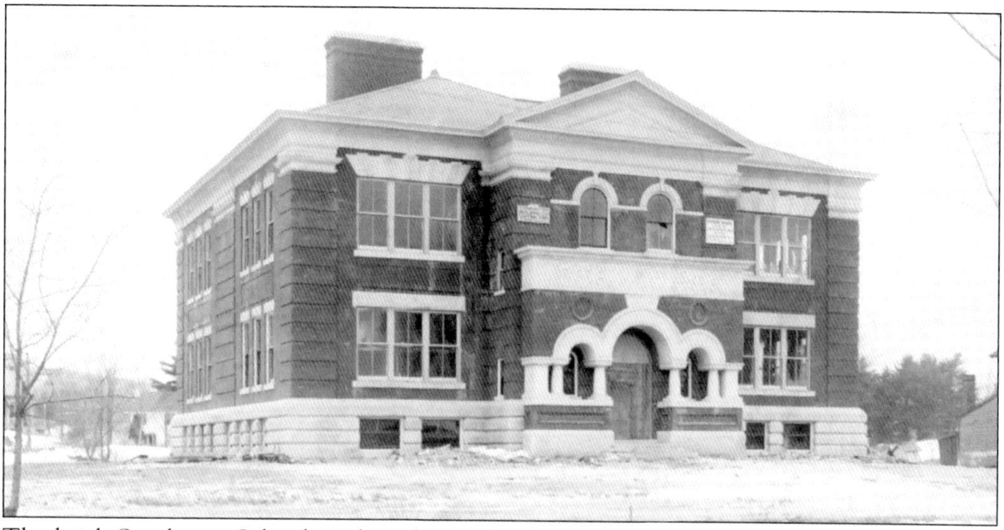

The brick Southwest School, with arches and columns of native granite, opened in 1905 on Litchfield Street with all the modern conveniences. The *Evening Register* reported that students could enjoy drinking fountains that released water "by the pressure of a button" and also a large indoor "dustless playground." Southwest was just one of several Torrington schools built at the turn of the century to accommodate the tremendous influx of children from immigrant families.

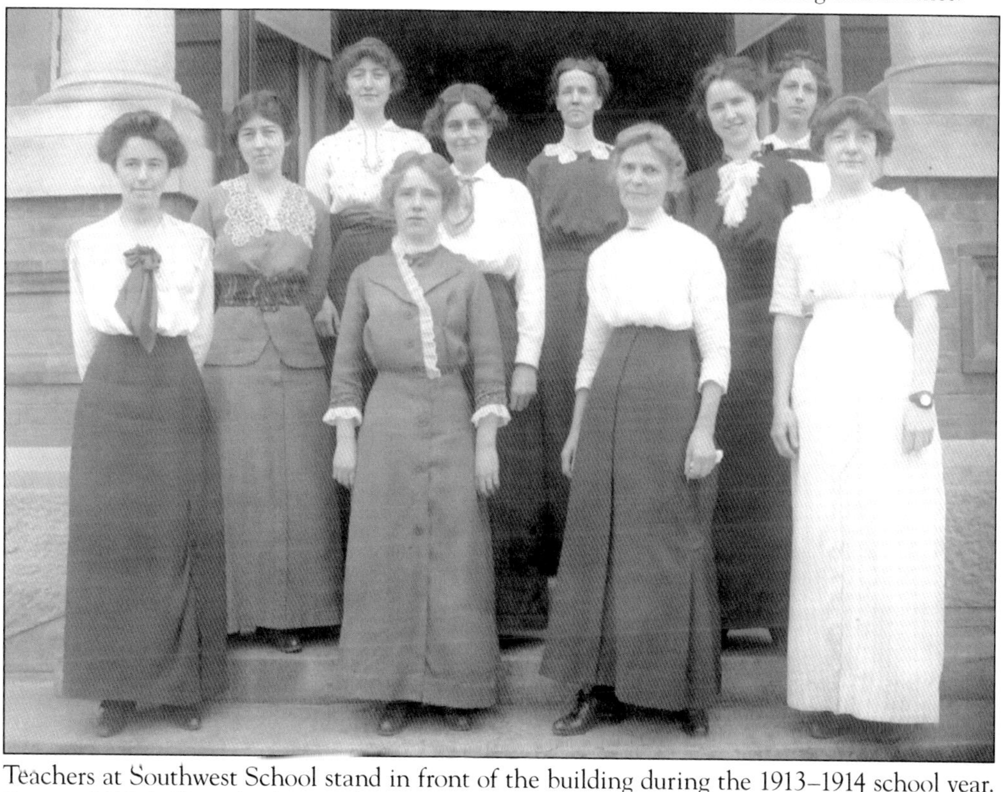

Teachers at Southwest School stand in front of the building during the 1913–1914 school year. Principal Edith Hine, looking rather stern, is in the center of the third row. At the time, most elementary school teachers in Torrington were young women. The annual teacher's salary in Torrington in 1914 was approximately $580.

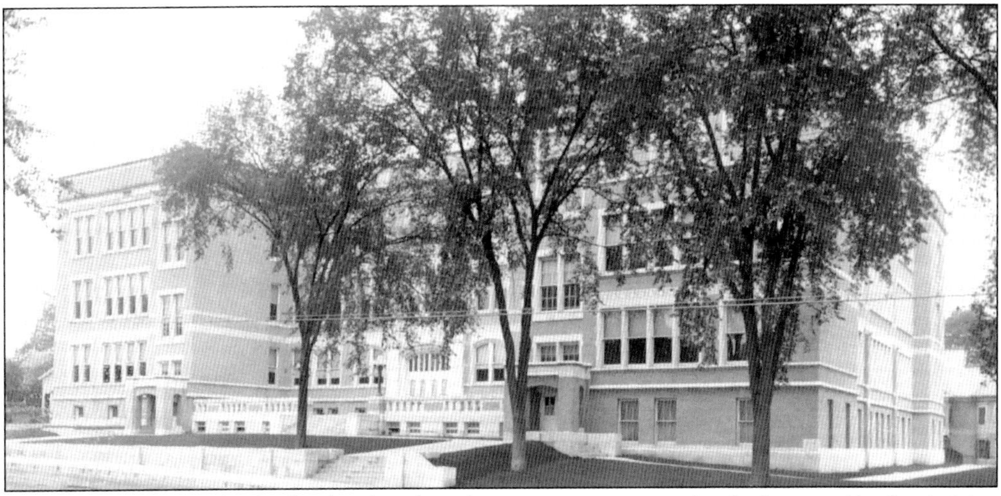

Torrington's old wooden high school and its observatory were completely destroyed by fire in May 1913. The new high school opened in September 1915 at the corner of Church and Prospect Streets with a capacity of 1,000 students. The building included the State Trade School, which enrolled enough boys to field six basketball teams and occupied several rooms in the basement. The name for the new building, "Torrington High School," was selected at a lively town meeting.

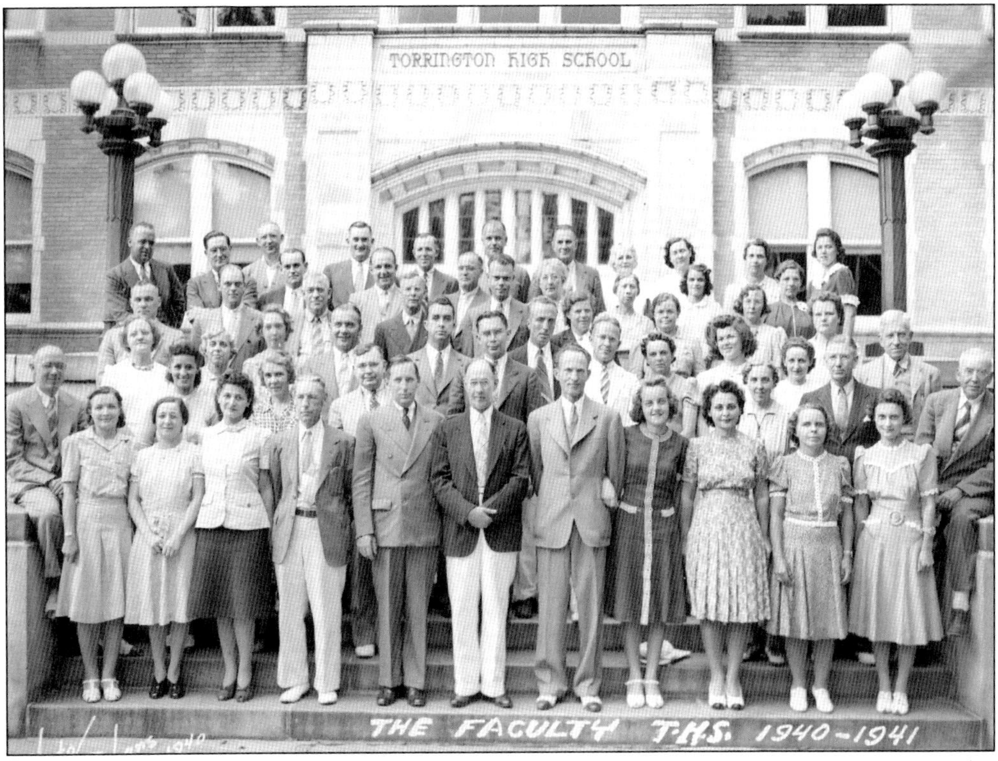

This photograph of the 1941 Torrington High School faculty includes several teachers who taught for decades in Torrington and became household names, including Tracy Conway, Clifford Mignery, Peter Dranginis, Inez Stoekert, and Connie Donahue. The sizeable staff shown here had more than doubled in 20 years because of a tremendous surge in high school enrollment during the Great Depression.

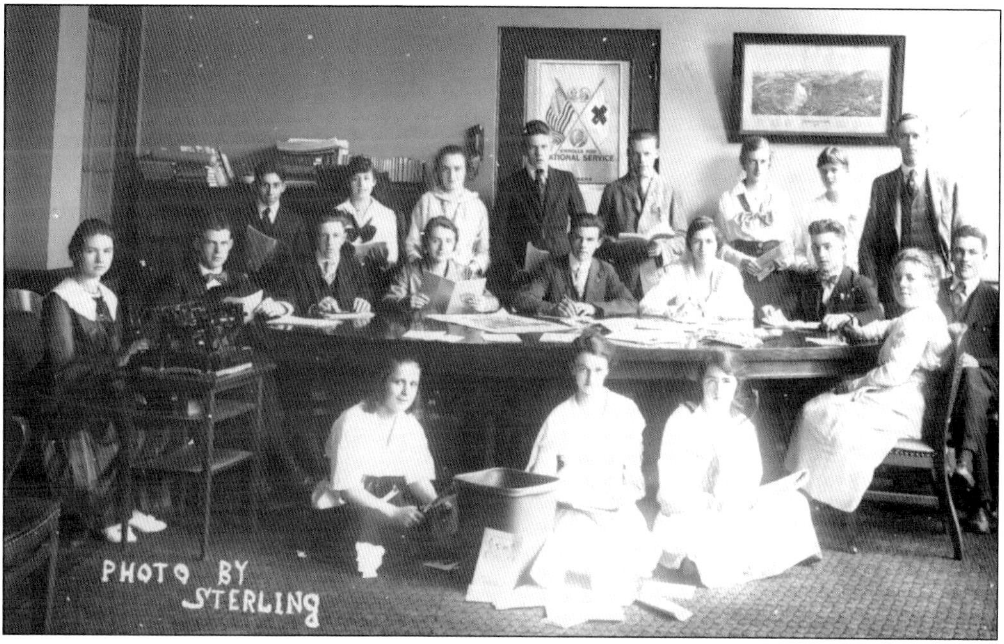

Reporters for Torrington High School's magazine the *Tabula* gathered for this group photograph. First published in 1893, the magazine included student, sports, and alumni news along with literary submissions. English instructor I. Burton Dunfield stands at farthest right in the third row. Next to him is freshman reporter Catherine Calhoun, future Torrington High School librarian and longtime director of the Torrington Historical Society.

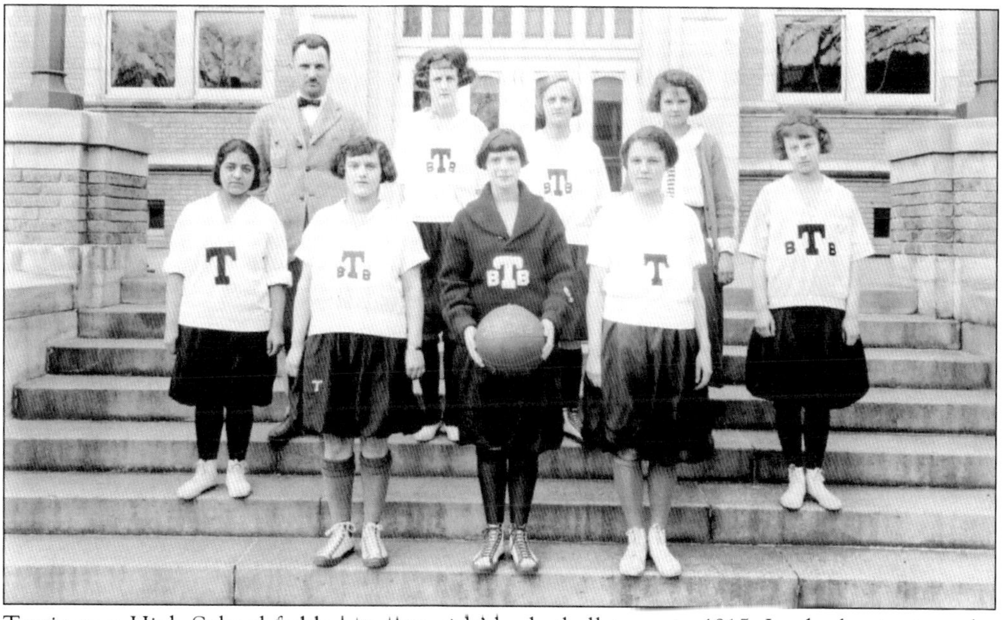

Torrington High School fielded its first girls' basketball team in 1915. In the beginning, the girls mostly played against each other. By the time of this 1922–1923 photograph, however, the team had a regular coach, Tracey Garey, and played other teams from around the state and from Torrington's recreation leagues. Inez Stoeckert (second from right in the top row) later taught business courses at the high school for 38 years.

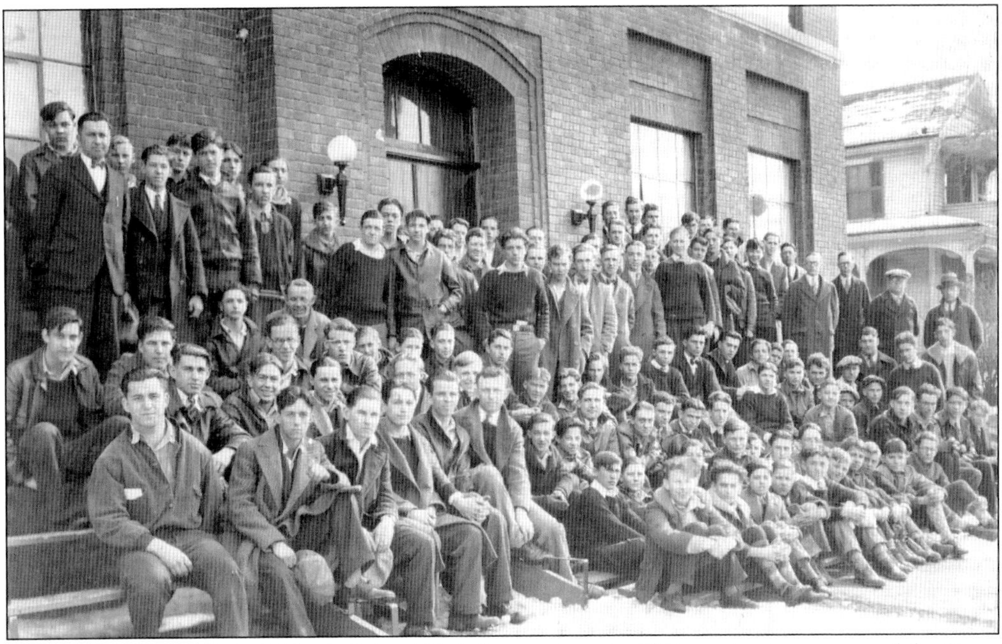

This photograph, labeled "Trade School Kids," was taken in 1931 on the front steps of the State Trade School on South Main Street. The building, which was designed and built in large part by the students themselves, was completed in 1926. Louis Basquin, the gentleman with the bow tie at upper left, was a machine shop instructor known for being "tough but fair." (Elizabeth Kaczmarcyk.)

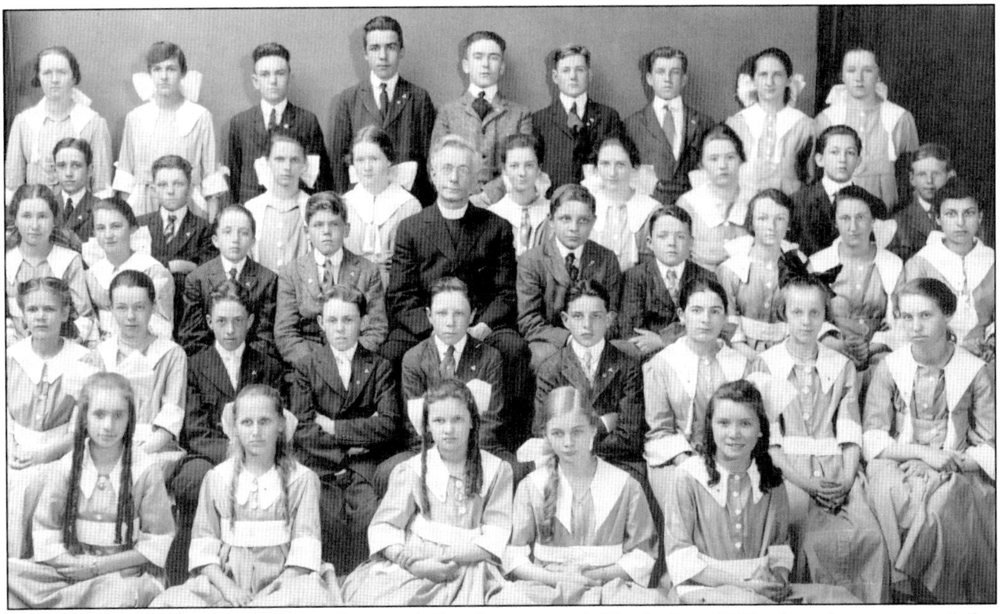

The 1918 graduating class of St. Francis School poses with Fr. Arthur O'Keefe, who presented the diplomas. The students were taught by the Irish Sisters of Mercy, including Sister Mary Loyola, who offered sewing lessons on Friday afternoons. In 1917, the girls made their graduation dresses for $1.05 apiece. St. Francis School, located behind St. Francis Church, opened in September 1893 with 391 students. It was Torrington's only Catholic school until Sacred Heart School opened in 1922.

Five

BUSINESSES

Torrington is a collection of neighborhoods. During the first half of the 20th century, these areas were particularly vibrant and anchored by neighborhood schools, taverns, drugstores, and family-owned markets. The north end, south end, east side, and west side each had its own character and convenient places to shop and socialize. The primary shopping district, however, was downtown on Main Street between Church Street and the Naugatuck River, with stores also clustered on Water Street to the west and East Main Street to the east.

Photographs from the 1860s show the beginnings of Torrington's downtown with several large inns and smaller stores in wooden buildings along Main Street. Gradually, the commercial footprint expanded, and multilevel brick buildings replaced the wooden structures. Local citizens and travelers enjoyed the proximity of downtown Torrington's wide variety of stores, banks, theaters, restaurants, and churches, as well as the library, city hall, and YMCA. The train depot was just a few blocks to the west, and after 1909, Coe Memorial Park offered a lovely green oasis a short walk over Center Bridge. Unfortunately, proximity to the river made downtown Torrington vulnerable to flooding. The August 1955 flood was particularly devastating to downtown businesses, destroying many and forcing the relocation of others.

The North End commercial district was another important shopping destination. The construction of the trolley line in 1897 along north Main Street led to an increase in housing and small businesses, including fruit and grocery stores, restaurants, shoe stores, barbershops, and pharmacies. Although the stores in downtown Torrington were larger, more numerous, and offered a wider variety of products, by 1930, North End shoppers could find pretty much all they needed without going to the city center. Anchored by the North School, St. Maron Church, and several factories, Torrington's North End became a desirable place to live and shop.

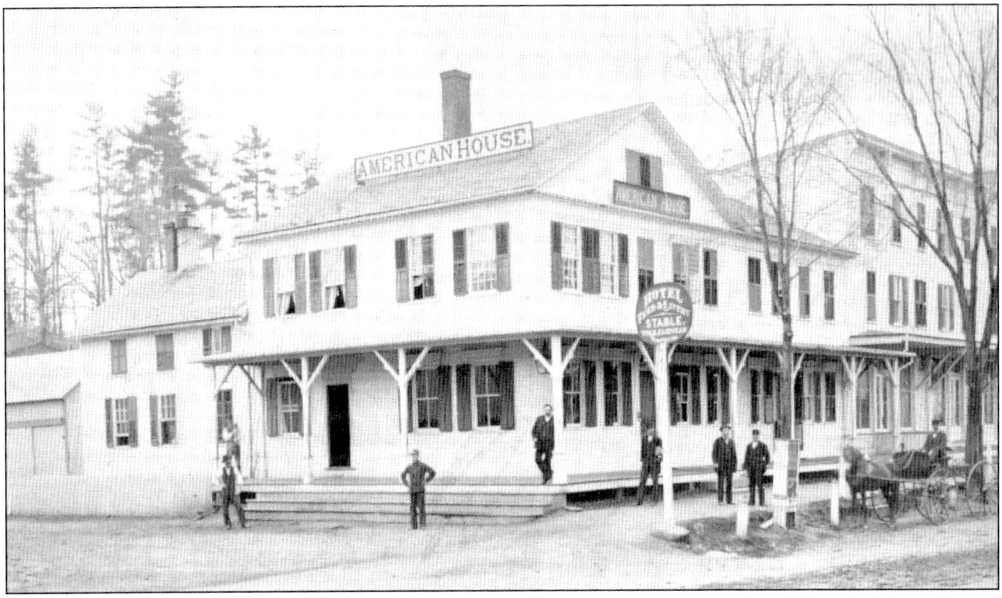

In 1826, Capt. Samuel Brady built the American House on the east side of South Main Street not far from Center Bridge. The hotel featured a spacious dining room and parlor and 25 "well-appointed sleeping rooms." It served short-term visitors as well as guests who boarded for years. By the time it was partially torn down in 1932, the American House was one of the few remaining wooden structures in downtown Torrington.

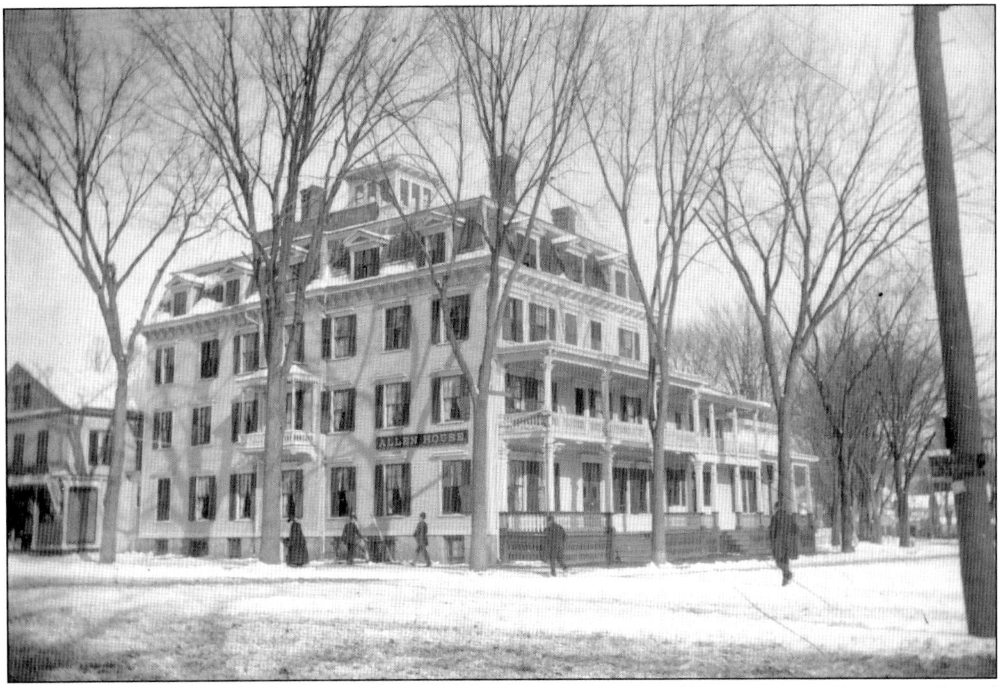

Long a landmark at the corner of East Main and Main Streets, the Allen House Hotel was purchased by Henry Allen in 1856. One of few hotels in Torrington, the Allen House was so successful that a third story was added to the building in 1868. It was demolished in 1935 after being severely damaged by a fire. Today, the site of the hotel is occupied by the Allen Block.

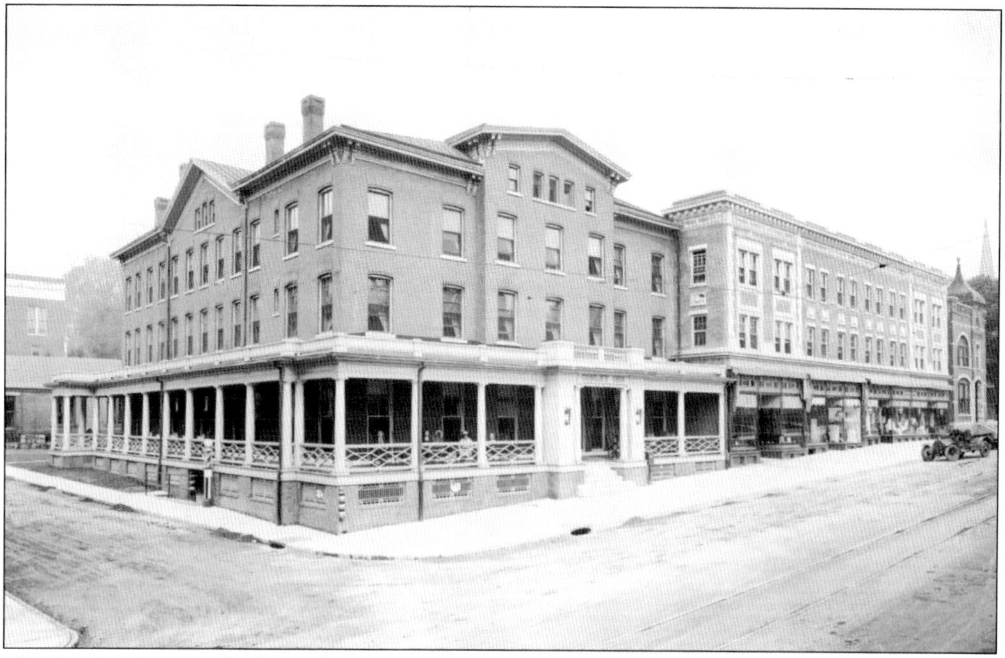

The Conley Inn was built on the corner of Main Street and Maiden Lane by Frank Conley and his wife, Alice Tryon Conley, former proprietors of the Allen House. The gala opening reception on July 18, 1891, drew over 1,000 guests. The inn boasted a billiard room and a parlor that was "a model of taste" and featured an elegant walnut piano and large writing desks. The dining room could seat 150 guests. The 52 uniquely furnished guest rooms were made even more comfortable with quilts made by Alice's mother, and the wainscoted halls, carpeted in velvet, added to the hotel's charm. The Conley Inn had its own stables and carriages to bring guests to and from the train depot, which was located just a short distance up the hill. The photograph below, taken by John Norton Brooks in the mid-1890s, shows one of the inn's carriages at the depot. In 1956, the lodging was renamed the Yankee Pedlar Inn.

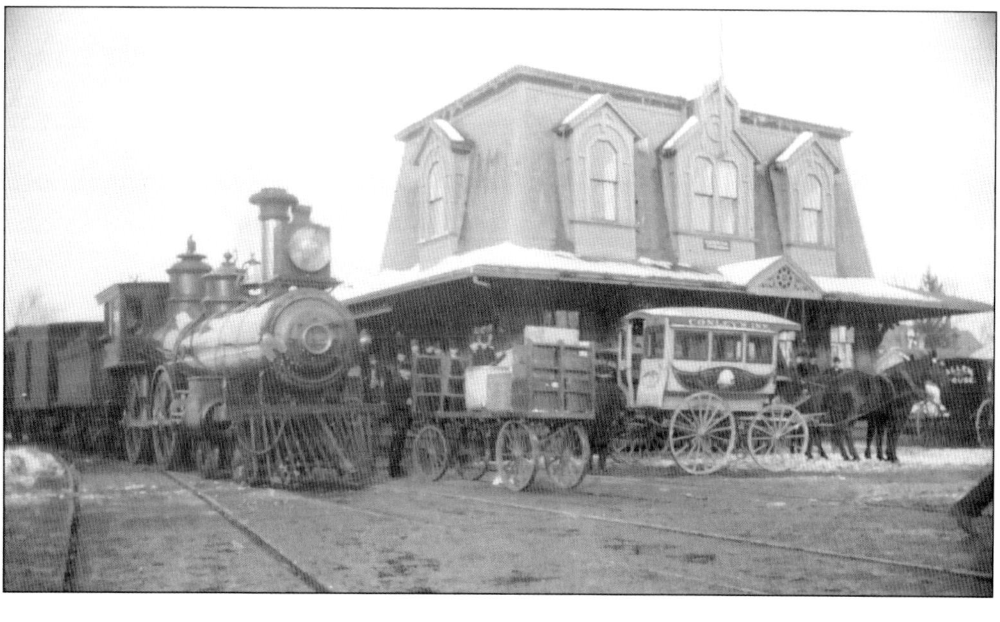

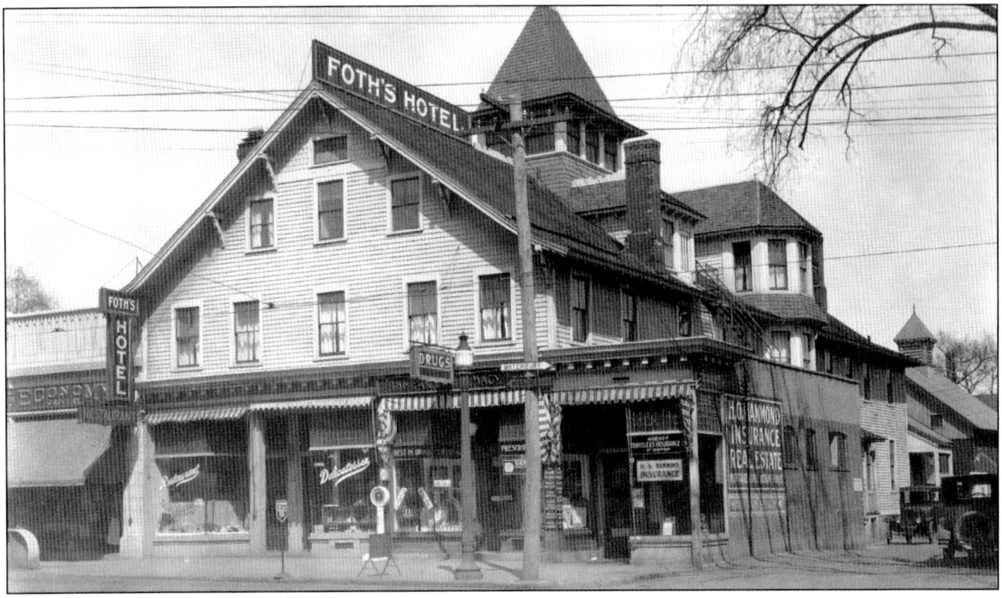

William Farnham, a popular businessman, converted an auditorium and roller-skating rink into the Farnham House Hotel on South Main Street just south of Center Bridge. The hotel, which opened in 1886, was destroyed in the 1955 flood (see page 60). The building underwent a significant remodel in 1920, when verandas were removed and storefronts were added. These changes are evident in this 1939 photograph taken when August Foth ran the hotel.

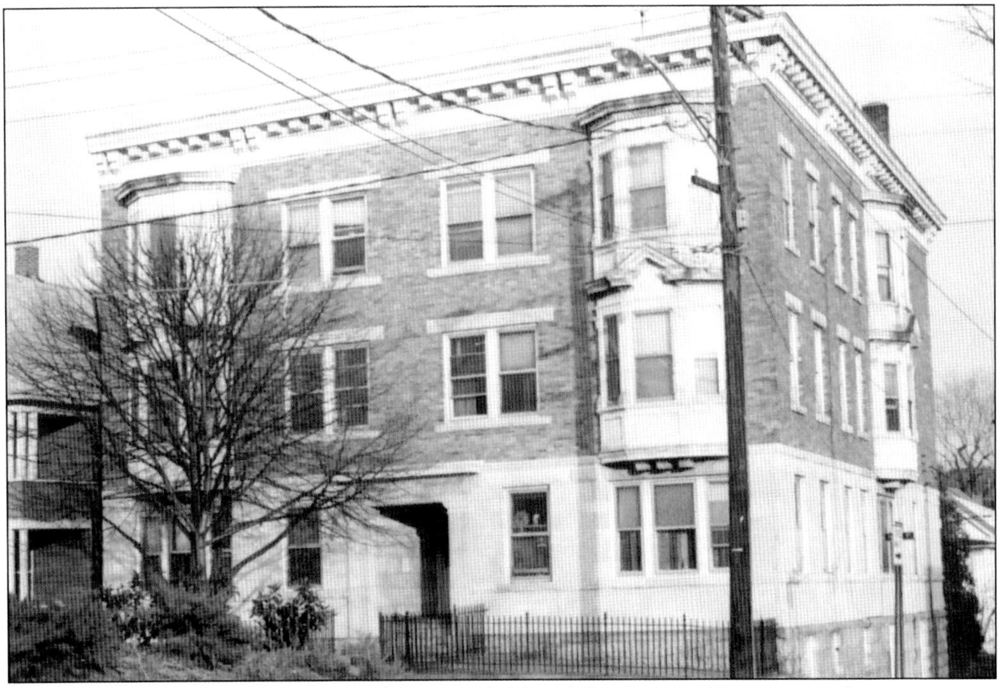

The Burmor, located at the corner of Main and Alvord Streets, was Torrington's first apartment building. Built by William Morrison and his wife, Ina Burton Morrison, in 1913, the Burmor offered seven spacious, sunny apartments and featured a lovely exterior of limestone, brick, and pressed metal ornamentation.

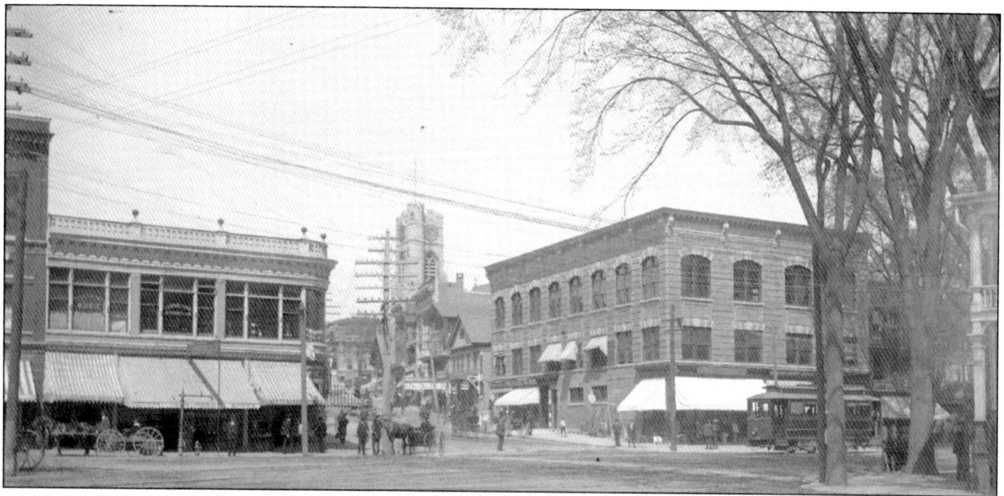

In the photograph above, the Torrington–Winsted trolley heads through Center Square. Construction of the 12-mile trolley route, including a steep spur to Highland Lake, began in April 1897 and was completed by August 1. According to *Rossiterville and the First Valley Road between Winsted and Torrington*, some had opposed the project, including Dr. Samuel Woodward, who opined that "no living creature could or would travel it save snakes, polecats, woodchucks and foxes." He could not have been more wrong. The 50-minute trip from downtown Torrington through the North End and on to Winsted was immediately popular, especially when people wanted to travel to football games or special concerts at Highland Lake. The trolley made its final run in January 1929; its demise was collateral damage resulting from the increasing popularity of the automobile. Jerry Canty, master mechanic with the Torrington-Winsted Trolley line, poses with his dog in the image below.

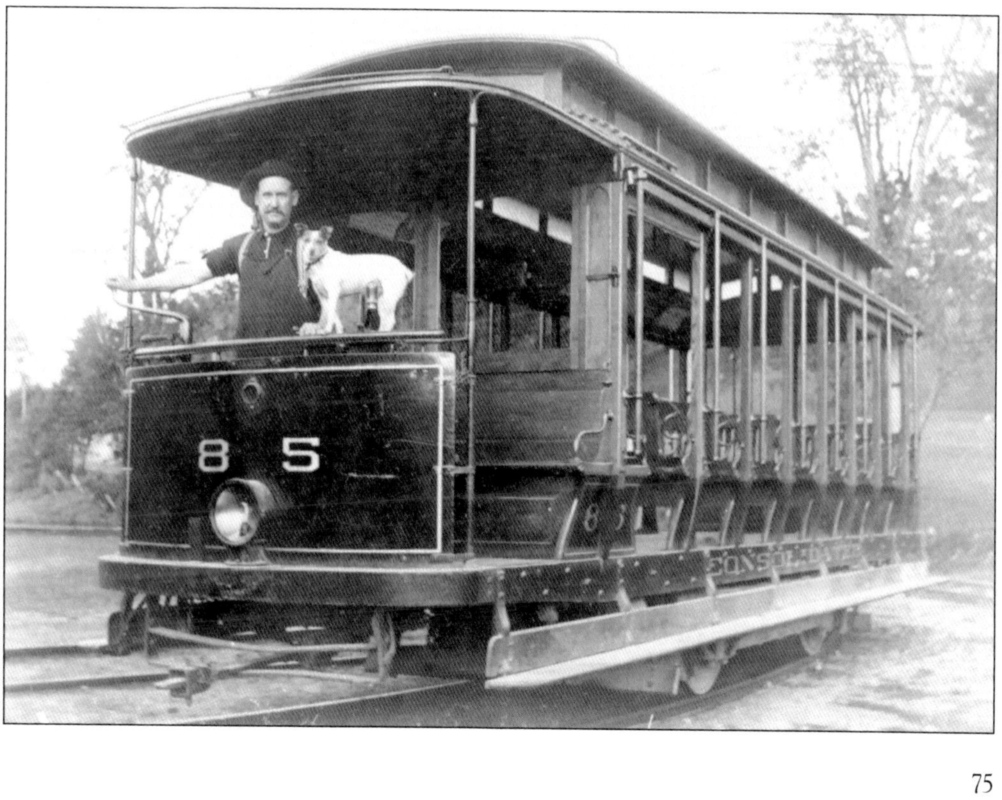

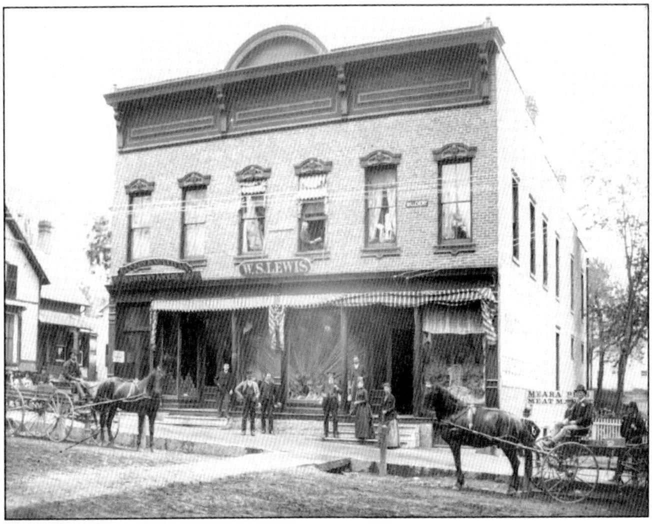

The W.S. Lewis Company, built by Walter S. Lewis on Main Street in 1883, was a marvel. It relied on its own power plant for electricity and featured inclined platforms in the rear to ease loading and unloading. Modern methods of merchandising were adopted, including separate departments within the store. Due to its large inventory, W.S. Lewis was known locally as the "Big Store." It was later taken over by Lewis's son-in-law, William W. Mertz, and renamed W.W. Mertz.

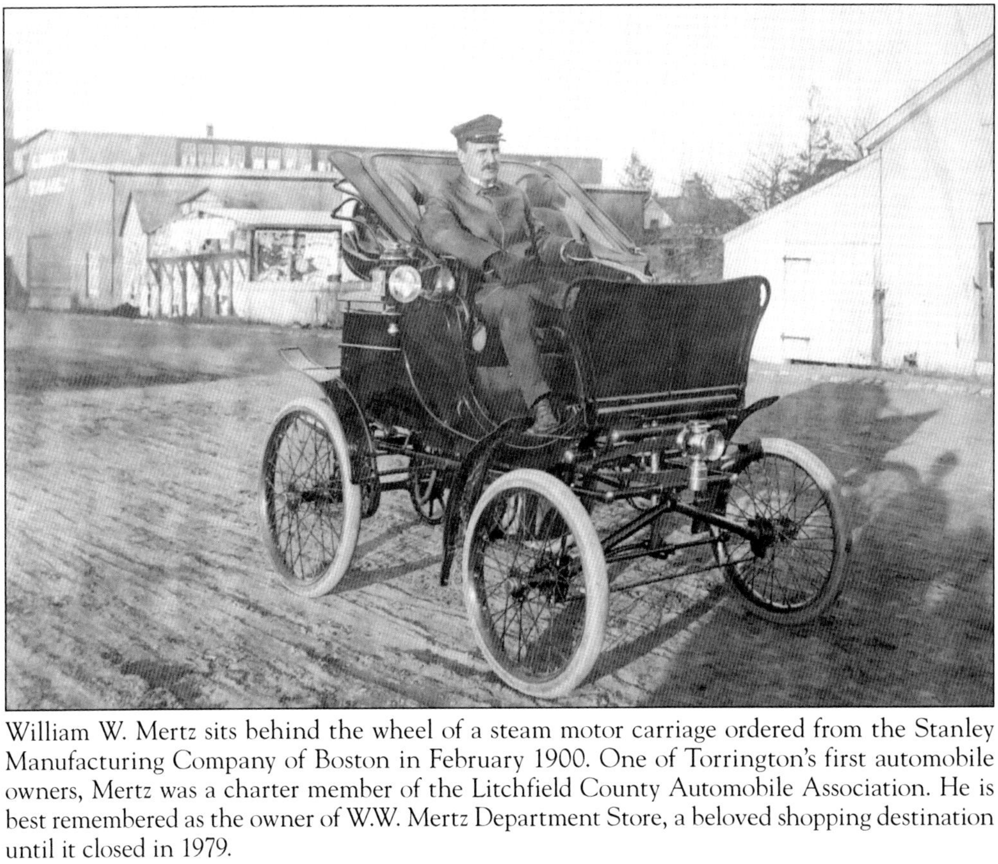

William W. Mertz sits behind the wheel of a steam motor carriage ordered from the Stanley Manufacturing Company of Boston in February 1900. One of Torrington's first automobile owners, Mertz was a charter member of the Litchfield County Automobile Association. He is best remembered as the owner of W.W. Mertz Department Store, a beloved shopping destination until it closed in 1979.

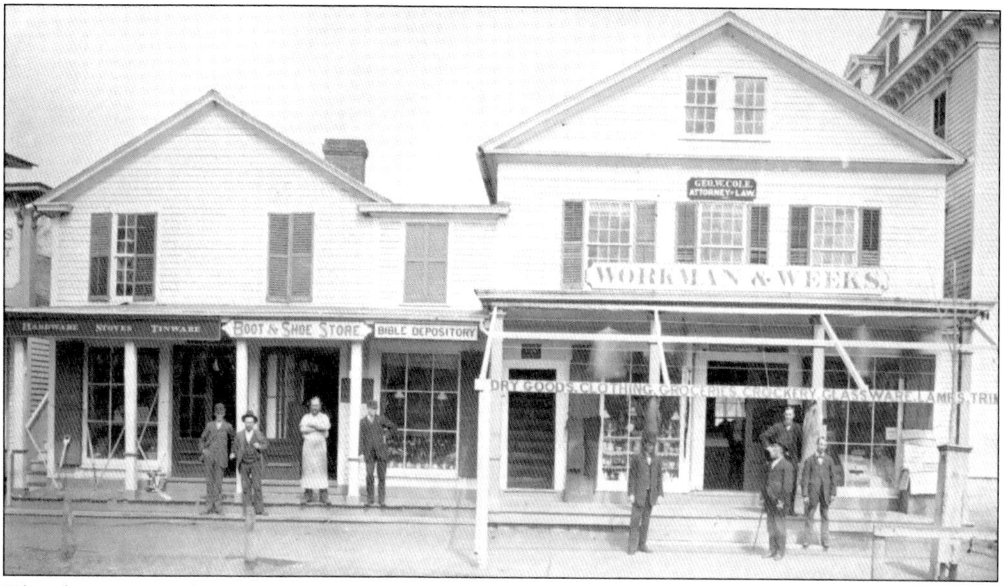

This late-1870s photograph features Workman & Weeks general store, which operated on Torrington's Main Street for several decades north of the intersection of Main and East Main Streets. Note the Bible Depository at center left.

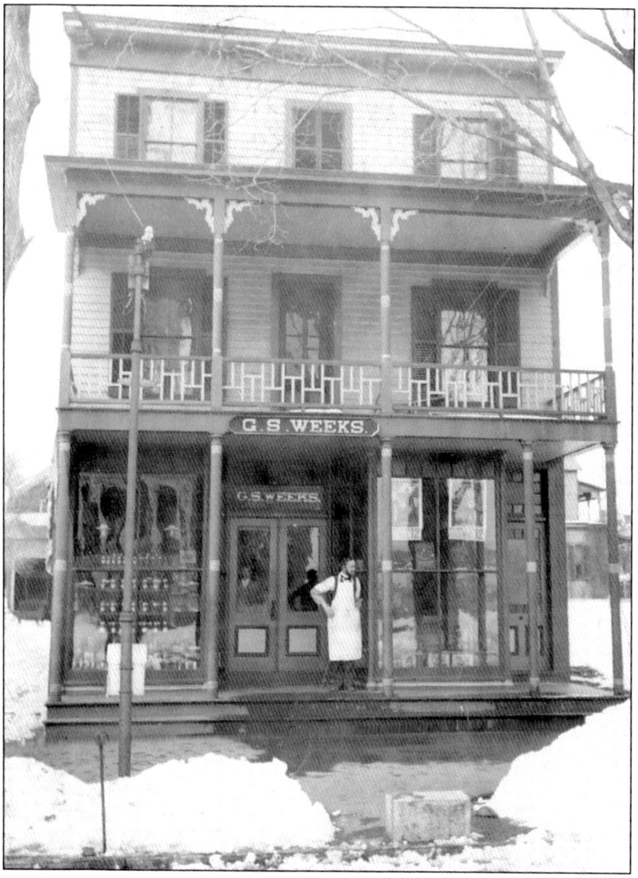

George Seymour Weeks opened his own grocery store on Main Street in 1889 and later constructed this wood-frame building, known as the Weeks Block, across the street from city hall. Weeks died unexpectedly in 1904 at the age of 57. His obituary notes that he was "a man of stainless reputation, with no enemies, honored and respected by all, a man who devoted every moment of time to his business."

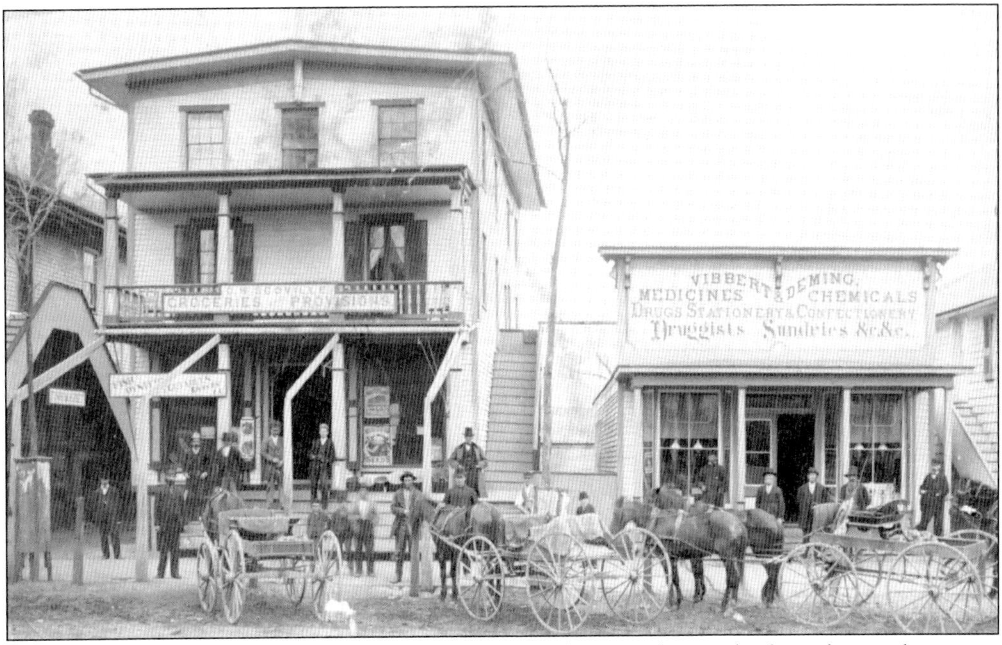

The Vibert & Deming Pharmacy, shown in this 1880s photograph, was the first of many drugstores to occupy this location south of the Warner Theatre. Charles Scoville built the one-story structure around 1870, and a second story was added in 1889. The last drugstore at this location, Opperman's Pharmacy, run by Ernest Opperman, closed its doors in 1998.

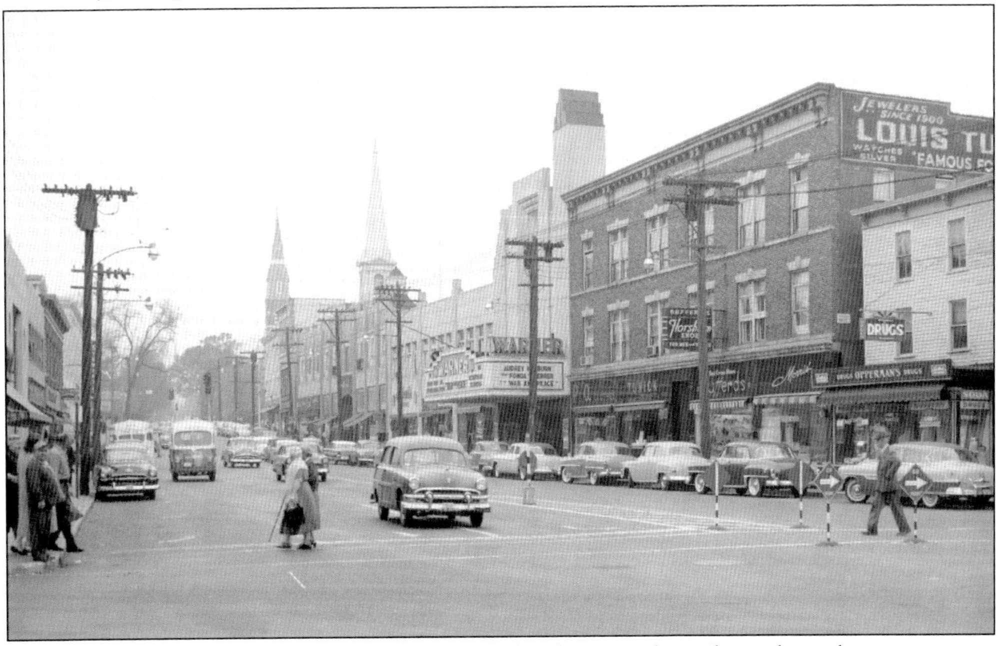

This photograph of downtown Main Street includes the area where the earliest pharmacies were located. Also visible is Torrington's Art Deco Warner Theatre. Built in 1930 by Warner Bros. at a cost of $700,000, the theater was saved from destruction in 1983 by a community campaign. A refurbished Warner Theatre, looking as good as it did in its heyday, now hosts concerts, plays, and other performances.

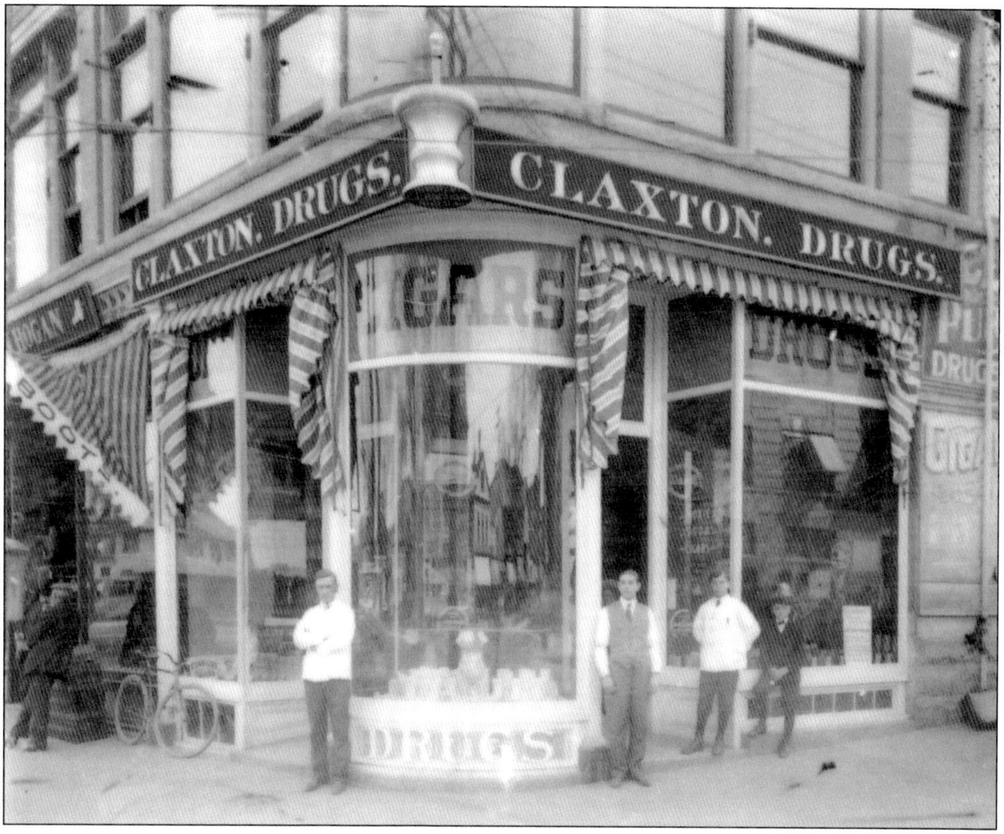

The photograph above shows Claxton's Drug Store at its corner location around 1915. Below, John Claxton (left) and his employee John Jarmosik pose behind the counter several decades later in a c. 1952 photograph. Claxton, who came to Torrington in 1887, began clerking at Lyons' Drug Store at the corner of Water and Main Streets. Lyons', with its onyx soda fountain and marble floors, was a busy, high-class establishment in which to learn the pharmacy trade. Claxton took over the business in 1912, and it thrived for four more decades, offering everything from ice-cream sundaes to medications and leeches. Photographer James Miller is visible in the mirror to the right of the two men.

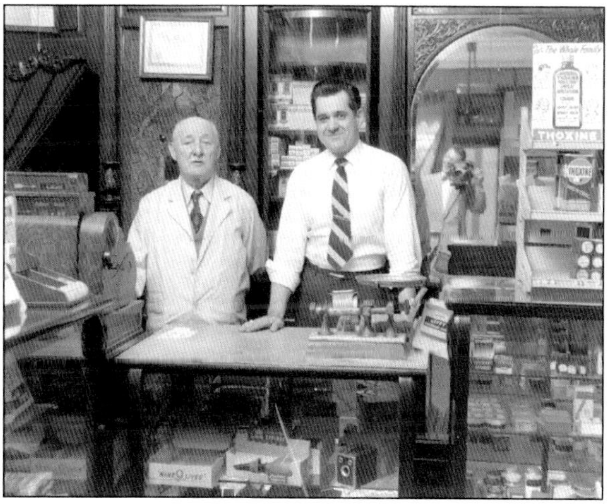

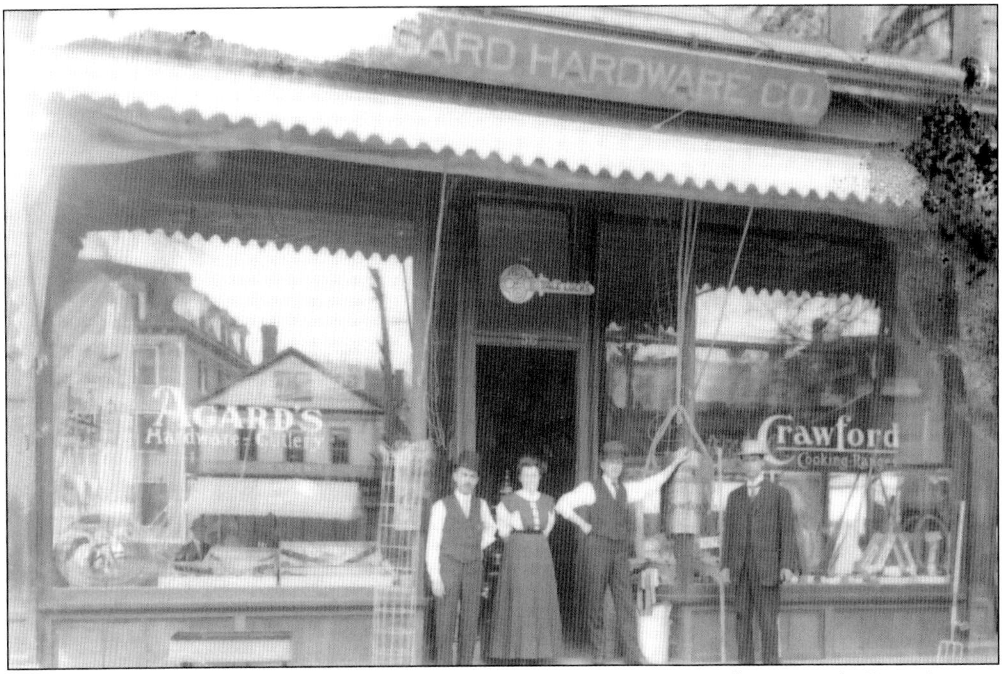

Agard Hardware Company opened in 1864 at the northwest corner of Main and Water Streets. In 1903, a new, modern brick building replaced the original wood structure. As this c. 1920 photograph shows, Agard sold a wide range of merchandise, including farm implements, hardware, cutlery, and stoves. After two damaging fires in the early 1930s, the Agard Block was remodeled and the third floor was removed.

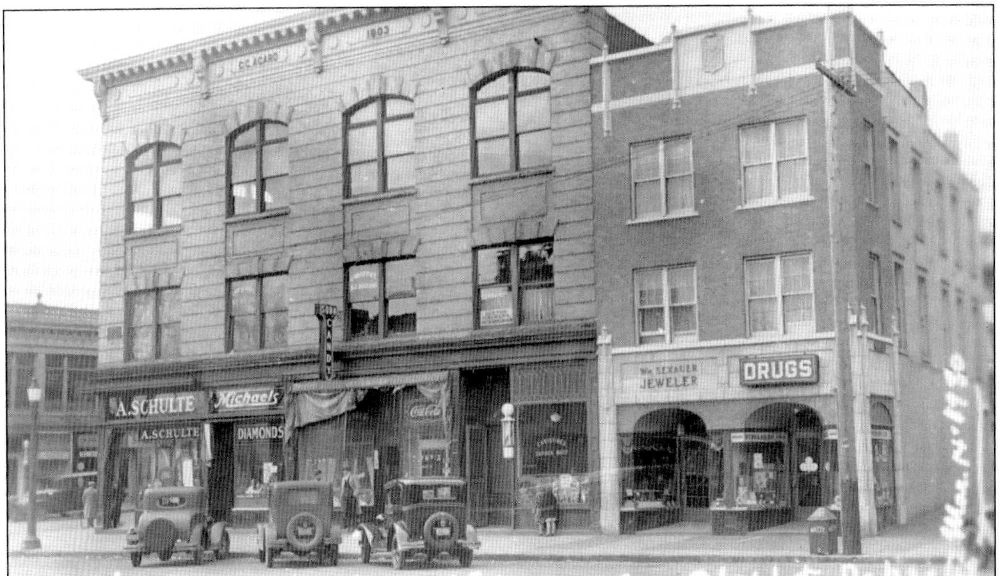

This 1930 photograph of the Agard Block also offers a glimpse of Michaels' jewelry store, which opened in Torrington in 1928 under the direction of Harry Michaels. During the Great Depression, the store gave away canaries as a promotion to attract customers. Michaels continues to operate as a family business not far from its original Main Street location.

The late 1890s saw the construction of many brick buildings along Water Street, including Morrison's Hardware at the corner of Water and Prospect Streets. Built in 1896 by William H. Morrison, a plumber and tinsmith who had moved to Torrington five years earlier, the firm remained in business until 2010.

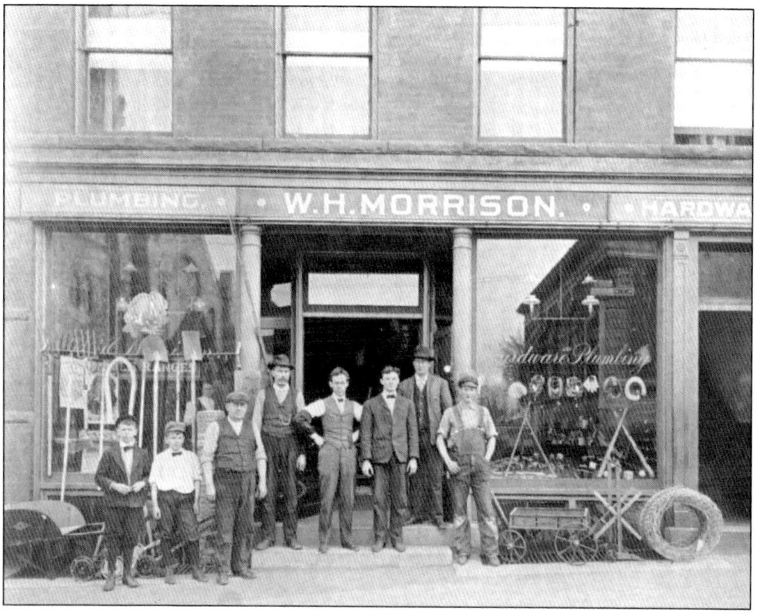

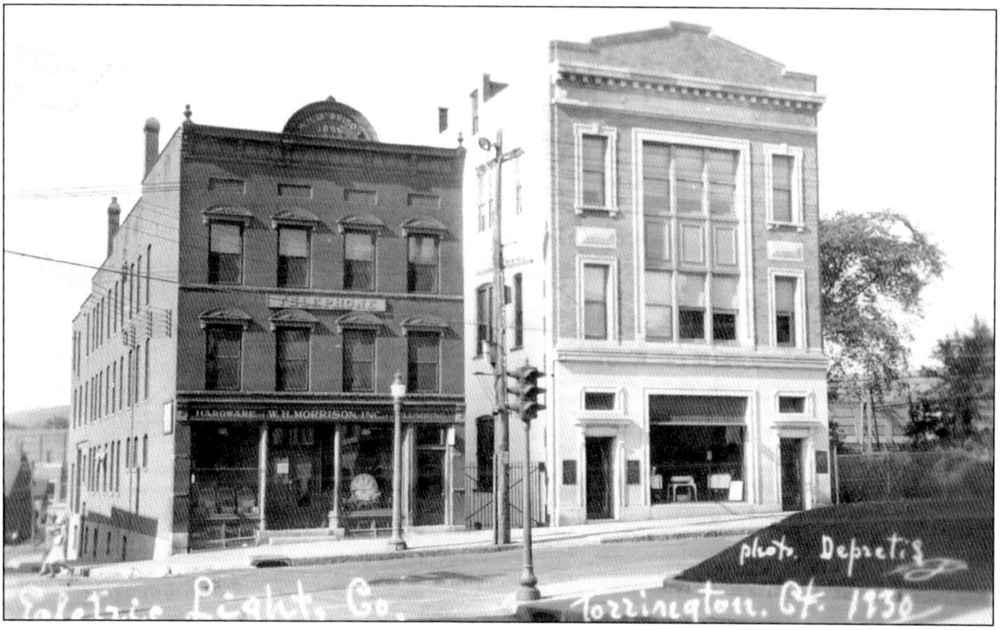

The insurance company Brooks, Todd, & McNeil is located at 69 Water Street in the building to the right of Morrison's in the photograph. The Torrington Electric Light Company, established in 1886, constructed the building in 1911 and had its offices there for many years.

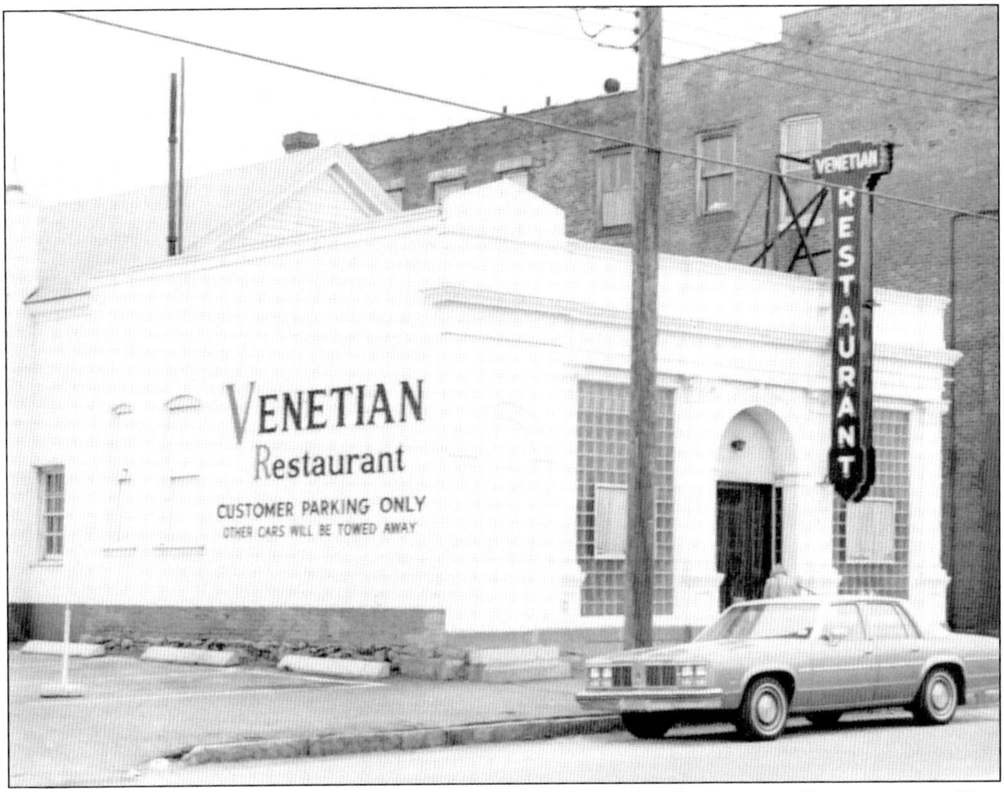

Charles and Antoinette Giampolo opened Torrington's landmark Venetian Restaurant on East Main Street in 1925, promising that "The Most Delicious Italian Foods Will Be Served." Since 1970, Michael DiLullo and his family have owned and operated the restaurant, which continues to be both a local favorite and a culinary destination for out-of-town visitors.

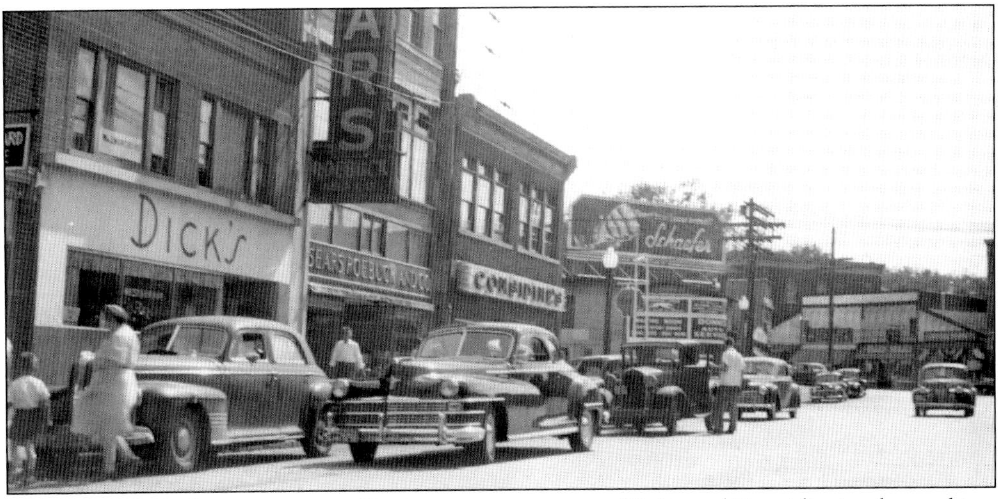

This photograph shows two iconic Torrington restaurants—Dick's and Considine's—located just down the street from the Venetian. In 1945, Richard T. Cooke opened Dick's at 26 East Main Street, promising "good food and excellent service" along with "modern furnishings and air conditioning." In 2008, then-owner Raymond Colangelo sold the business, disappointing many loyal customers, some of whom had eaten at Dick's for decades.

Angelo Scarpelli, along with George Fritch, started Scarpelli's as a roadside hamburger and hot dog stand on South Main Street in 1934. Fritch left a year later, but Scarpelli continued to sell hot dogs for a nickel apiece from his food truck. Scarpelli's, located on Migeon Avenue since 1947, still offers family dining. Angelo Scarpelli's son, Joseph, poses in front of the restaurant.

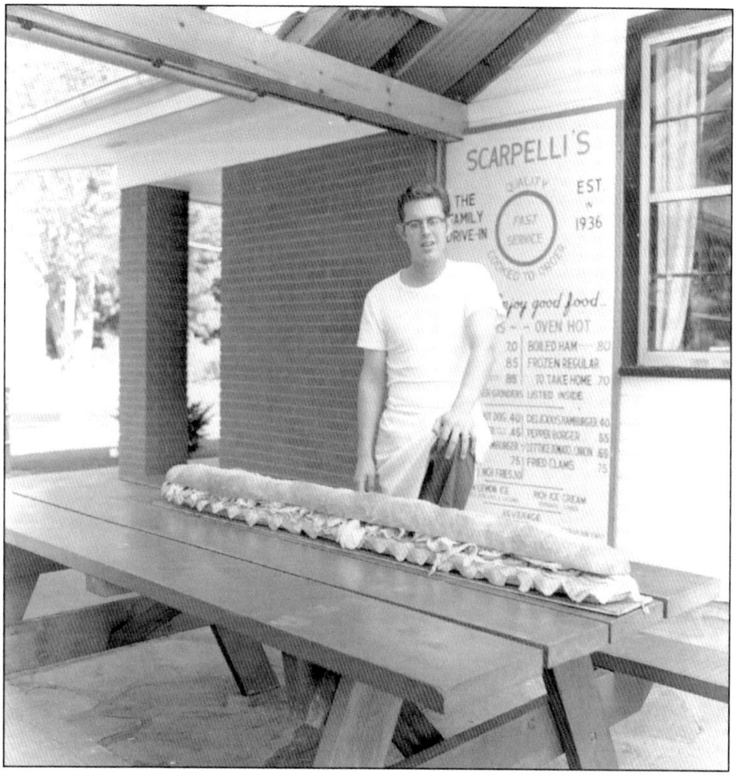

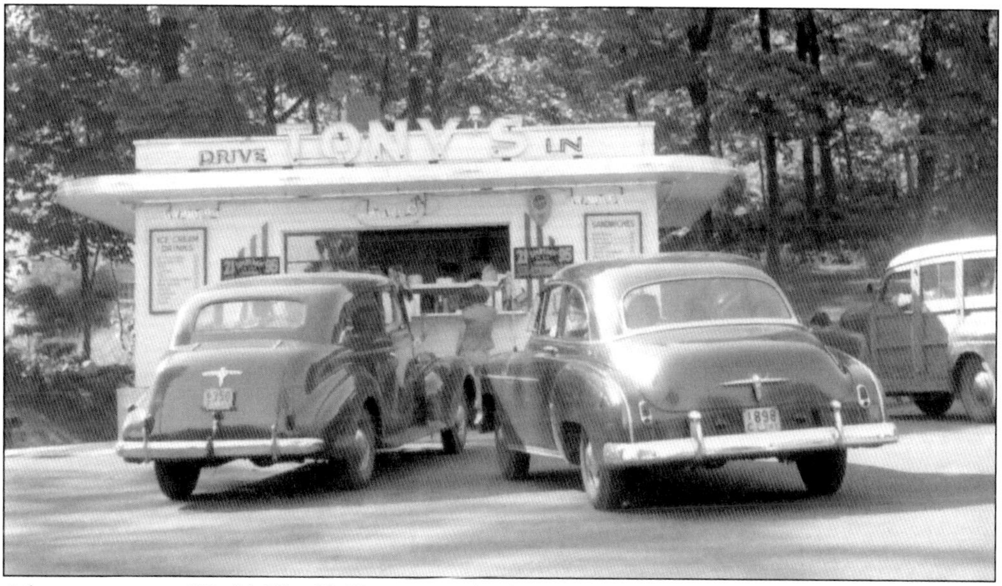

After serving in World War II, Tony Miscikoski returned to Torrington and opened Tony's Jumbo Stand on Butler Street in 1946, serving hot dogs, hamburgers, and grinders. In 1949, just a few years before this photograph was taken, Miscikoski moved the restaurant to its current location on Migeon Avenue and renamed it Tony's Drive-In. With his good fast food and colorful personality, Miscikoski made Tony's Drive-In one of Torrington's most popular dining spots. (Miscikoski family.)

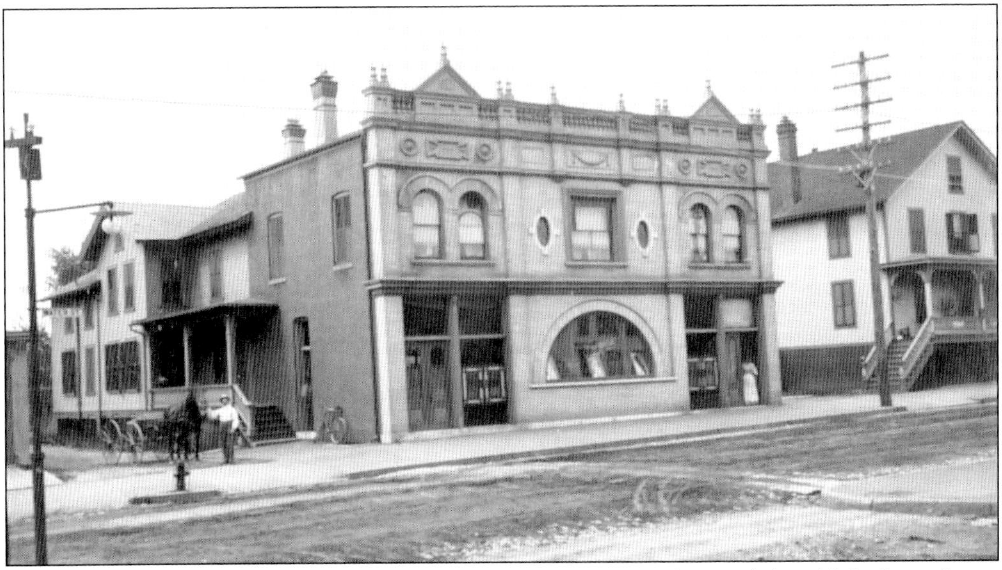

Pictured here around 1900, this building at 131 Water Street (west of the old firehouse) was home to a succession of businesses. In 1934, the Polish National Home purchased the structure and celebrated with a parade from St. Mary's Church and a dance in the ballroom. Most local ethnic groups operated clubs like this, where people could socialize informally at the bar and large parties could also be accommodated. A handful of these clubs still exist in Torrington. (Zbigniew Rozbicki.)

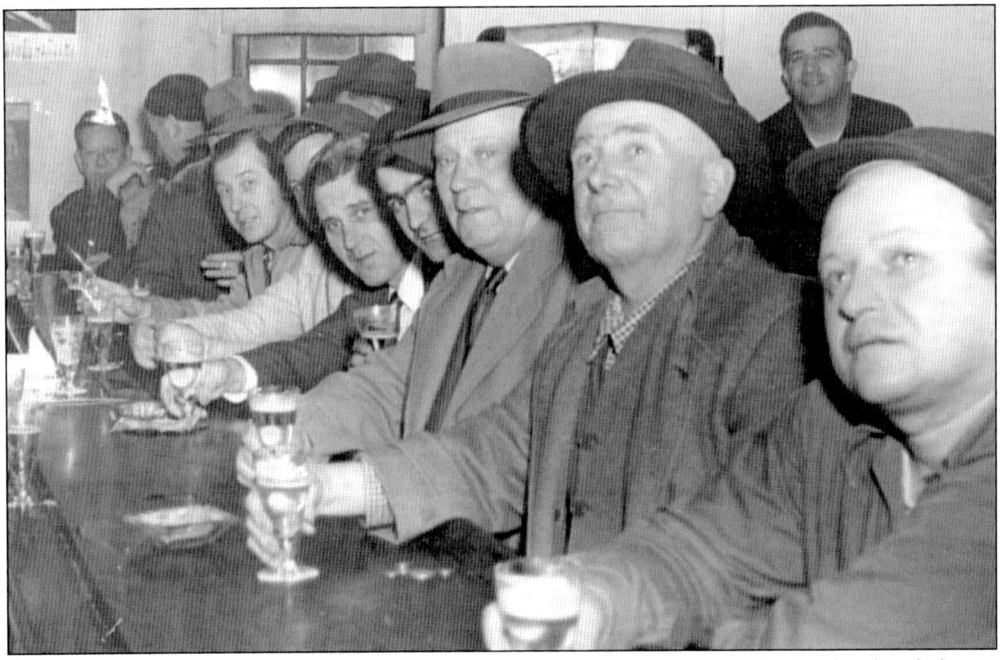

When Prohibition ended in 1933, Gus Giarnese converted the stable attached to his family home on Washington Avenue into a small tavern. Known as Gus's Stables, it was very popular with musicians. The Stables, the longest-running tavern in Connecticut, is currently owned by Michael Hand and his wife, Bonnie, and is still going strong. This photograph is believed to have been taken when the Barella family owned the business. (Michael Hand.)

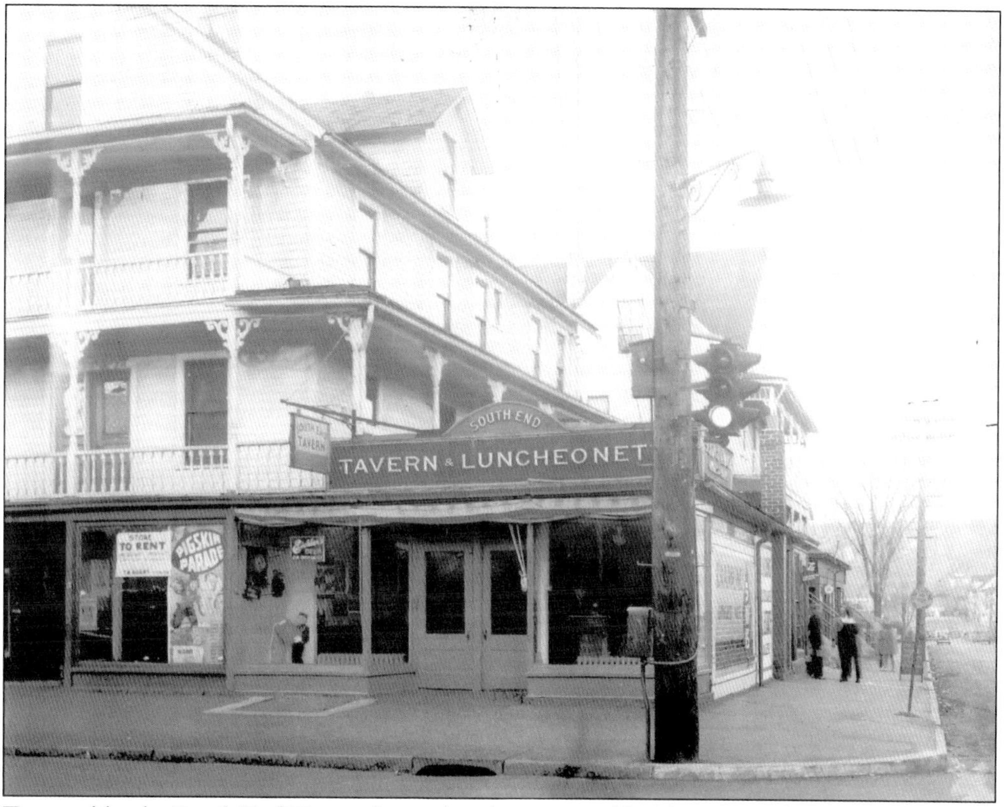

Taverns like the South End Tavern, located at the corner of South Main and East Albert Streets, were once a familiar sight in Torrington's neighborhoods. In 1936, when these photographs were taken, Torrington had more than 36 taverns—low-key places where workingmen stopped in after their factory shifts to have a beer and chat with friends. Alexander Radzevitch owned the tavern at the time of these photographs.

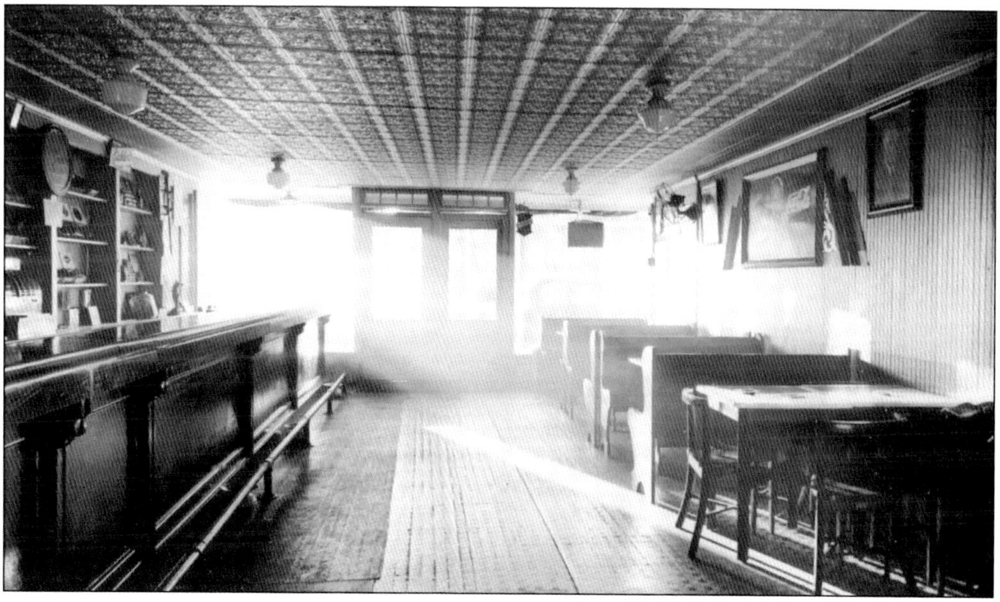

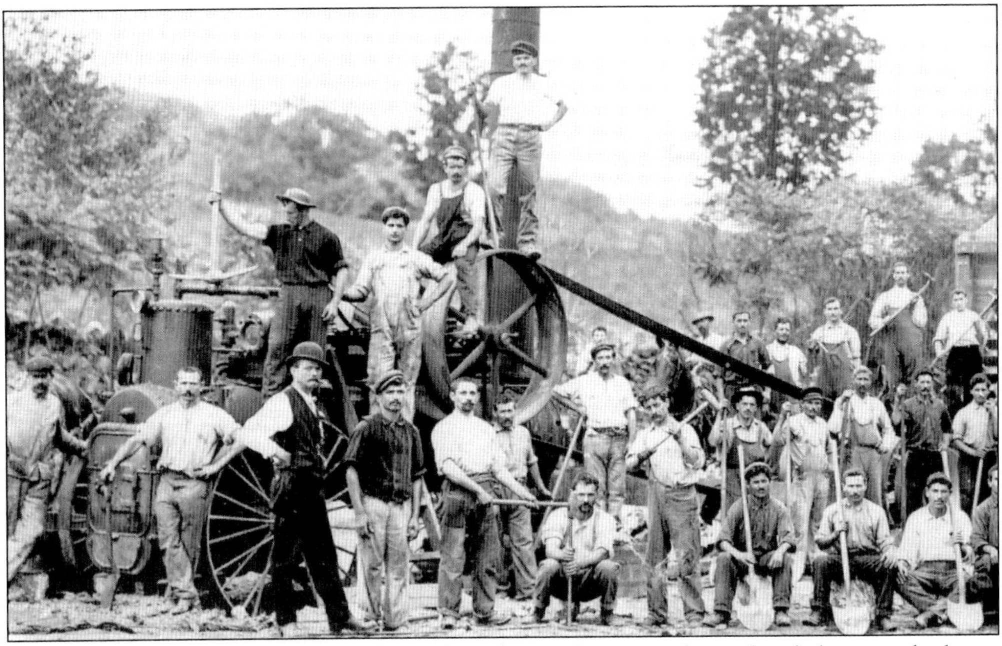

Joseph Mascetti (wearing bowler hat) stands with a work crew in the undated photograph above. Mascetti, a trained stonecutter, came to Torrington from northern Italy in 1897. By 1901, he had learned English, obtained American citizenship, and was bidding on road-grading contracts. In 1916, he partnered with Irving Holley, and for many years, Mascetti & Holley was one of the most respected roadbuilding companies east of the Hudson River. Mascetti employed many compatriots. He also mentored several men who went on to establish their own successful businesses, including master mechanic Andrew Oneglia and Flaviano Gervasini, pictured from left to right below in an early-1920s photograph. The Oneglia family still runs O&G Construction, a multimillion-dollar business headquartered in Torrington.

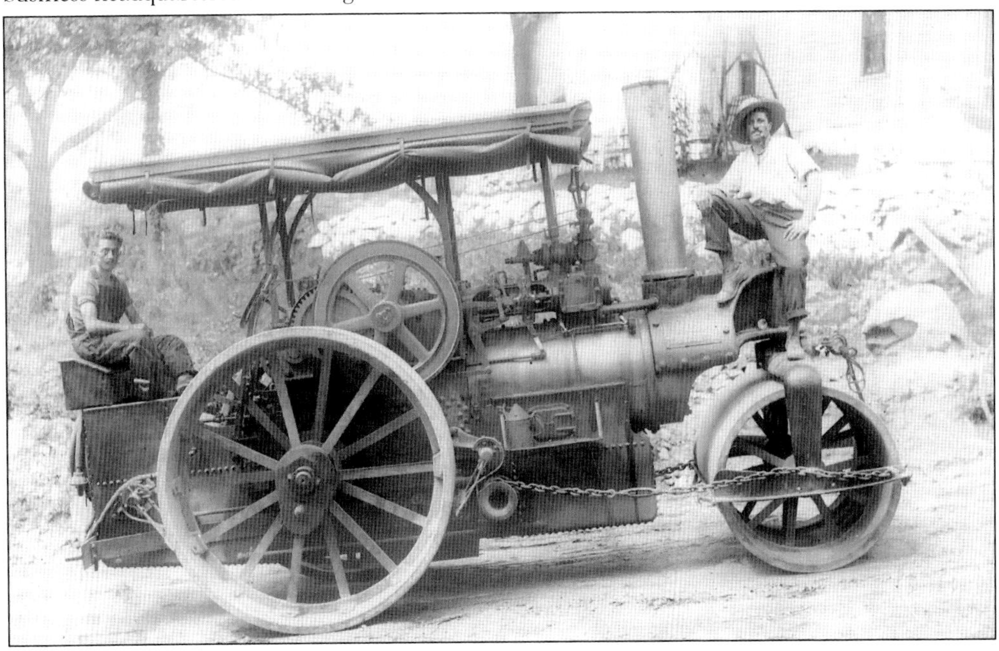

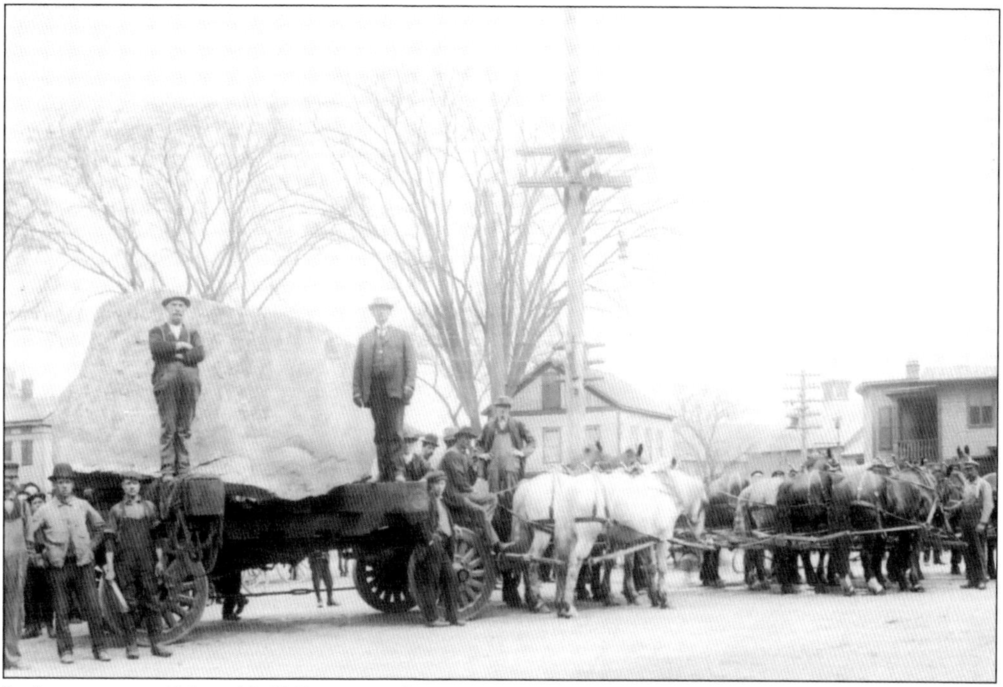

Irish immigrant Edward J. Kelley arrived in Torrington in 1860 and immediately began working for the railroad station. He recognized the need for a business that transported goods and established the Edward J. Kelley Transit Company. In this 1908 photograph, Kelley, his employees, and a team of horses stop for a break in the midst of hauling a 40-ton boulder from Migeon Avenue to its new home in Coe Memorial Park.

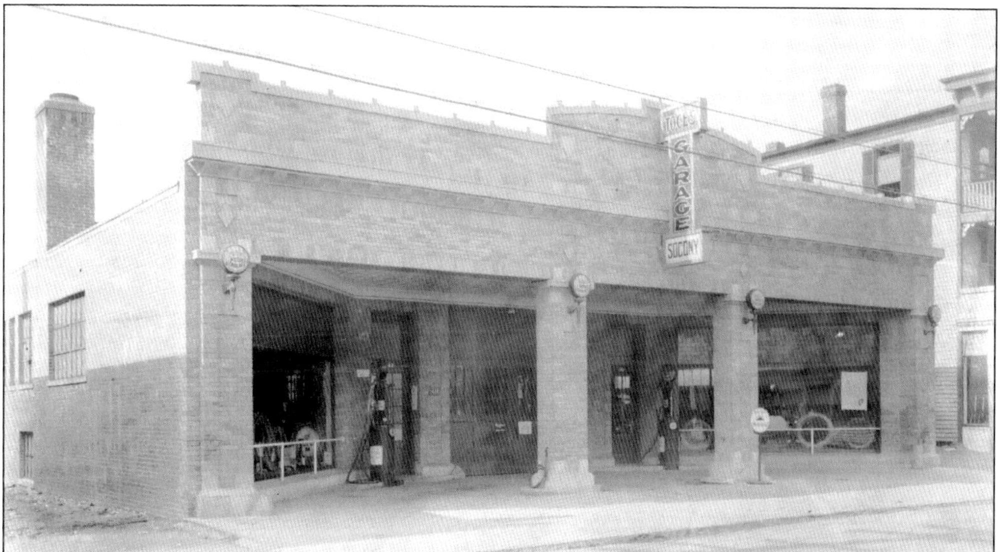

The Toce brothers—Frank, Louis, Dominic, and Joseph—started their tire business in this handsome garage at 143 East Main Street in June 1924. The 1923 structure, with its multihued beige brick and a drive-in portico, is a good example of early automobile-related architecture. Toce Brothers is still a family-owned business and operates at the same landmark location. (Debra Lapardo.)

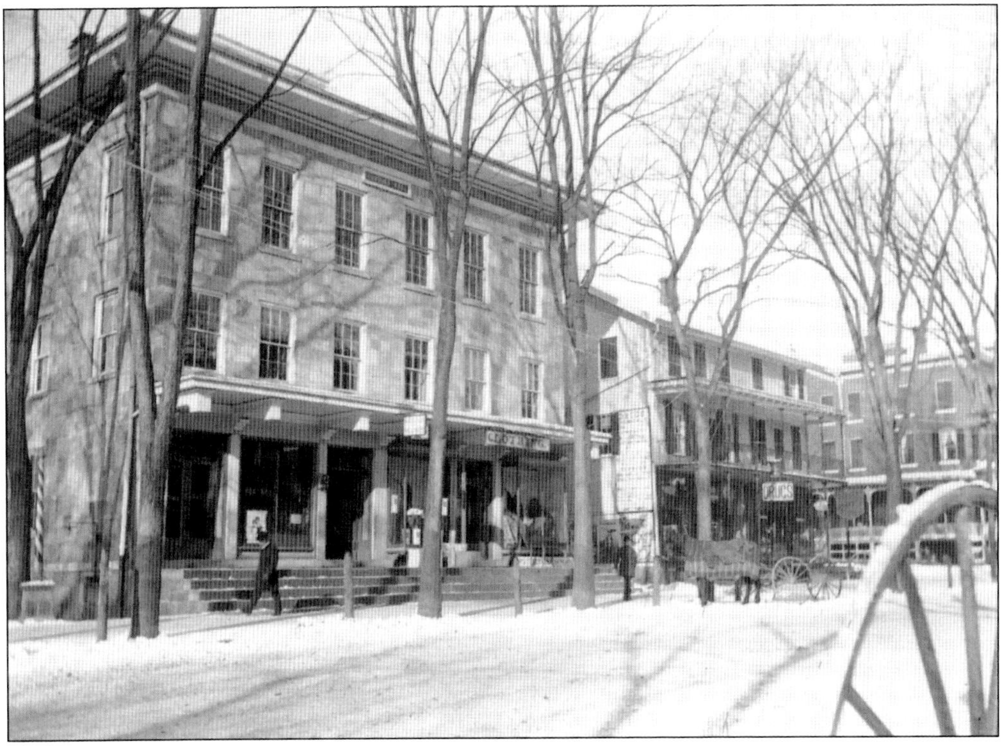

The Torrington Savings Bank, chartered in 1868 as the Wolcottville Savings Bank, spent 70 years in the Granite Block (shown here) built by George D. Wadhams. The Brooks Bank and Trust Company, founded in 1872 by Isaac W. and John W. Brooks, shared the Main Street space, eventually taking over the entire first floor. I.F. Hungerford had law offices on the second floor.

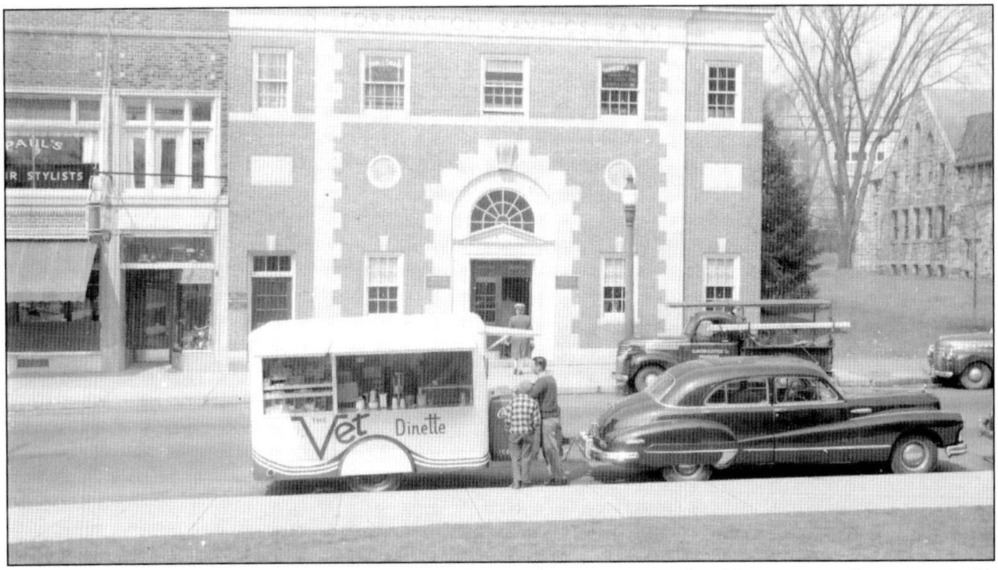

In 1938, the Torrington Savings Bank moved into this impressive building across from city hall. The native brick and limestone structure, with its mahogany entrance doors and simple Colonial Revival design, remains a striking presence on Main Street. This 1947 photograph features an early food truck parked across from the bank.

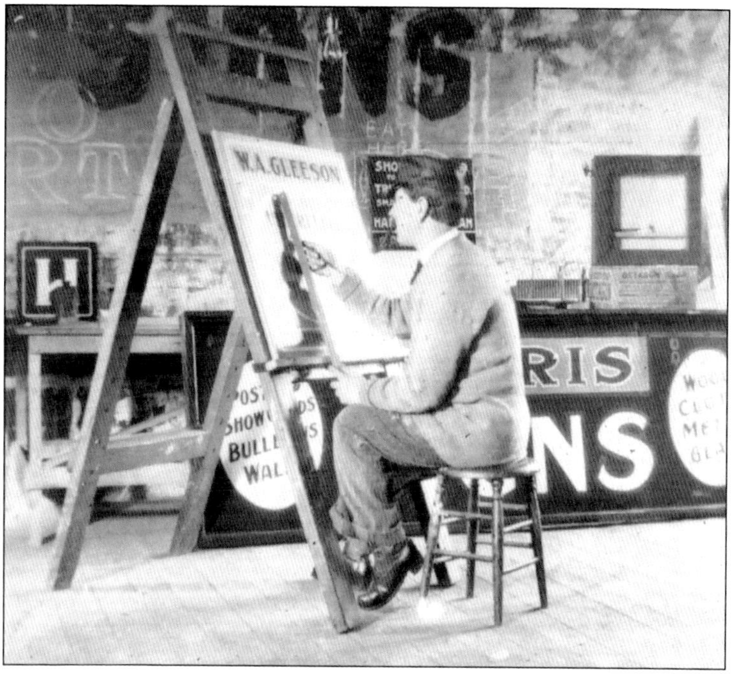

Charles Harris, photographed working in his sign shop, moved to Torrington from Lewiston, Maine, in 1912. The following year, he bought out the T.C. Cark business and established Harris Advertising Service. In 1926, the *Torrington Register* noted that about 80 percent of Torrington's business signs featured Harris's name "in small letters in the lower right hand corner," adding, "and they are good signs."

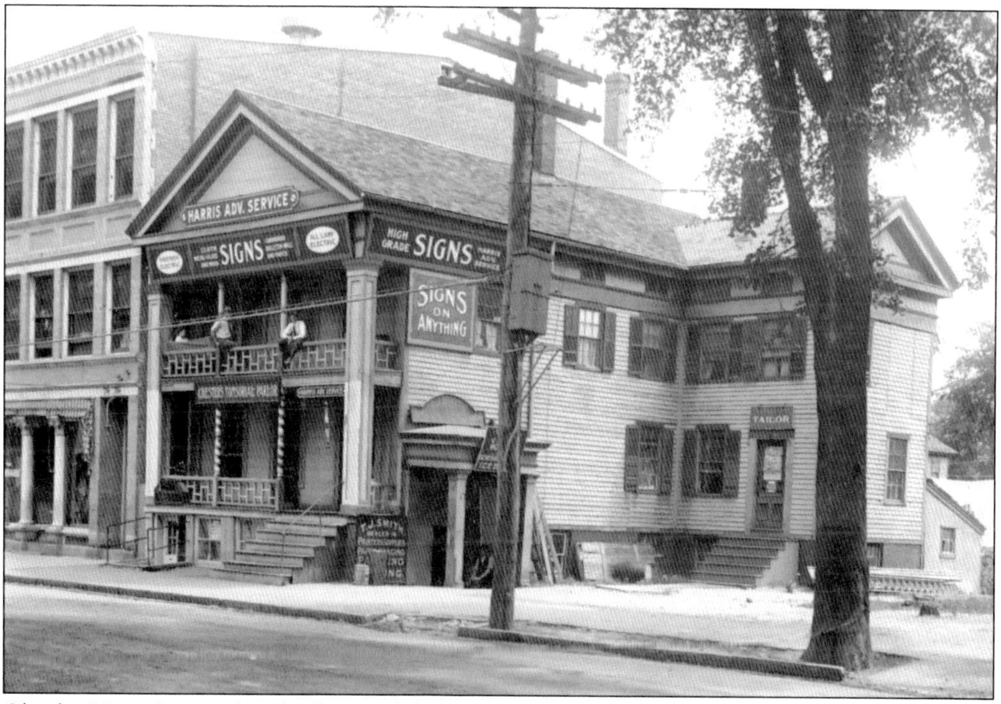

Charles Harris's sign shop had several different locations, including this attractive building on East Main Street next to the Ashborn Block. When Harris died in 1932, his wife gave up the shop and returned to her home state of Maine.

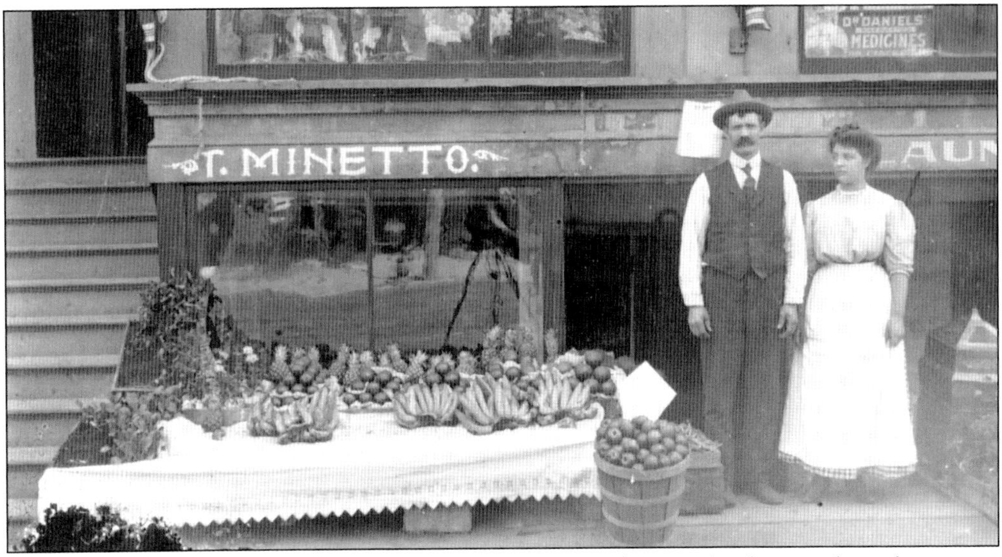

Thomas Minetto came to the United States in 1887 and opened a fruit and confectionary business in 1896. He married Amelia Crovo a few years later. One of Torrington's first candy and ice-cream makers, Minetto erected his own building on the corner of Church and Water Streets in 1912. He retired in 1930 and was long remembered for his ice-cream cones, which cost 1¢ for a small one.

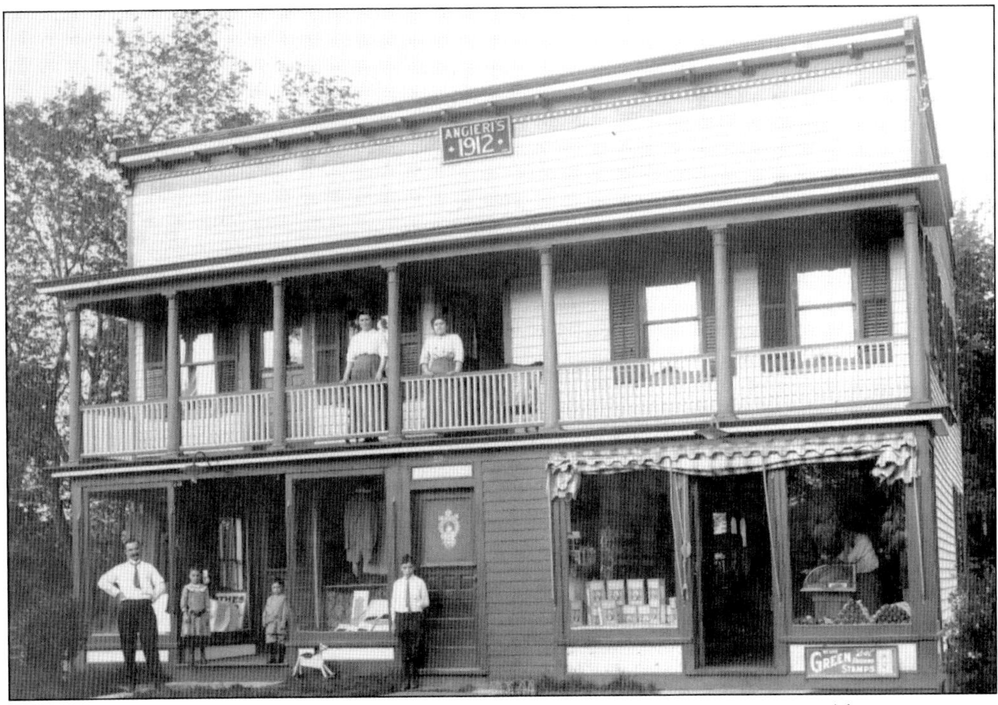

Eduardo Angieri, custom tailor, constructed this building at 298 Main Street (the current site of Besse's Paint and Decorating). Angieri lived with his wife, Maria Mennella, and children Domenico, Salvatore, and Filomena on the second floor above the tailor shop. In 1912, Angieri advertised "Suits and Overcoats to Order $20.00 and Up." The shop even had a telephone and its own number: 451-5.

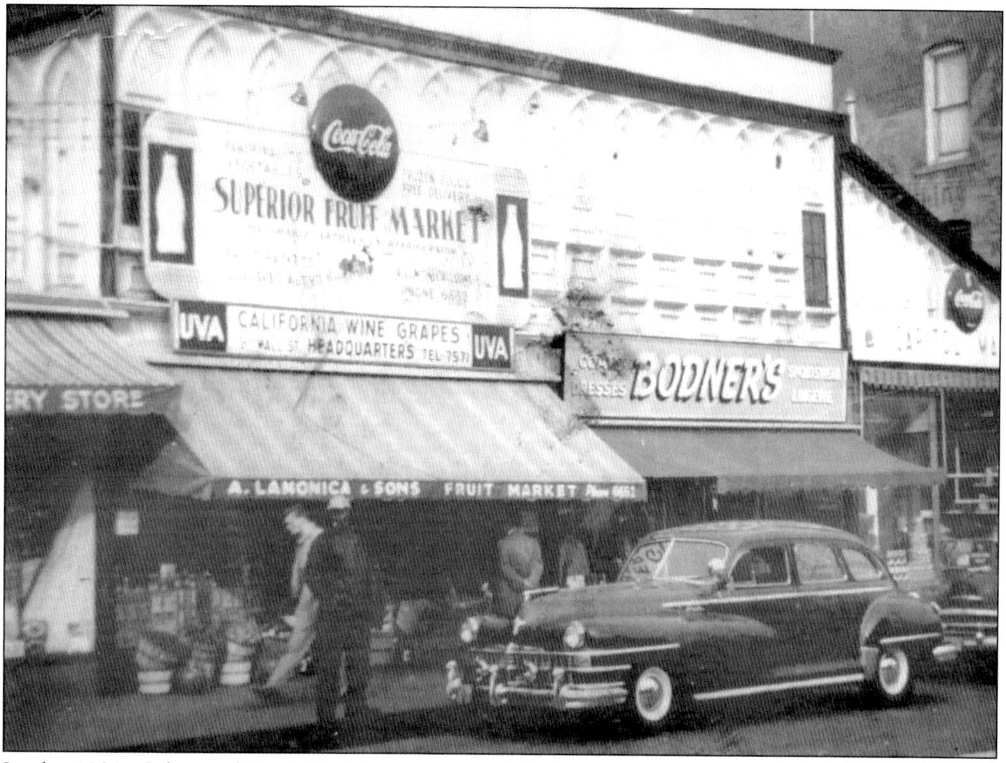

In the 1930s, John and David LaMonica, sons of Sicilian immigrant Angelo LaMonica, opened the fruit market pictured here on Torrington's Center Bridge. The 1955 flood washed away the bridge and LaMonica's, but the family opened another store on Migeon Avenue, where it now thrives as a restaurant and catering business. (Angelo LaMonica.)

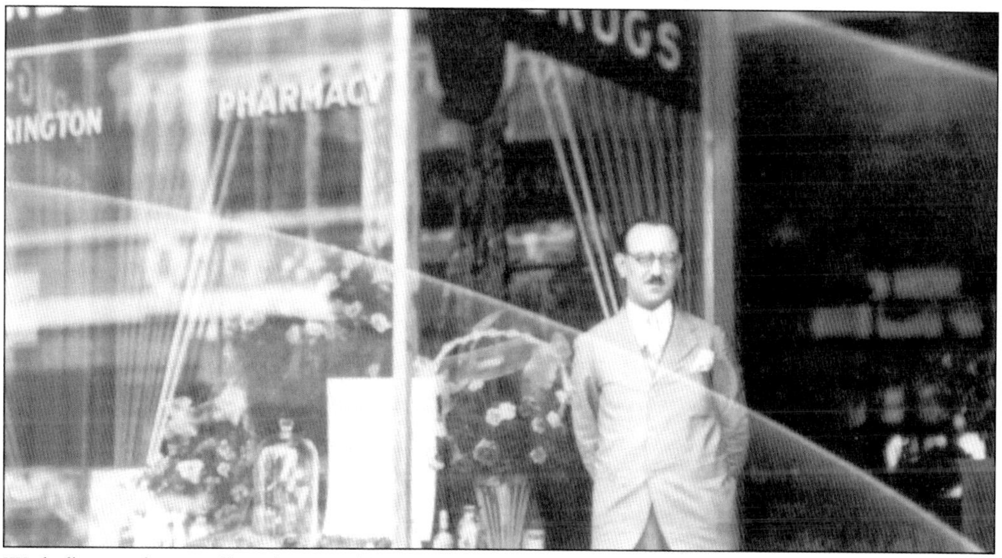

With flowers from well-wishers visible in the window, Fiore Petricone stands outside his Torrington Pharmacy on opening day in 1930. Petricone was active in the community and became a prominent school board member. His descendants continue to run the lower East Main Street business, which is now known as Petricone's Pharmacy. (Joseph R. Petricone Jr.)

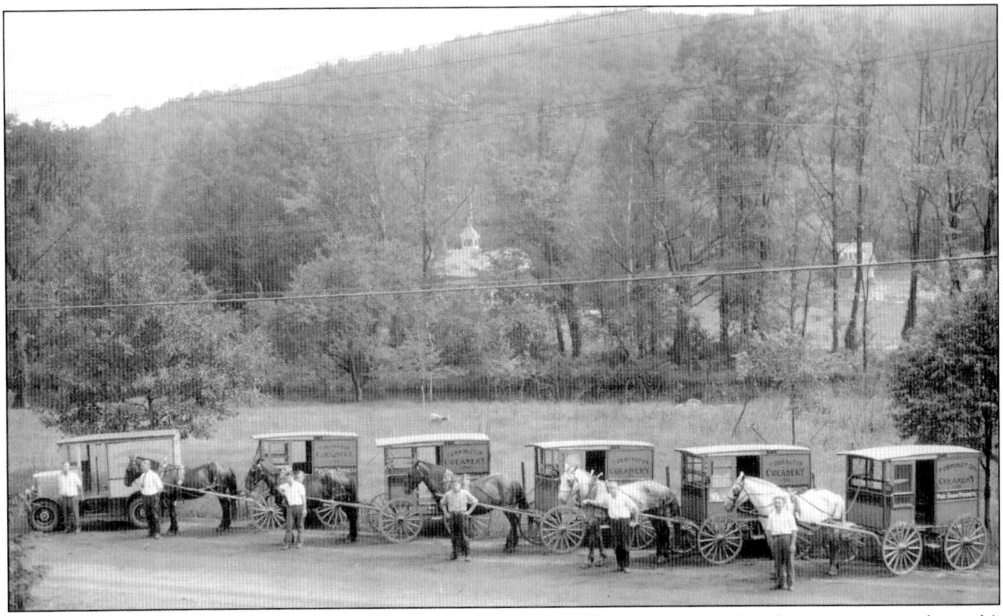

Torrington Creamery deliverymen pose with their horse-drawn wagons (and one motorized truck) in this 1930s photograph. The Riverside Avenue creamery was purchased by George Weigold in 1900. His son Arthur turned it into one of the largest, most progressive dairies in northwest Connecticut. The Torrington Creamery was the first in the area to use refrigerated trucks and the first in the country to sell commercially homogenized milk.

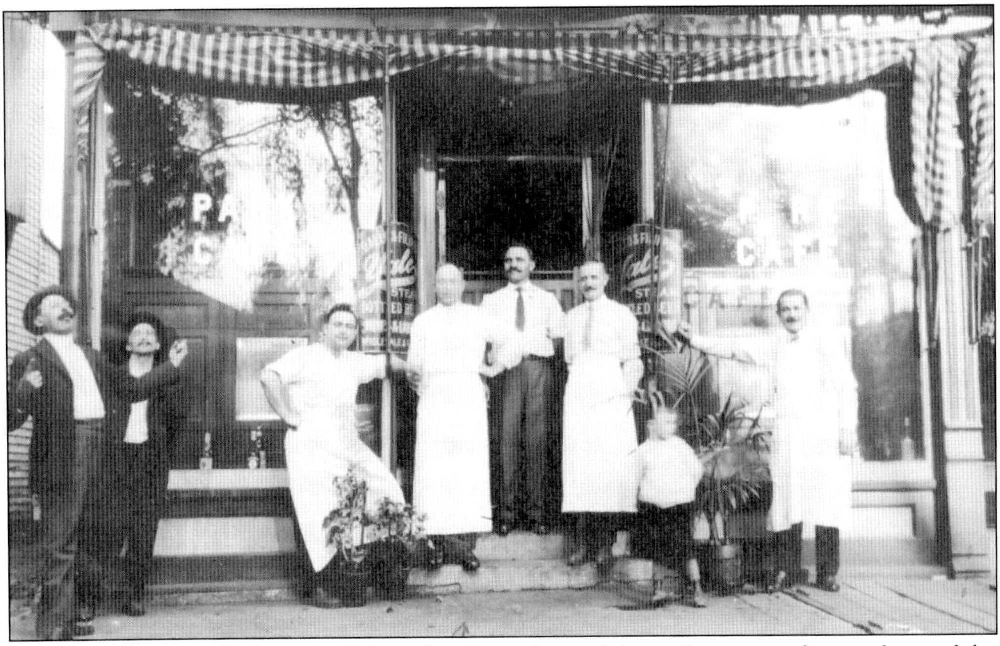

Luigi Gallo, "the Gallo boy," and "Bartoletti" are three of those shown standing in front of the Park Café at 29 South Main Street. Gallo and Luigi Filippini operated a drinking establishment here in the early 1920s, sharing the space with a compatriot's restaurant. Because saloons were not allowed during Prohibition, Gallo and Filippini, like others, simply called themselves "beverage purveyors."

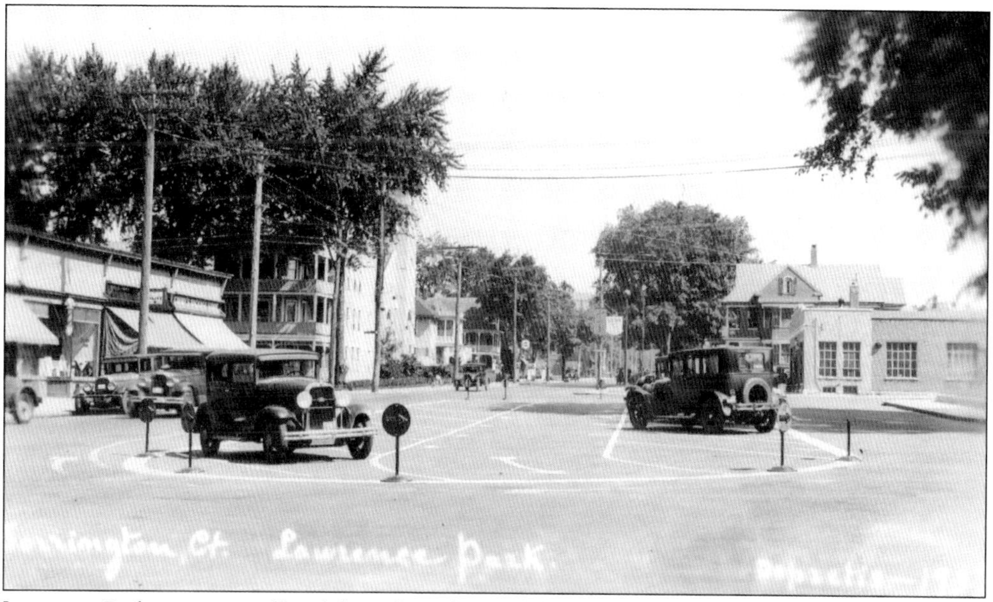

Laurence Park is a piece of land directly in front of the old North School in Torrington's North End. It was donated to the city in 1903 by Adelbert H. Hine. In 1908, the park was named in honor of Hine's son Laurence, who had been killed in an accident. Once a green space, Laurence Park was later reconfigured as a traffic rotary with interior parking spaces. In 1932, the name was officially changed to Laurence Square. Both the park and square are sometimes misspelled as Lawrence.

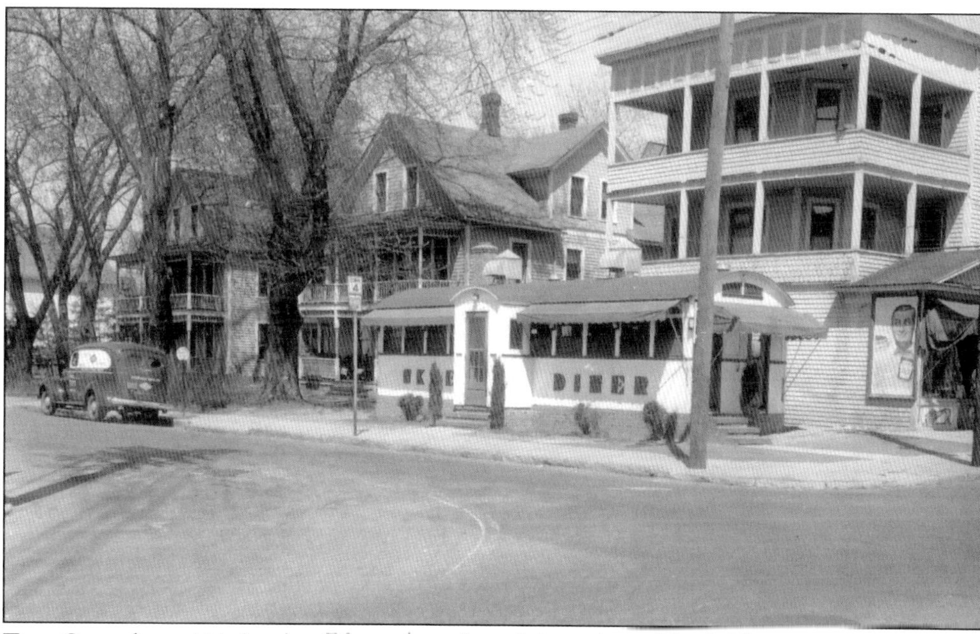

Tony Cisowski and his brother Edmund purchased their classic North Elm Street diner in 1946 and gave the restaurant its now iconic name, Skee's. The brothers, who ran the diner for almost 30 years, offered quick, quality meals at affordable prices. Skee's, which served its last customer in 2001, was listed in the National Register of Historic Places in 2002. The diner is currently owned by the Torrington Historic Preservation Trust and is undergoing restoration off-site.

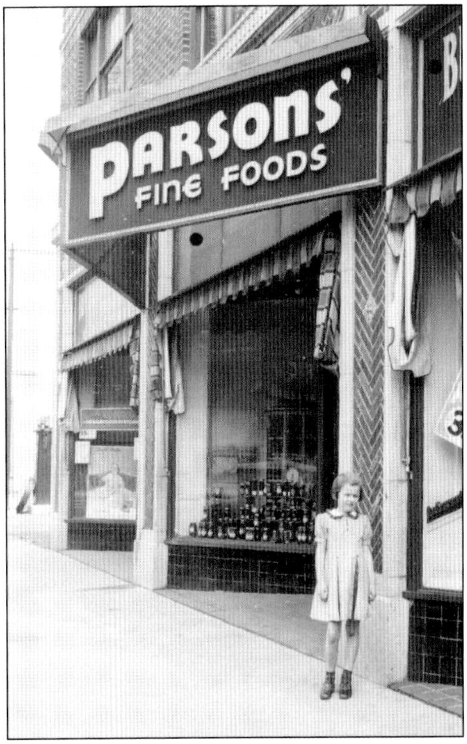

Eleanor Mae Parsons poses in front of her grandparents' grocery store in the North End in 1937. Frank and Nellie Parsons' market was in business until the early 1940s, when a fire at the Arcade Bowling Alleys on the second floor forced them to close the store. The Parsons family went on to run the popular hot dog stand Parsons' Puppy Palace off upper East Main Street. (Eleanor Parsons Potter.)

Ganem Jacob (right) poses with his wife, Katherine, and their son Joseph at a display highlighting his ice-cream shop. Jacob began manufacturing his own ice cream—three flavors of it—in 1930, and his North End shop, complete with soda fountain, was a popular gathering place for decades. He sold the business to Clover Dairy in 1957.

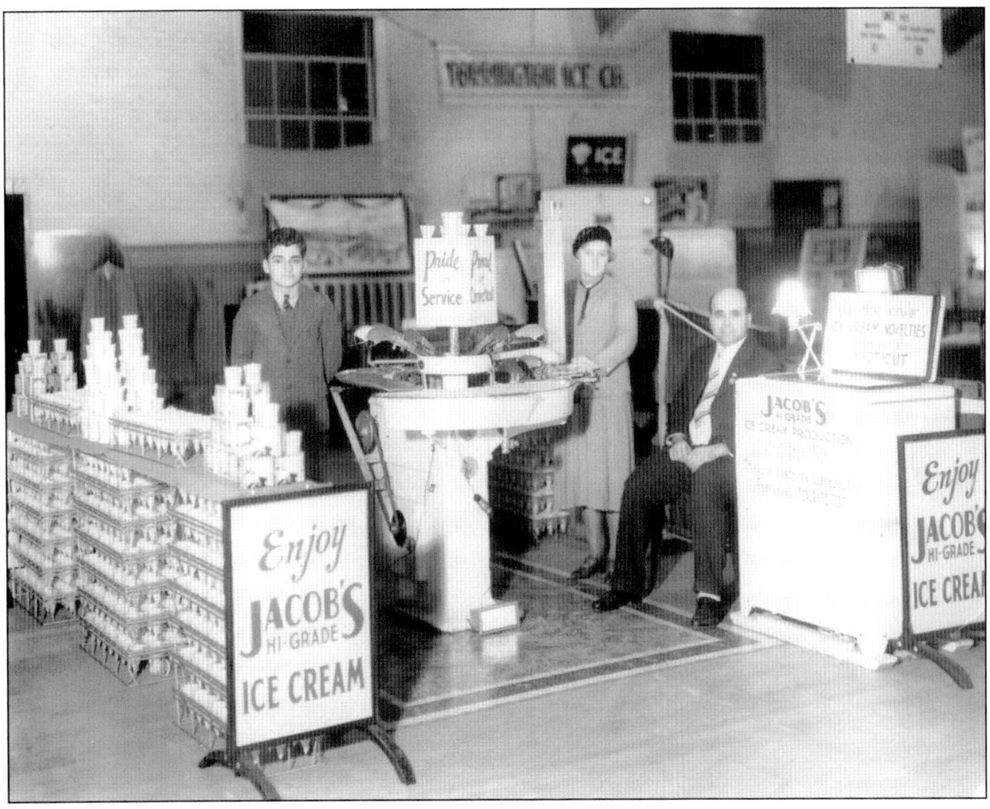

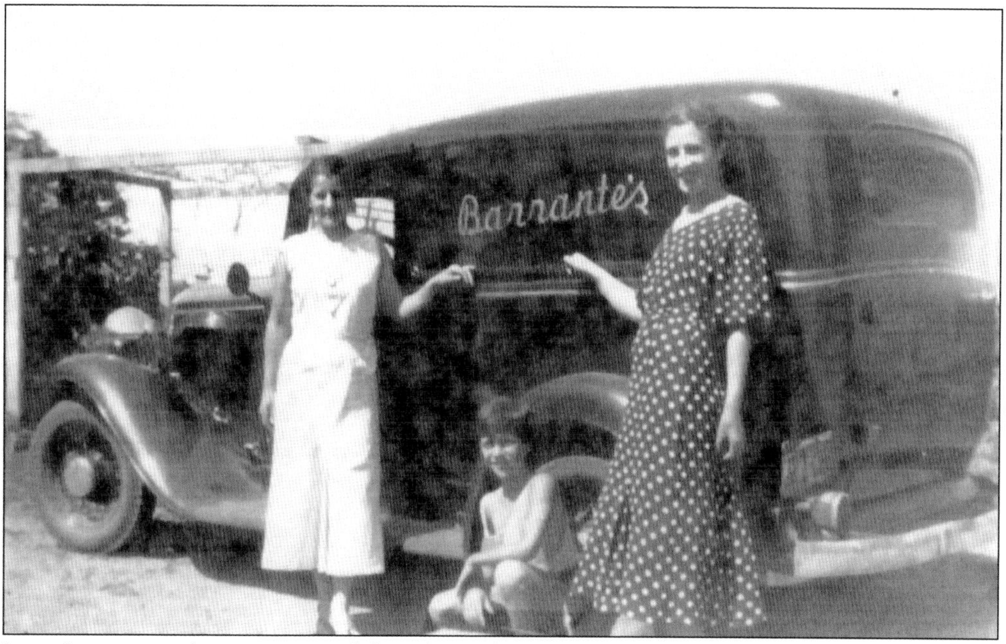

In earlier times, when customers did not have the luxury of owning their own automobiles, they expected pickup and delivery services to be offered by local merchants. Here, a child and two unidentified women pose with the Barrante's delivery van. (Ron Barrante.)

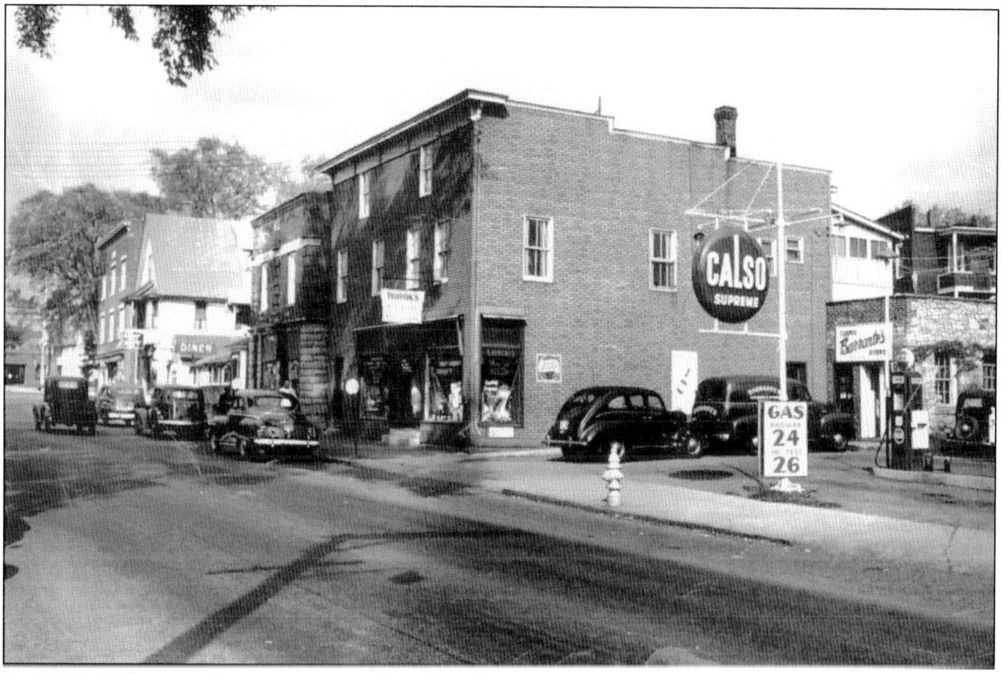

In 1923, Salvatore Barrante opened a dry cleaning business in the building behind Torok's Package Store. This photograph shows Barrante's on the east side of Main Street in Torrington's North End. The shop has since relocated but remains a local family business. Ron Barrante, who started working at his father's store almost 70 years ago, still stops in every day to press clothes. (Ron Barrante.)

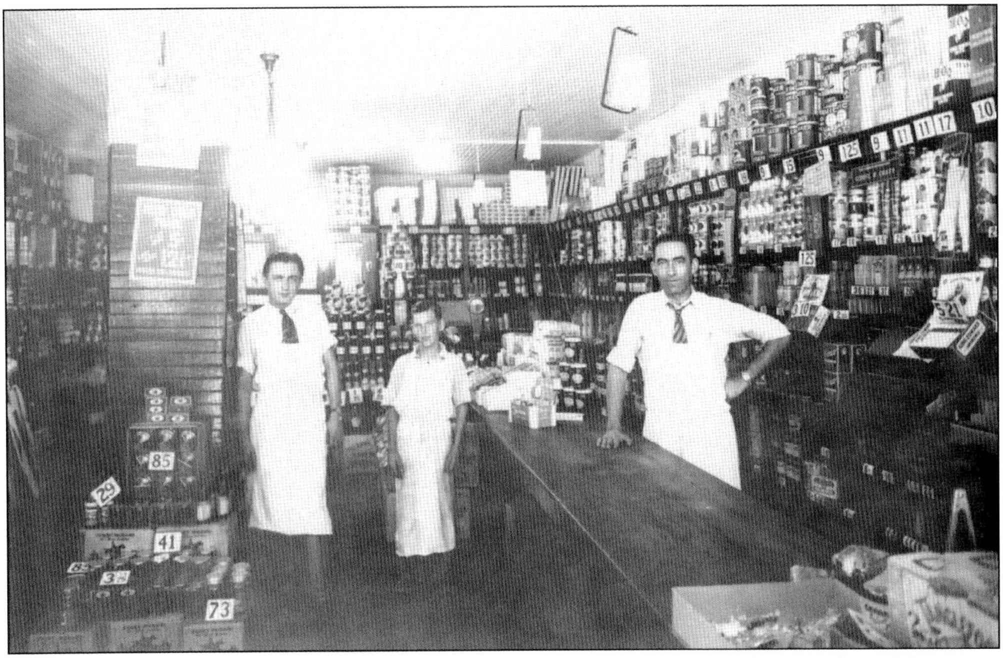

Douglas Colligan (at left in the photograph) probably began working at this North End Economy Grocery Store in the late 1920s. Economy opened its first store in Torrington in 1916. By 1920, there were eight Torrington locations, each offering low prices, "no premiums," and a sample of high-grade coffee on opening day.

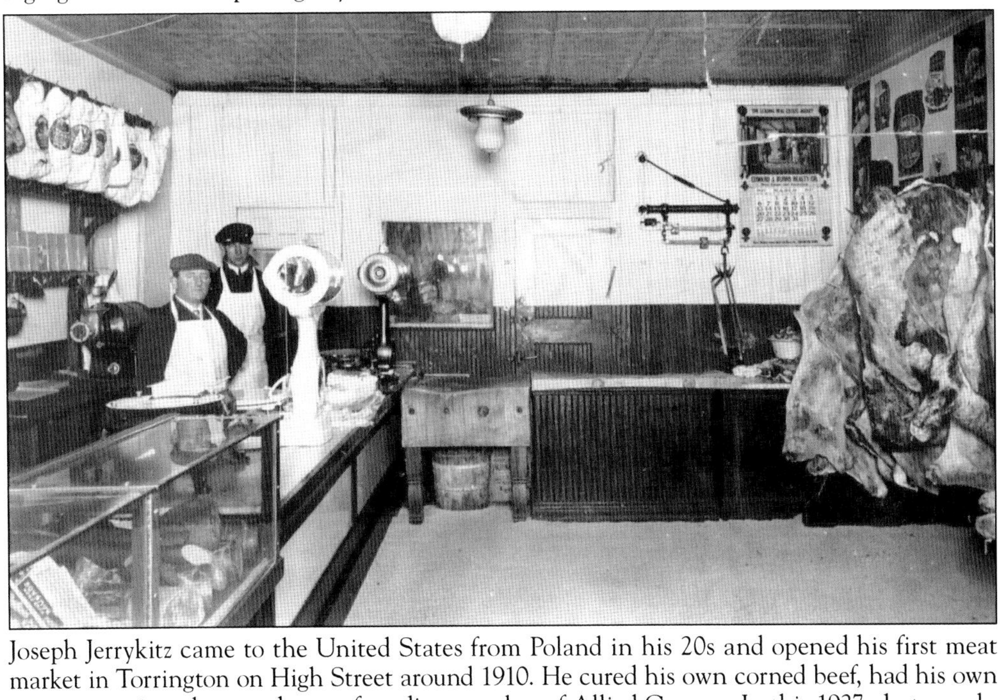

Joseph Jerrykitz came to the United States from Poland in his 20s and opened his first meat market in Torrington on High Street around 1910. He cured his own corned beef, had his own meat-processing plant, and was a founding member of Allied Grocers. In this 1927 photograph, Jerrykitz (left) stands with Pete Ficere at his shop, Jerrykitz Market, at 546 Main Street in the North End. His sons Stanley and Edward continued the family business. (Robert Jerrykitz.)

Six

RECREATION

Leisure activities bind neighbors and communities together, and the range of pastimes enjoyed by Torrington's citizens during the 19th and early 20th centuries was really quite remarkable. Amateur theater groups and musicians, as well as traveling performers, played to packed houses. Notices were posted every week for dances, lectures, and card parties. Adults attended sporting events, took evening classes, and joined organizations ranging from the Temperance League to the Bald-Head Club of America. Surrounded by beautiful rolling hills, Torrington also offered a perfect setting for outdoor activities of all kinds. Early photographs capture locals bicycling, hiking, hunting, boating, skating, and swimming in local ponds and rivers. Torringtonians gathered arbutus and blueberries, climbed Ivy Mountain, and visited John Brown's birthplace—excursions diligently reported in the *Torrington Register*. Many prominent citizens passed their summers in cottages at nearby Highland or Bantam Lakes.

All year long, churches, schools, clubs, factories, and neighborhoods fielded sports teams of all kinds. Factory outings included games and competitions for both men and women.

Torrington's children were always out and about—sledding on the city's steep hills, whizzing by on Union Hardware roller skates, or playing baseball and marbles. In the 1920s, local women expanded Torrington's neighborhood playground movement, offering thousands of children free supervised summer activities close to home. Eventually, this grassroots effort evolved into Torrington's Department of Parks and Recreation, which has continued to offer programs over many years.

Between 1915 and 1940, Torrington benefitted from generous gifts of parkland from local philanthropists. In 1917, John F. Alvord donated the land for Alvord Park in the north end of town, and the following year, Frederick F. Fuessenich gifted a large tract of land just south of downtown in memory of his wife, Elizabeth Blake Fuessenich. Maj. William E. Besse donated Besse Pond in memory of his mother and later donated parklands in the western part of the city. Alvord Playground, home to Christmas Village, was a gift from Helen Alvord in 1940. Decades later, these lovely public spaces are still being enjoyed by the community.

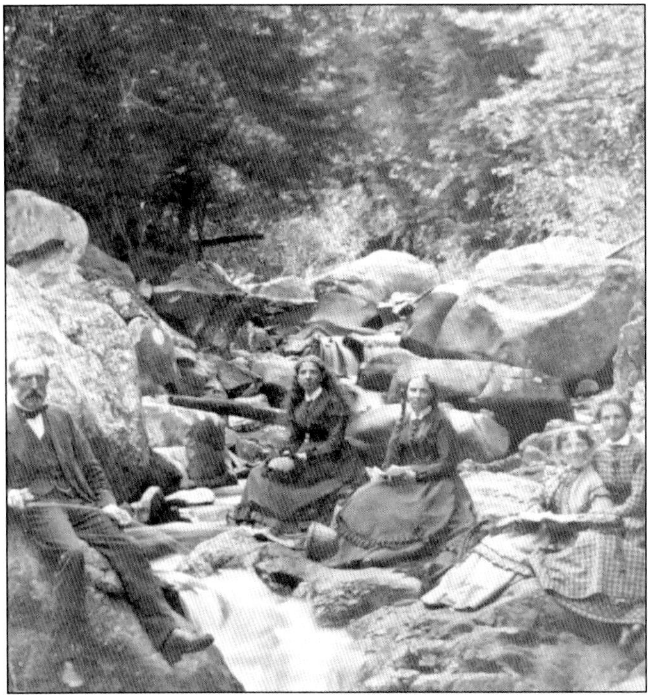

In this photograph labeled "Cowles' Falls, Torrington," an unidentified group enjoys the scenery in West Torrington. During Victorian times, local residents, including women, were nature lovers and intrepid explorers despite their cumbersome clothing. Bird-watching; butterfly collecting; and flower, berry, and mushroom gathering were all popular pastimes.

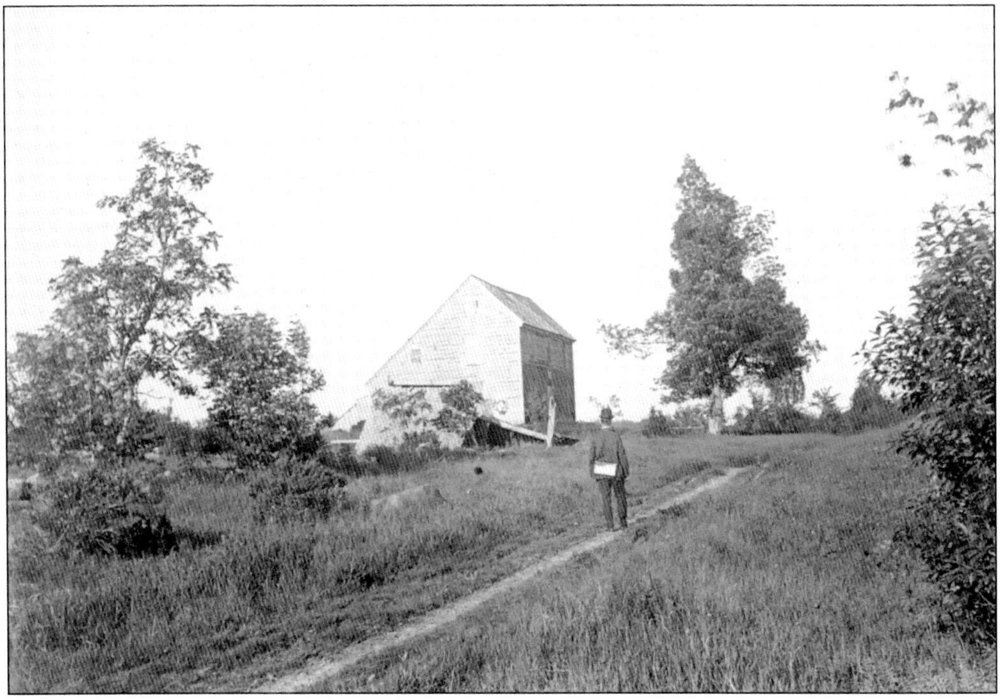

A solitary walker heads toward the John Brown Birthplace on John Brown Road. The missing chimney and boarded-up windows indicate that the photograph was taken before the house's reconstruction in 1902. The homestead was a popular destination for those traveling by foot, bicycle, and carriage. The house was destroyed by fire in 1918, but the site, now owned by the Torrington Historical Society, is part of the African American Freedom Trail and still draws visitors.

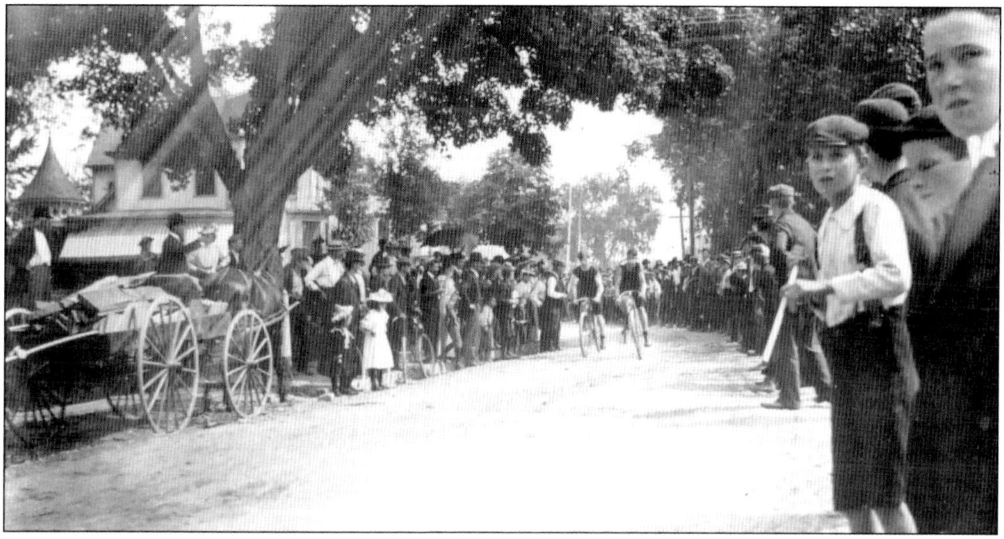

This photograph taken near the corner of Migeon Avenue and Church Streets during the 1890s captures the finish of a local 20-mile bicycle race won by John Cameron. Bicycle races were also held at Treat Street Park. Competitors even raced from Torrington to East Litchfield and back.

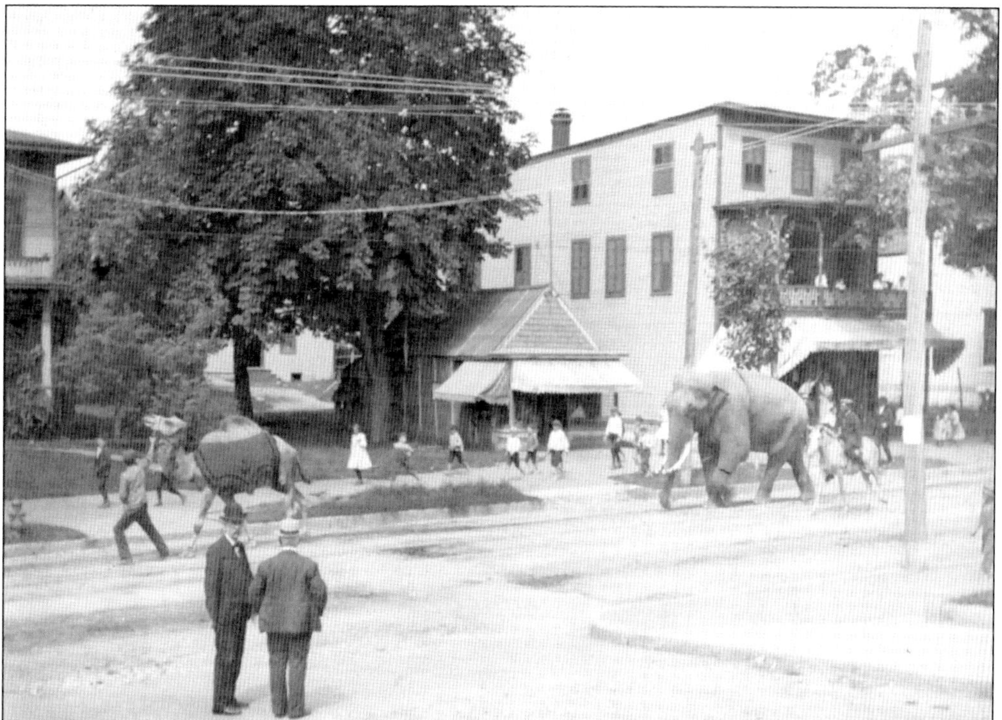

This 1905 photograph shows a circus parade making its way down Torrington's Main Street, probably from the railroad station. The three-story building on the right is Weeks' dry goods store, located about where the Torrington Savings Bank is now. Smaller traveling truck circuses also came to town and set up in local neighborhoods, including at Stefurak's lot, site of the current post office.

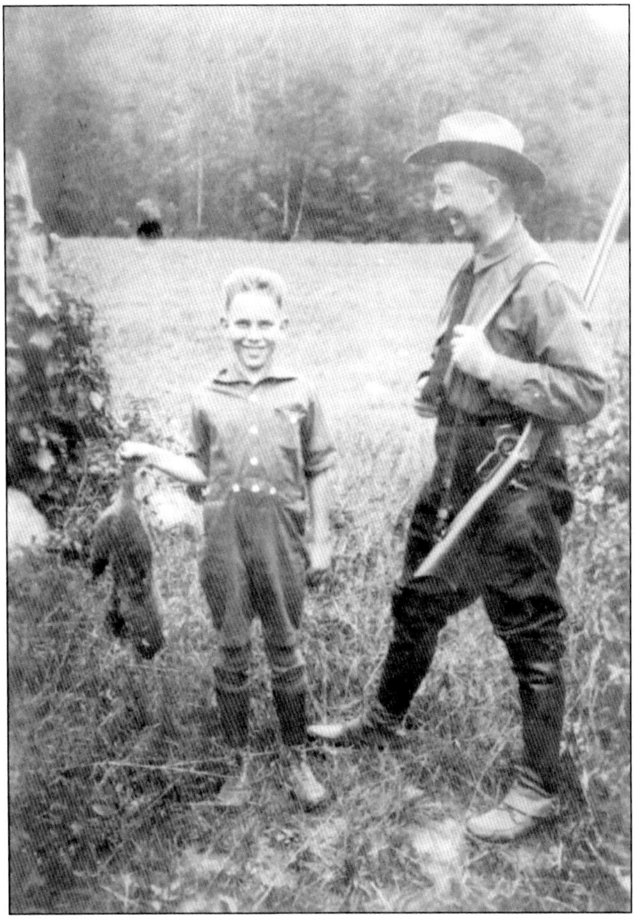

"Woodchuck" Jack Tuttle (left) poses here with Maj. William Besse after a successful hunting expedition. Hunting and trapping were enjoyed by men and boys of all ages. Enterprising locals—even children—could make money selling pelts, including muskrat, to local furriers.

Torrington's first two Boy Scout troops were organized one Saturday in March 1904 at the YMCA. Soon, other troops were established. During the 1920s, local Scouts competed at large meets in challenges such as knot-tying and signaling. In this undated photograph, Jane Ford Coe, a Boy Scout benefactor, stands at far left with the Boy Scout Drum & Bugle Corps, possibly at one of the aforementioned meets.

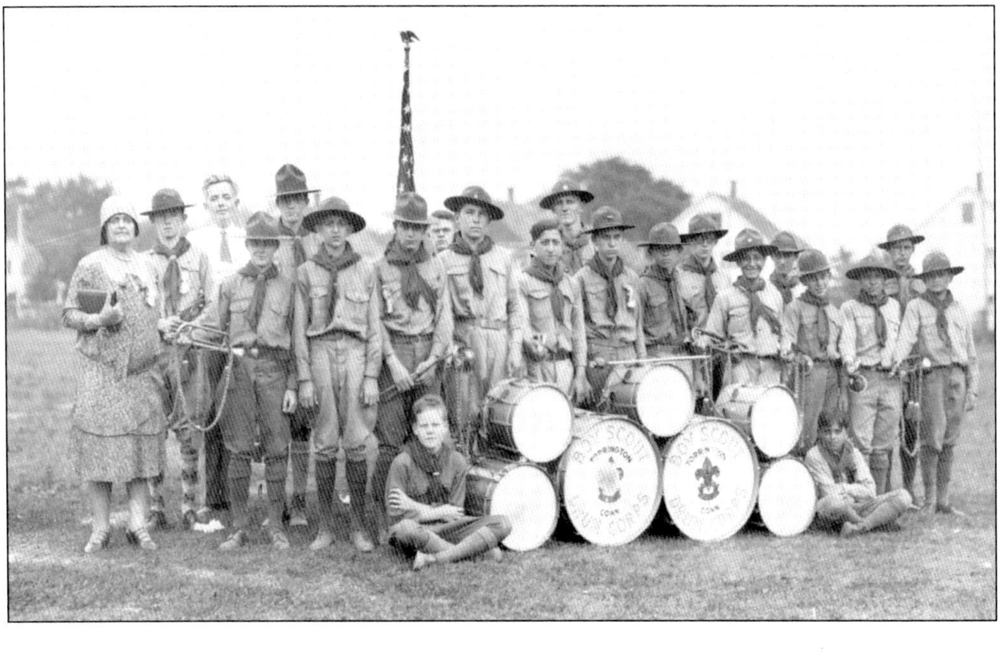

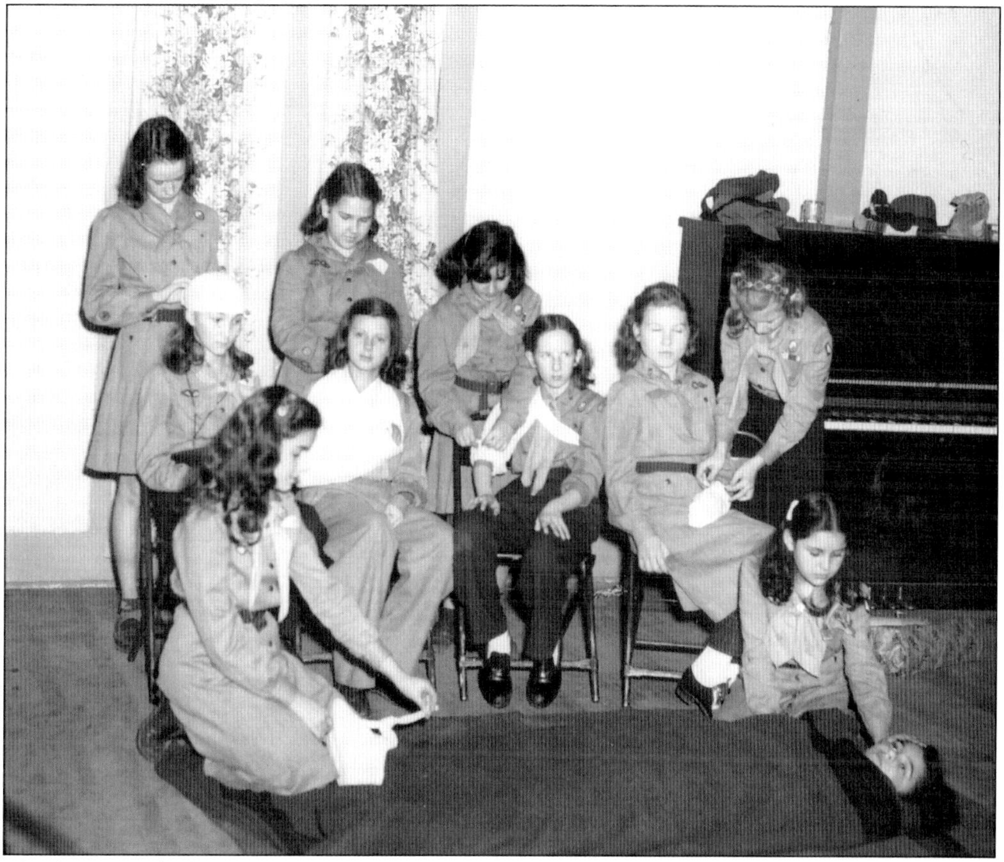

The first record of Girl Scout activity in Torrington was in 1924. In 1931, Maria Blake Pratt, one of Girl Scouting's staunchest supporters, helped to establish a Girl Scout Council to promote local scouting. By 1933, there were 23 troops in Torrington. Above, Troop No. 4 receives first-aid training at St. Peter's Community House in 1948. Marlene Gallichio is lying on the floor while Elaine Wolfe bandages her feet.

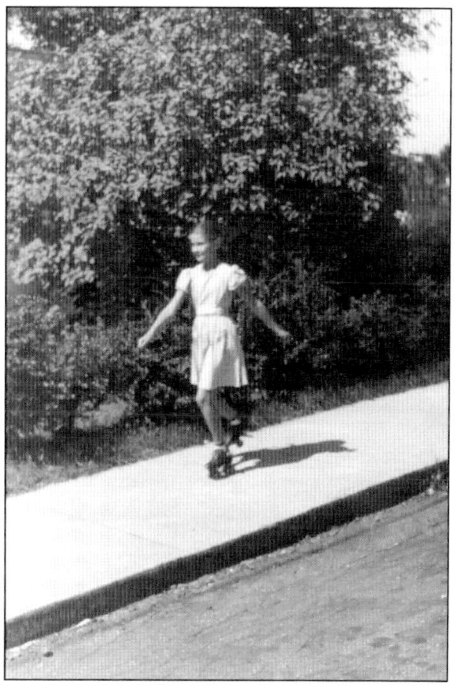

Elaine Borzani flies along French Street on her roller skates in this late-1930s photograph. Sidewalks were rough then, and girls were still not allowed to wear pants, even for play, so skinned knees were always a threat. Torrington's Union Hardware Company made both ice and roller skates, and some enterprising youngsters earned spending money by testing out new skate models for the company.

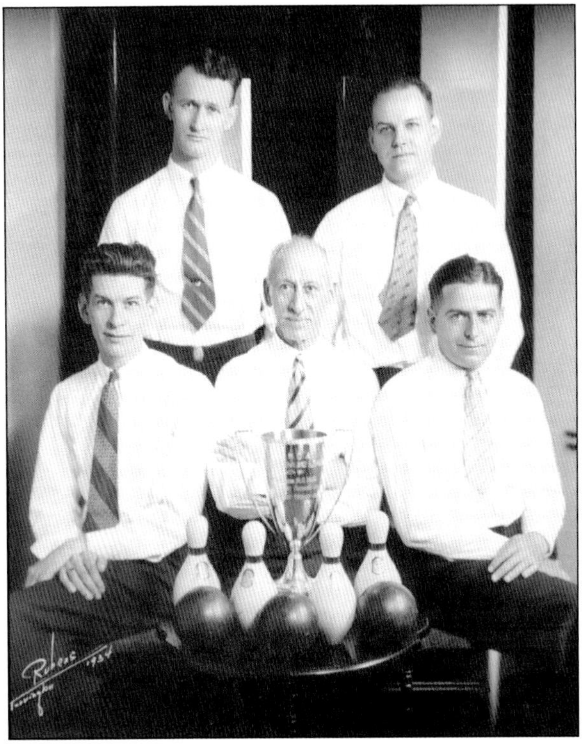

William E. Bennett (first row, center) poses with Calvary Baptist Church's men's bowling team, which won the city church league championship several times in the 1930s at the YMCA bowling alleys. Bennett, a widower with two young sons, served as church clerk from 1904 until 1956. For many years, he also did light repairs for the church and kept the furnace going free of charge.

Torrington women were avid bowlers in leagues sponsored by churches, shops, and factories. Recreation Alleys on Maiden Lane set aside lanes specifically for women and even advertised that ladies would always be treated with courtesy. Here, Sacred Heart League teammates Gertrude Palker Tomala (far left) and Dorothy Lucas Zaharek (second from left) celebrate with their trophies at an unidentified bowling alley.

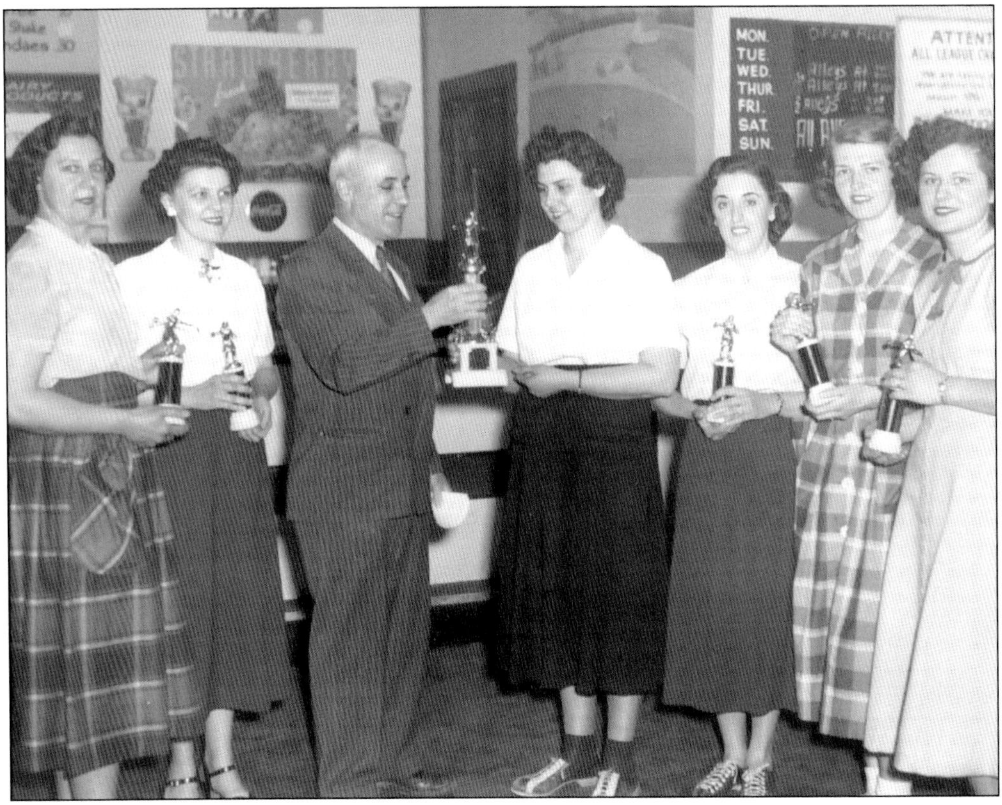

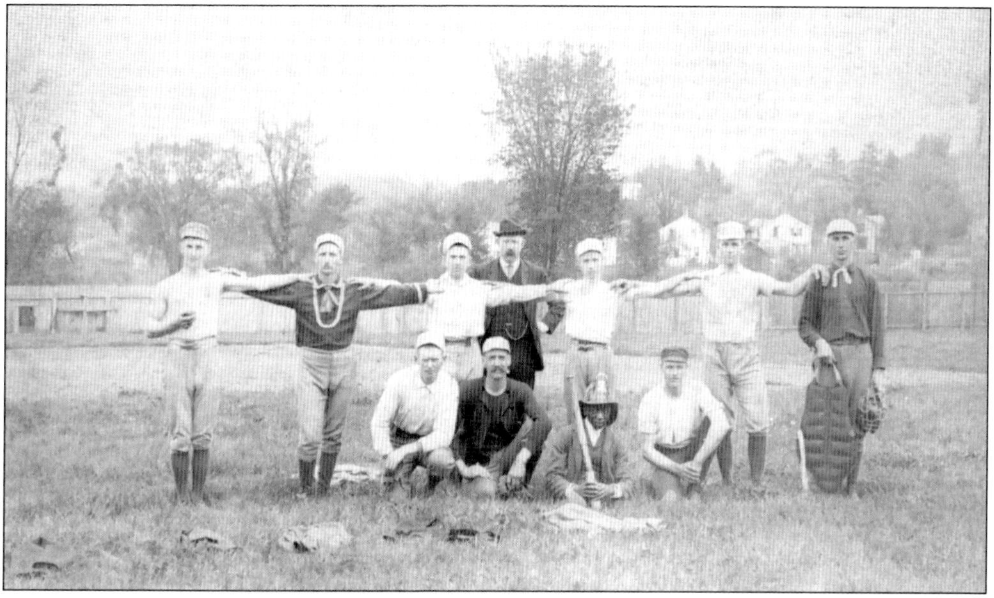

The Mutual Volunteer Fire Department Baseball Team poses at the athletic grounds on Franklin Street in this c. 1890 photograph. The Mutual VFD was formed in 1888 by consolidating the two existing volunteer fire companies. E.J. Kelley is at far left in the first row. Hubert Harrison is wearing the fireman's hat.

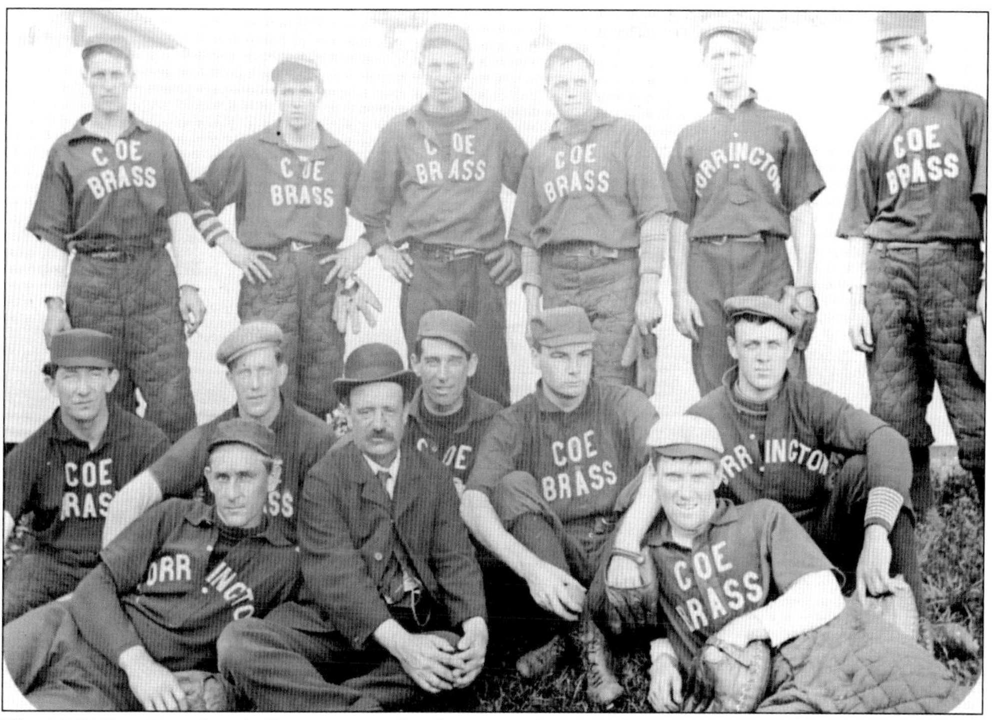

The 1903 Coe Brass baseball team poses for this team photograph. Factory-sponsored teams had loyal followers, and the games were enthusiastically covered in the *Evening Register*. In 1903, Eagle Bicycle, Hendey, Excelsior Needle, and Coe competed for the local baseball championship. The opening game of the series, which was eventually won by the Needles, drew unprecedented crowds.

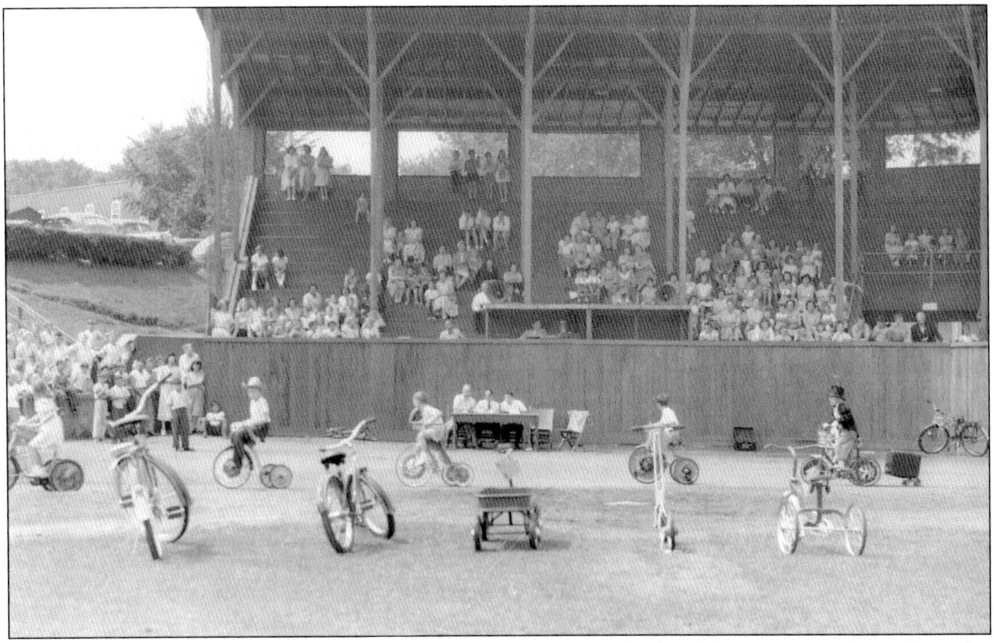

In November 1918, Frederick F. Fuessenich donated Elizabeth Blake Fuessenich Park to the Town of Torrington in memory of his wife. Originally known as League Park, the 7.5-acre parcel located just south of downtown has been used for decades for factory league baseball, high school athletics, playground contests, firework displays, Wild West programs, youth soccer, and much more. Fuessenich's gift insured that the park would forever belong to the people of Torrington. Above, in an undated photograph, some children participate in a Torrington Parks and Recreation program. The grandstand, which was torn down in 1989, is in the background. Below, a 1910 baseball team takes the field. Note the cars and horse-drawn carriages at left.

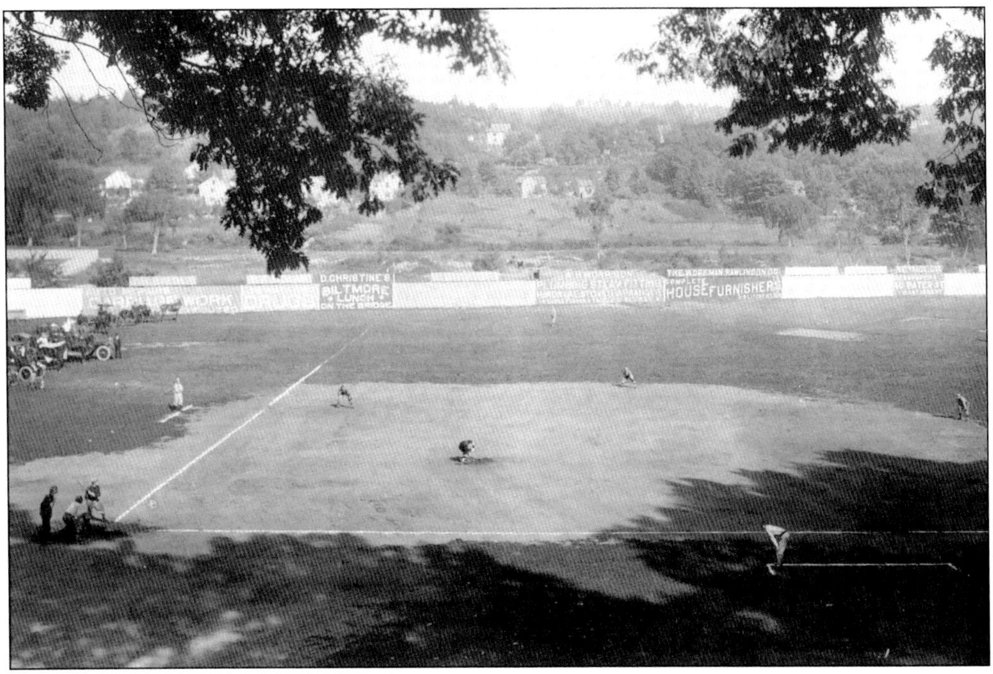

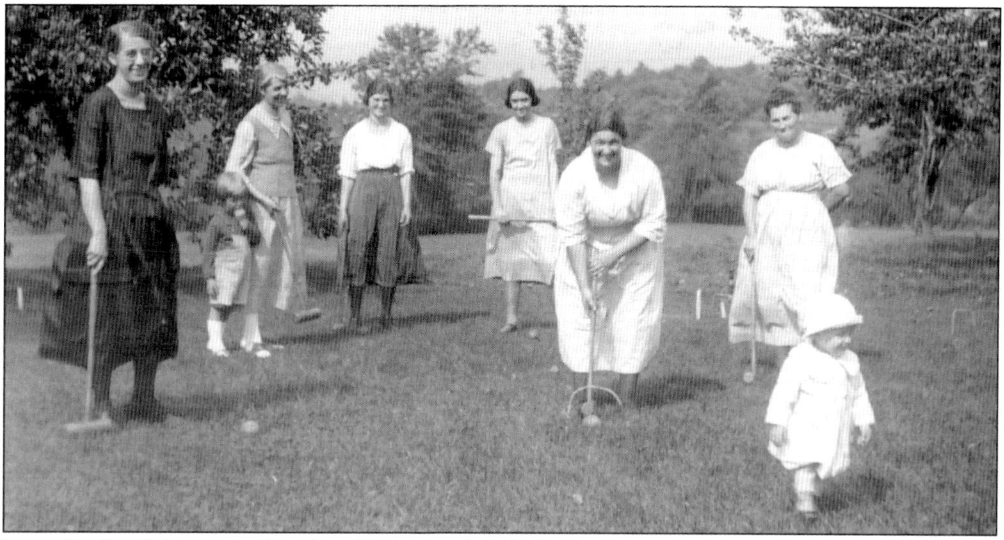

Laura Richard (wearing the white blouse and dark skirt) enjoys a game of croquet at the Richard Farm with some relatives from the Mougenot and Bolomey families. Other outdoor games like tennis, bocce, and golf also had loyal adherents in Torrington. (Richard family.)

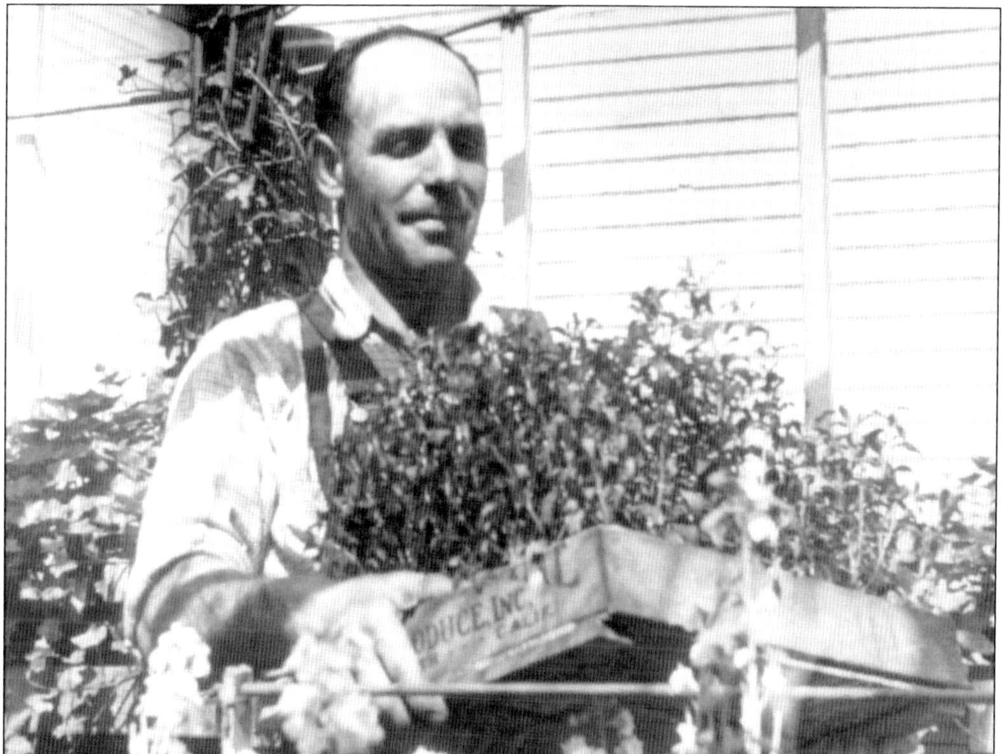

Here, a smiling Joseph Moscarillo poses with a box of plants. Moscarillo's greenhouse has provided Torringtonians with bulbs, seeds, plants, and gardening advice since the early 1900s. Before World War II, most residents filled their yards with vegetables, flowers, and fruit trees. Moscarillo, an avid gardener himself, enjoyed stopping by the formal gardens at the Hotchkiss-Fyler House and consulting with Gertrude Hotchkiss in his free time. (Maria Moscarillo.)

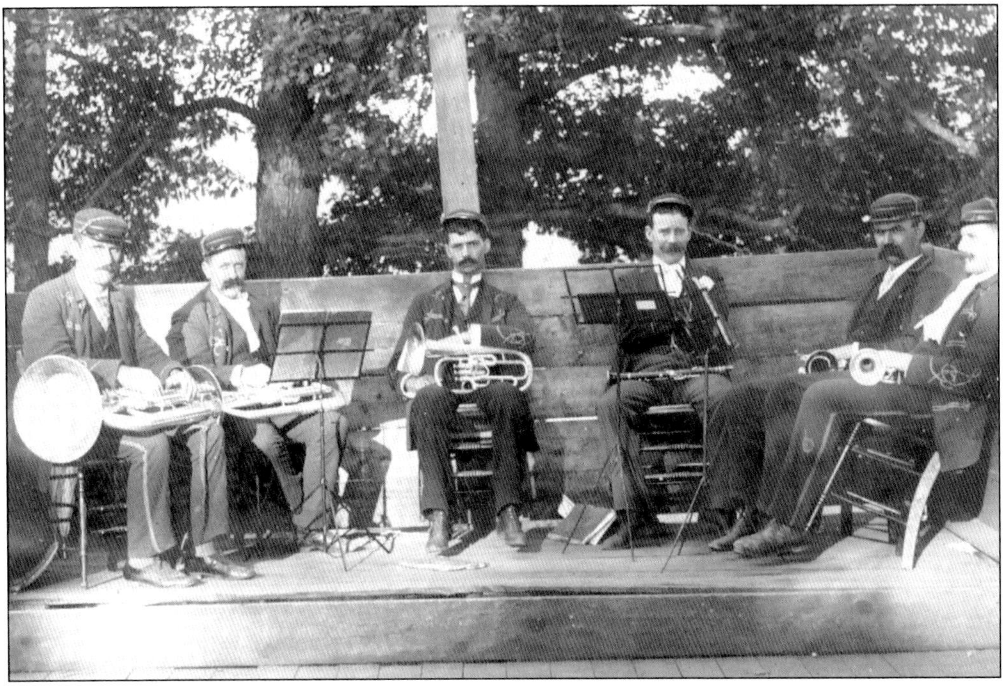

The Dance and Picnic Band, including leader James Palmer, takes a breather in this undated photograph. In the 19th and early 20th centuries, no outing was complete without live music, and band concerts were very popular. There was an eight-sided bandstand downtown where people gathered to dance or listen to music on a summer evening. Palmer was the leader of several local bands, including the Winsted, American, and Slovak Bands.

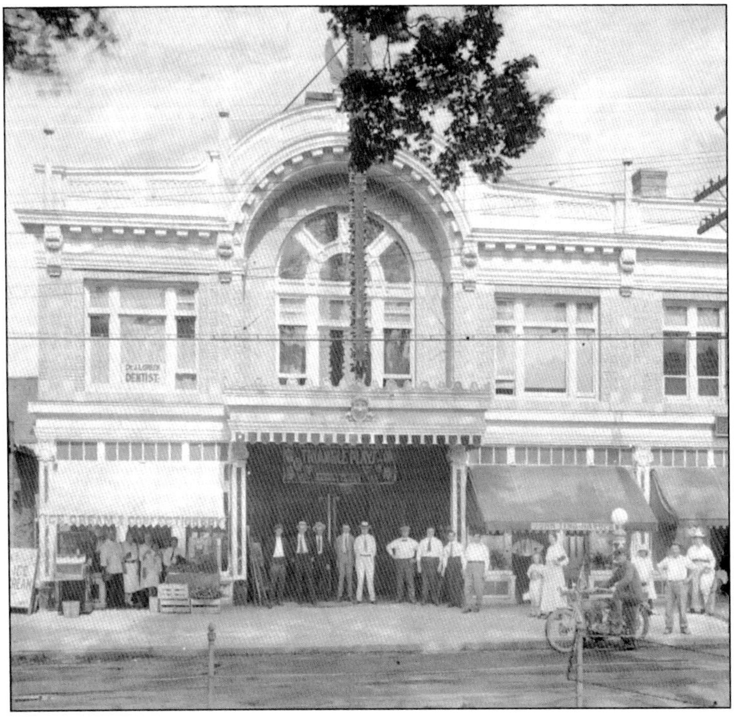

The Alhambra Theater, built on South Main Street in 1915 by Slovak businessman Nicholas Ostrofsky, was the entertainment center of Torrington for decades, offering vaudeville shows, popular films, serials, and well-known plays performed by touring companies. Weekend specials sold out, and in the early 1940s, children's 5¢ summer matinees were a favorite. The Alhambra was destroyed by fire in 1949.

Dr. Thatcher S. Hanchett relaxes on Bantam Lake in this c. 1900 photograph. T.S. Hanchett began practicing in Torrington in 1865, when the town had a population of about 2,500. For many years, he did all of Torrington's surgical work and had a large obstetrics practice as well.

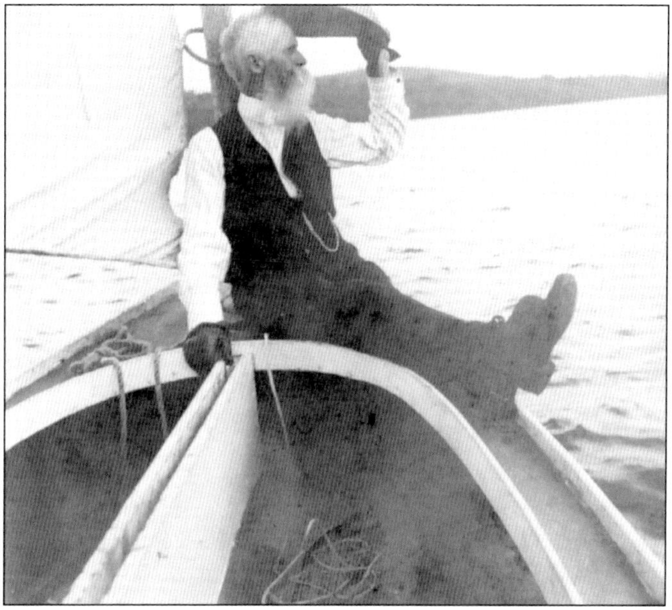

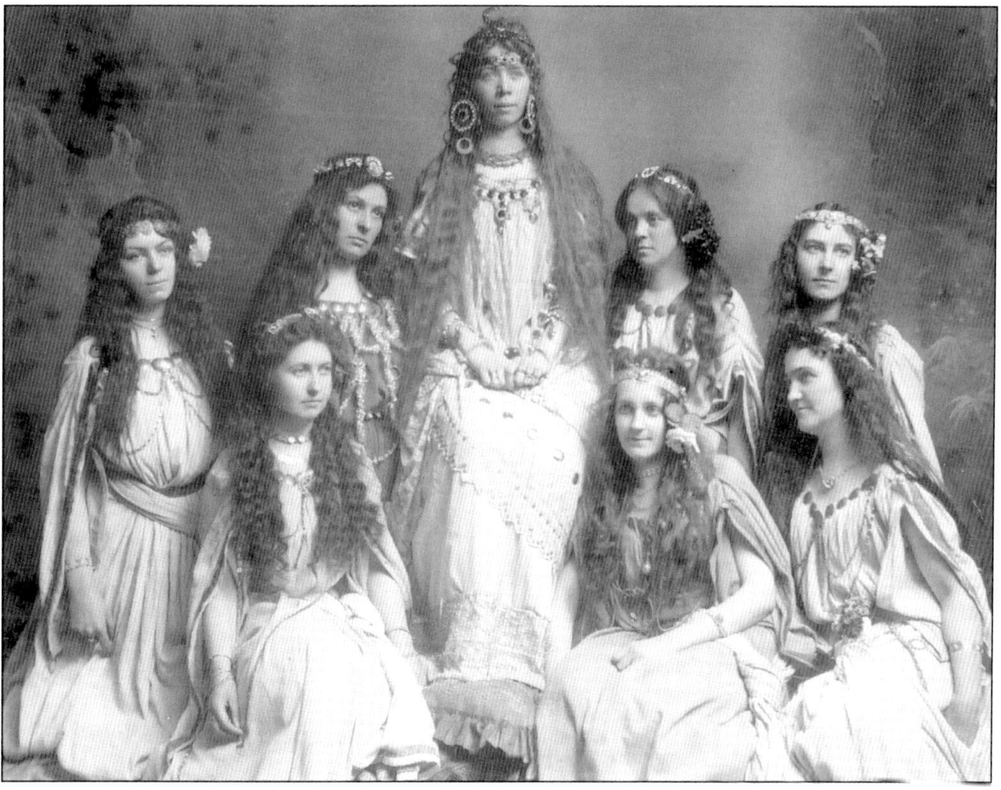

Cast members from the opera *Egypta*, which opened on May 1, 1902, at the Union Theater, pose for this photograph. Over 500 local people appeared in the production, as angels, fan-bearers, and Egyptian priests, or in the chorus of 200 children. Matinee tickets cost 15¢. Although *Egypta* was more extravagant than most, amateur theatricals and musicals played an important role in Torrington's social life throughout the 20th century.

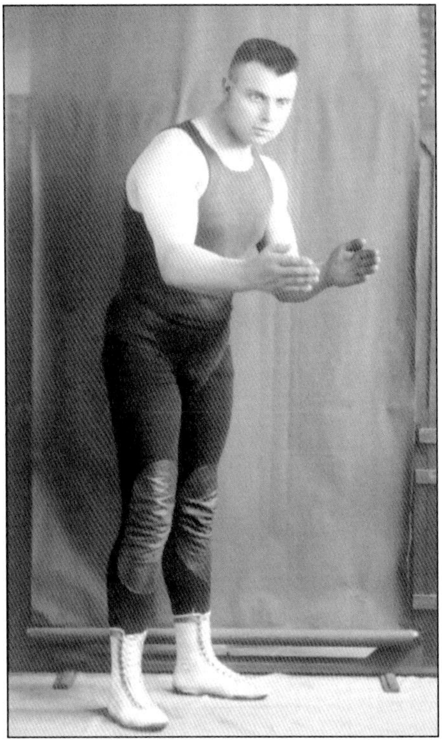

Tranquilo "Lilo" Nardi, Torrington's Italian heavyweight wrestling champion, wrestled professionally in the 1920s and 1930s. Fans turned out to see him at Fuessenich Park in June 1936 at the city's first outdoor wrestling match. Nardi, a butcher, eventually opened Nardi's Market on Highland Avenue. (Ernest Nardi.)

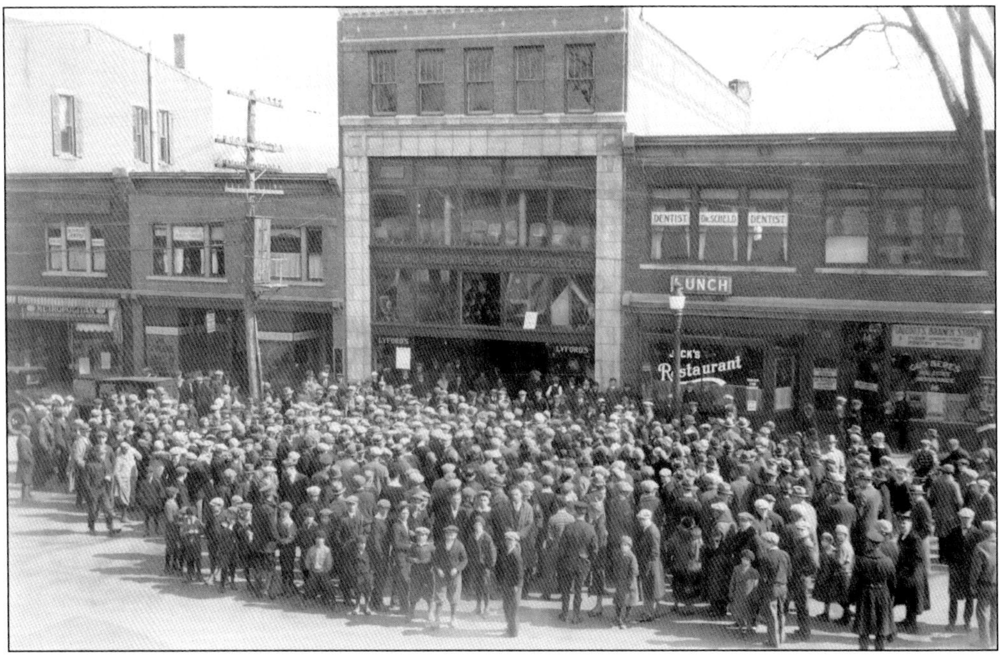

To keep fans seeking updates on game day from clogging its telephone and telegraph lines, Torrington's local newspaper, the *Register*, sometimes arranged to have important sporting events broadcast live. In this 1926 photograph, fans gathered on East Main Street to hear broadcast coverage of the Torrington–West Haven basketball game direct from Yale gymnasium via a "ten-horn Bristol audiophone" installed by radio expert Ted Lyford.

Seven

Public Service and Civic Engagement

Torrington's citizens have always played an active role in the life of their community and their country. During the American Revolution, able-bodied men joined the militias and fought in significant battles, including the Battle of Saratoga. Torrington also supplied equipment and livestock to feed George Washington's army. Seven African American men were among the 150 Torrington soldiers who fought in the Civil War, while almost 1,500 Torrington residents served in World War I. During World War II, Torrington lost 85 servicemen. At home, residents founded relief organizations, planted Victory gardens, gathered scrap metal, and purchased war bonds. With factories in full-time war production and men serving overseas, women stepped up and entered the workforce.

Domestic security was a matter for local police and fire departments. An appreciative community supported these public servants with modern equipment, new buildings, and larger staffs.

The progressive ideas and generous gifts of local philanthropists have also had a great impact on Torrington's civic life. William Besse, Frederick F. Fuessenich, John Alvord, and the descendants of Lyman Coe are among those who donated land for city parks. Uri Hungerford's generosity built Charlotte Hungerford Hospital. Torrington's library was a gift from Elisha Turner. Charles F. Brooker set up the Maria Seymour Brooker Memorial on the family homestead on Litchfield Street. Gertrude F. Hotchkiss provided a permanent home for the Torrington Historical Society when she bequeathed the use of her Main Street property to the society.

Many of Torrington's churches exist because of the early support of local benefactors who donated land, paid off mortgages, or financed the construction of church buildings. The first YMCA was built on a parcel of donated land. The Torrington branch of the University of Connecticut, now closed, was made possible through a gift from Julia Brooker Thompson.

Carl Bozenski made Torrington's Christmas Village a reality, and local doctors like Elias Pratt not only served individual patients but also worked tirelessly to improve public health and sanitation. The contributions of these citizens—and countless others, many of whom are unnamed and unknown—continue to enrich and inspire.

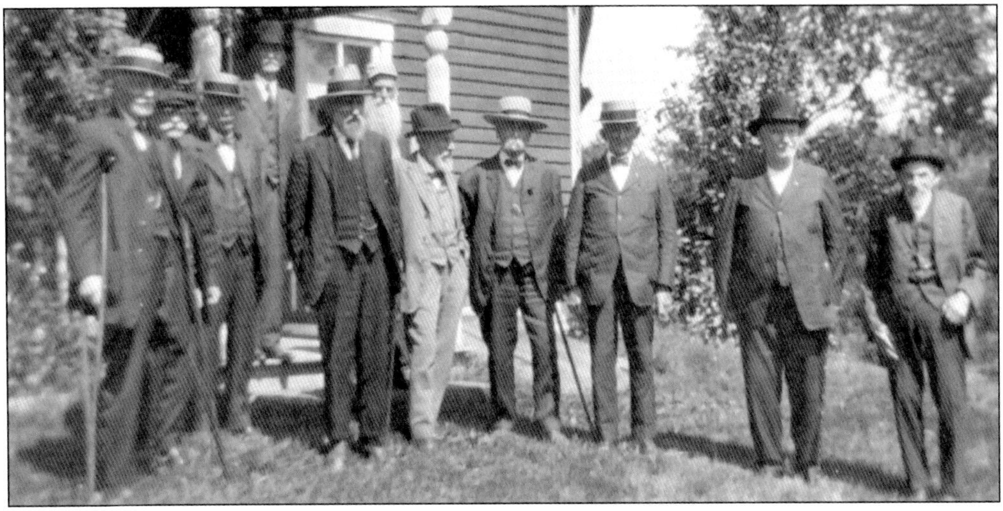

Torrington's remaining Civil War veterans pose for this photograph around 1912. Torrington soldiers were present at almost every significant battle in the war, and about 30 of the 200 who enlisted or were drafted were seriously wounded or killed. Civil War veterans were held in high regard upon their return and honored throughout the years in parades and commemorative ceremonies. Andrew Workman stands third from right.

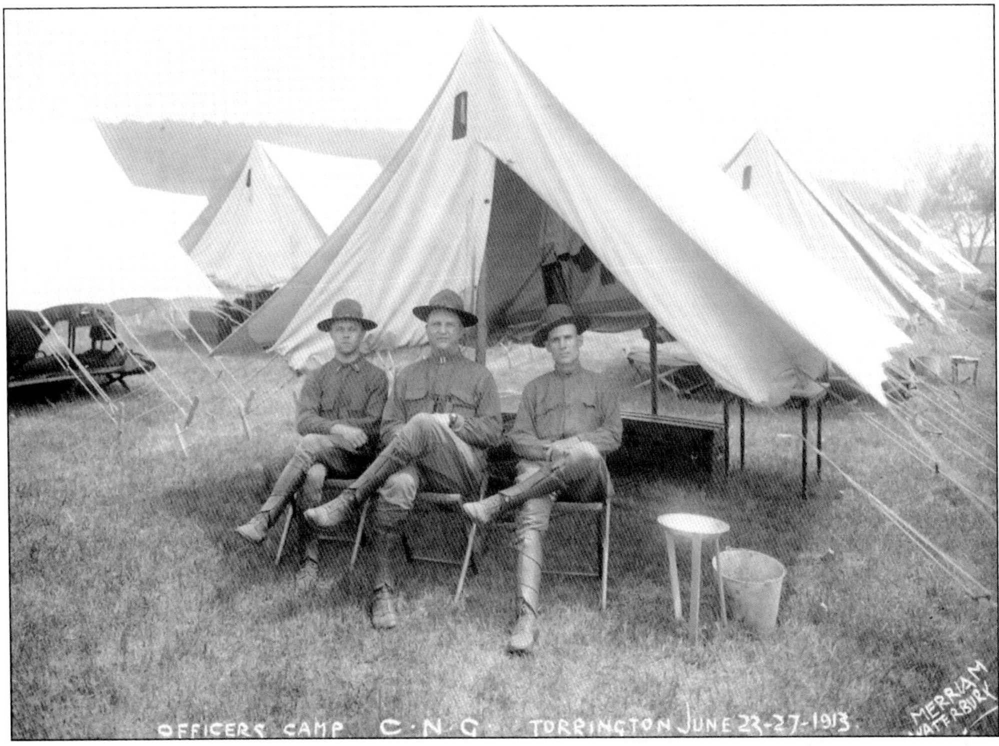

Torrington's Company M of the 2nd Infantry Connecticut National Guard was organized in 1903. In June 1913, officers from around the state, including Torrington's Capt. L. Cleveland Fuessenich (center), gathered on Schibi's land on the Torrington-Winsted Road to practice their rifle skills. From its founding, Company M took its military training seriously and was recognized for its drilling and marksmanship.

Six Torrington men gather around a "St. Louis fellow" and his dog in this 1918 photograph taken in Mehun, France. All of these World War I soldiers safely returned to Torrington, including Ernest Opperman (second row, far left), who opened his Main Street pharmacy in 1923. Dennis Ungvarski (second row, second from left) retired from American Brass in 1950.

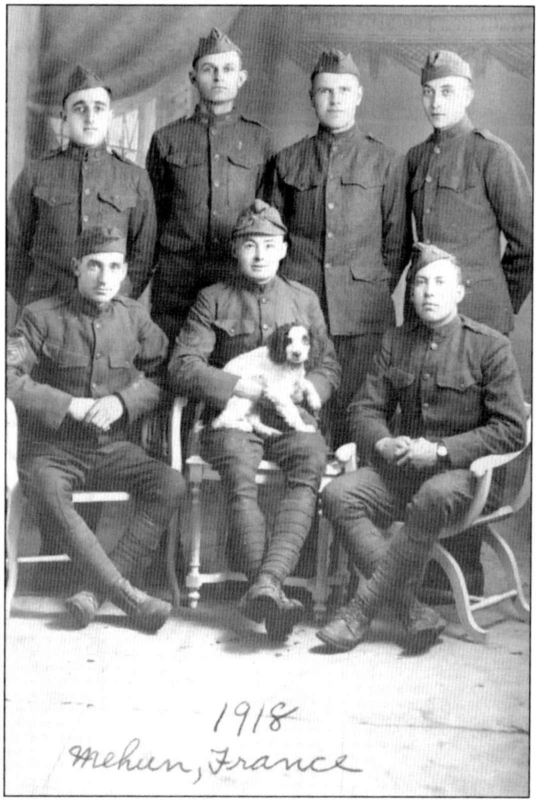

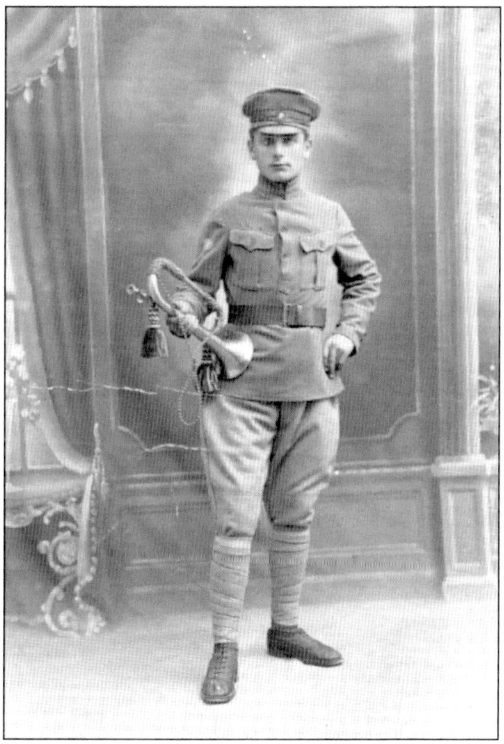

Bugler John Lauf was one of 13 Slovak recruits who left Torrington in December 1917 to join the Czecho-Slovak army during World War I. Escorted by the Slovak Band, the men were given a rousing send-off at the train station. Prior to the United States' entrance into the war, a number of Torrington's Slovaks and Poles volunteered to fight with the European allies. (Elizabeth Kaczmarcyk.)

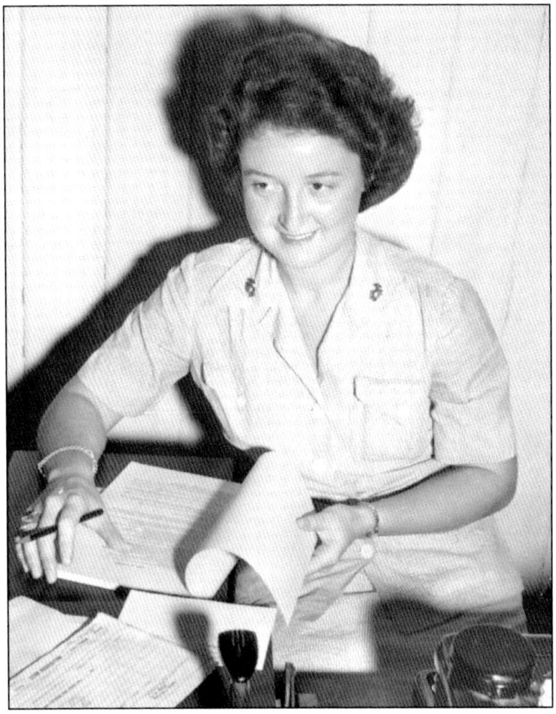

Elizabeth Agnes Whalen, one of several women from Torrington who served in the military during World War II, enlisted in the Marine Corps in January 1944. A 1938 graduate of Torrington High School, she was among the first female Marines to be stationed overseas. Her brother Francis served in the Navy.

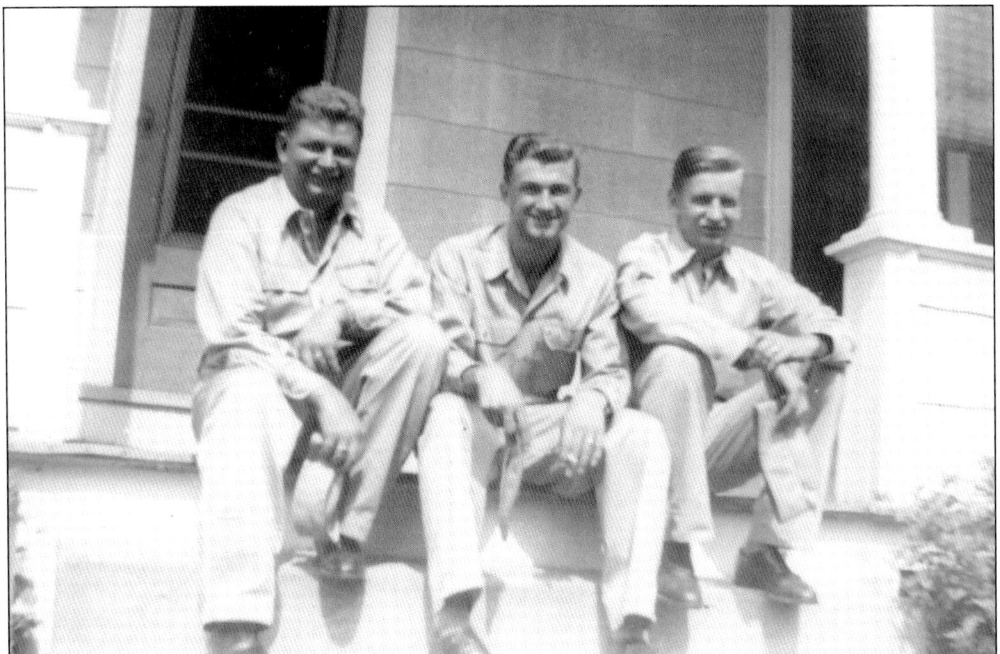

George (left), Michael (center), and Joseph Amrich sit on the front porch of the family home on Kinney Street. The three brothers, along with their older brother Stephen, all served in World War II, as did many other Torrington siblings, including Alexander, Henry, and Edward Kaczmarcyk and John and Raymond Avenia. Having multiple family members in the military put a strain on families but also bolstered community support for the war. (Elizabeth Kaczmarcyk.)

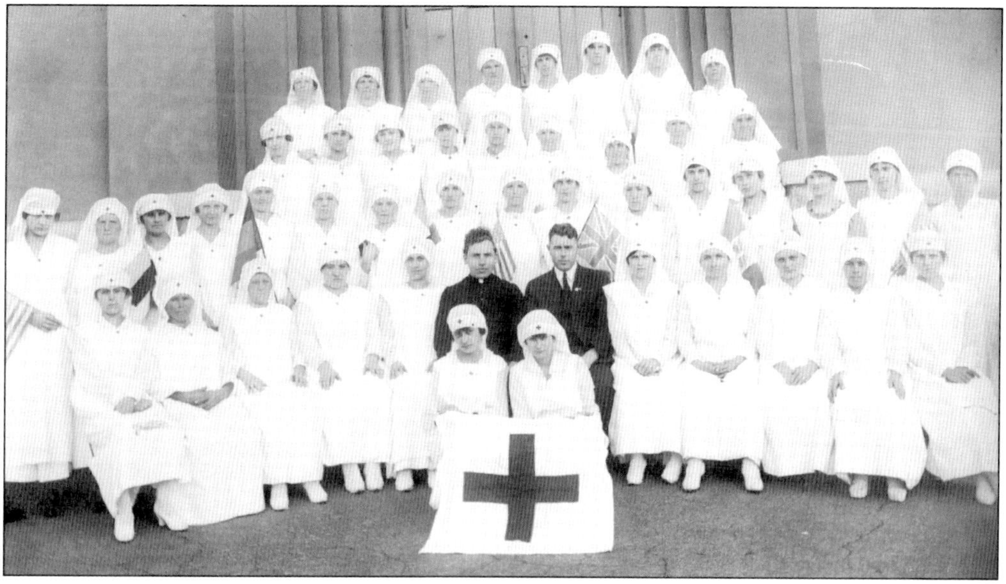

Slovak relief workers gather in front of Sacred Heart Church in this undated World War I photograph. At the time, many local ethnic groups and churches formed service organizations, usually affiliated with the Red Cross. The groups knit blankets and clothing and made bandages and surgical supplies. The totals reported in the newspaper were impressive: one woman made 100 pairs of socks.

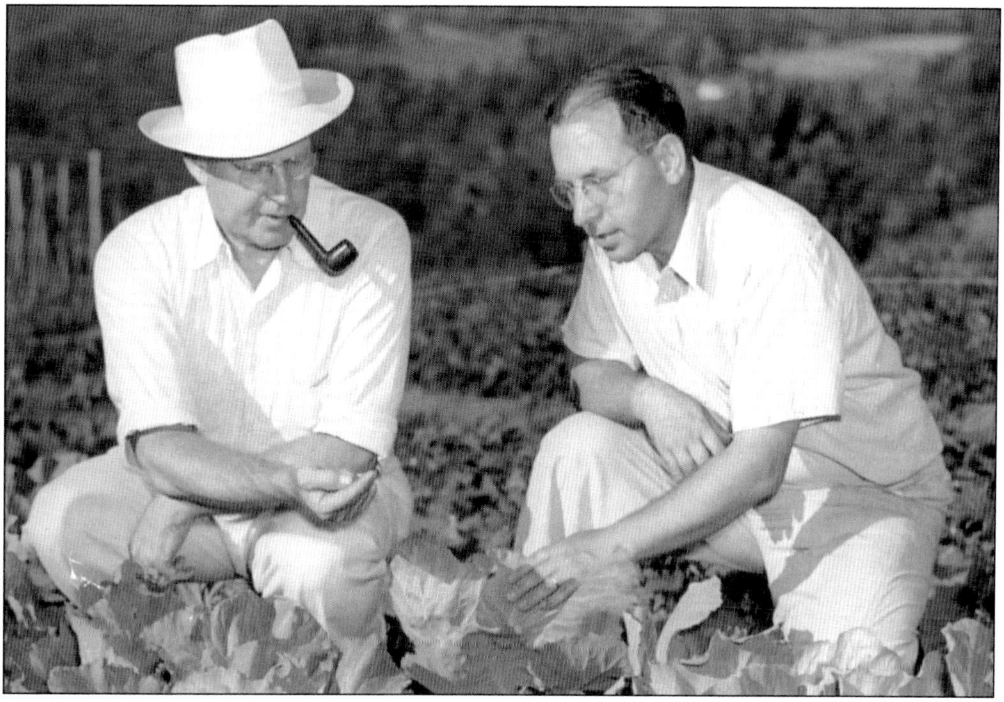

During World War II, more than 5,000 Torrington residents volunteered for Civil Defense or with the Red Cross. Others aided the war effort by donating blood, buying war bonds, or collecting scrap metal. Here, Mayor Ernest Novey (left) and Rev. Adam Tangerone inspect produce from a 1943 Victory garden.

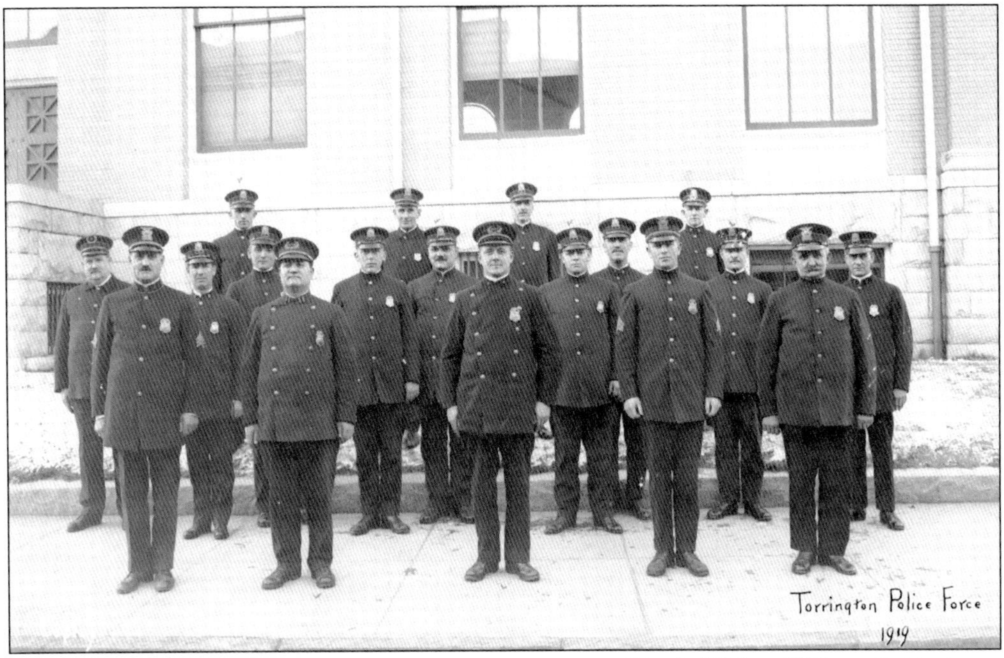

Chief of Police William E. Nevin (center) stands with his Torrington Police Department in this 1919 photograph. Appointed in 1917, Nevin was a modernizer who kept the station house open 24 hours a day and secured up-to-date equipment for his officers.

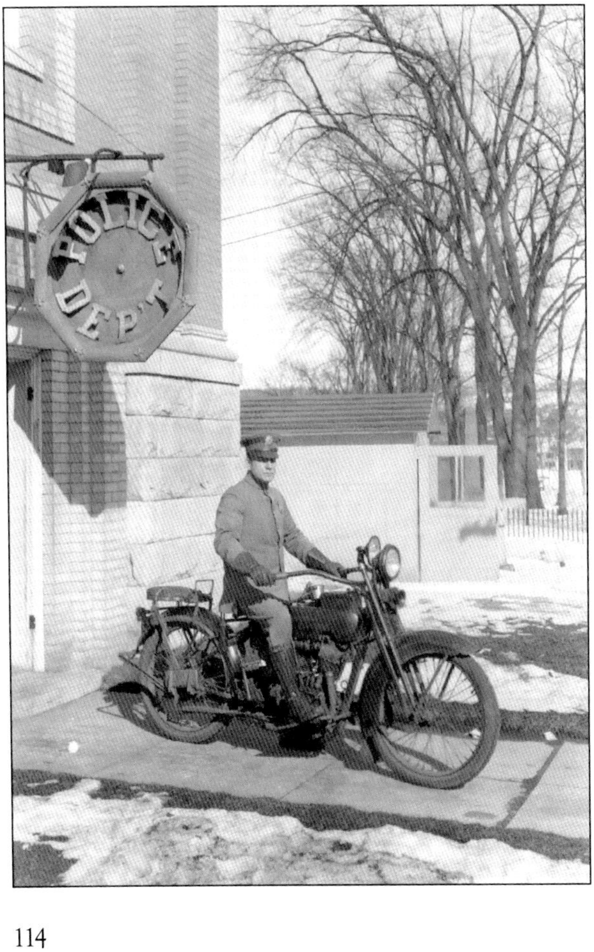

A Torrington police officer sits astride his motorcycle in this undated photograph. Soon after taking the helm in 1917, Chief William E. Nevin purchased a motorcycle for the department. A night patrol car was added later.

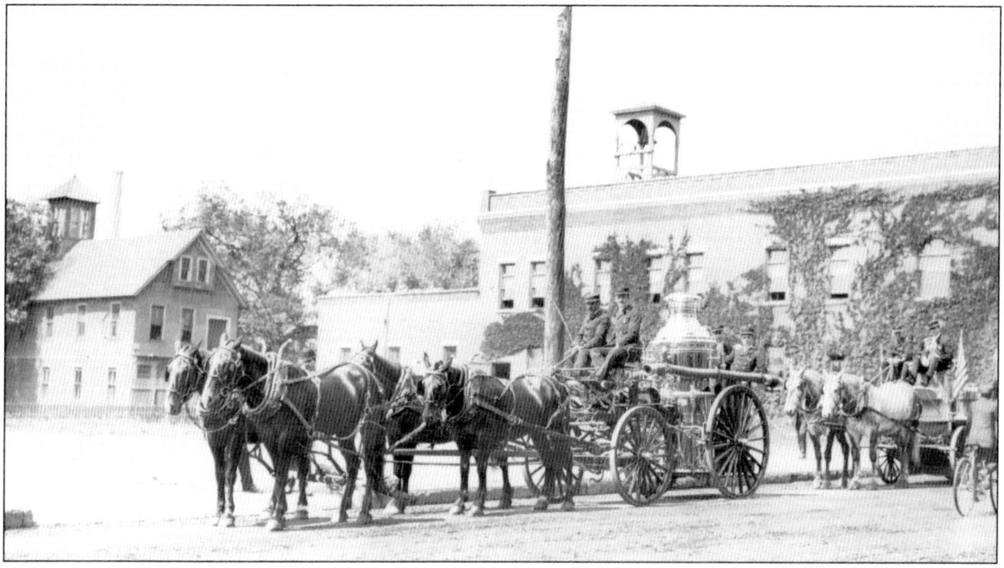

Torrington's original firehouse (in the background at left) was built on Water Street in 1887. The wood-frame building, conveniently located near Torrington's business and residential districts, is dwarfed by the newer firehouse (in the background at right), which was constructed in 1900. Chief John Palmer found the firehouse so comfortable that he made it his home for 28 years, only moving out when he married in 1929.

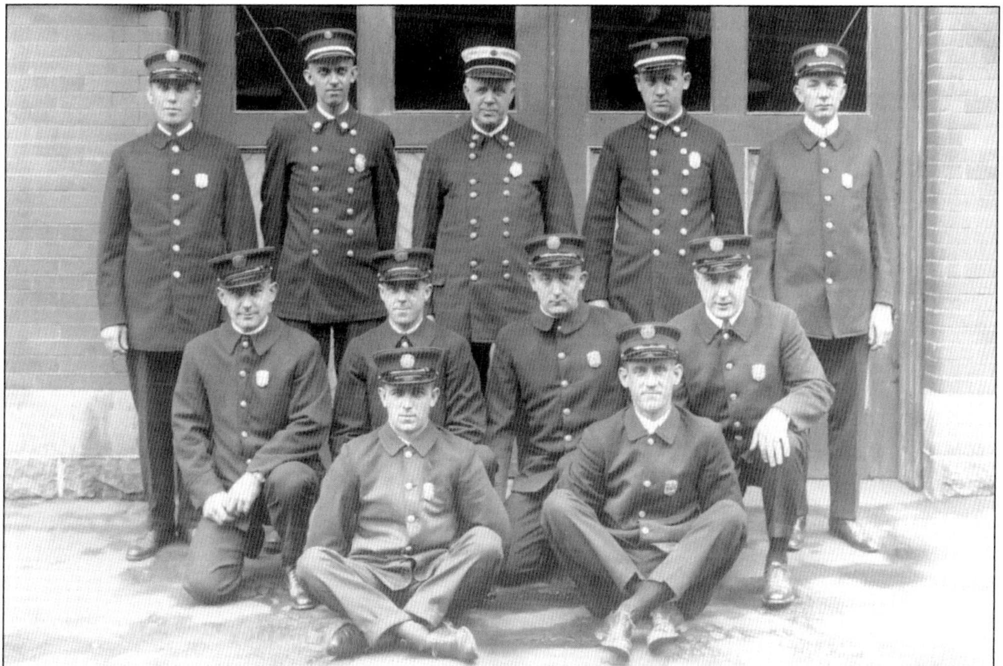

John A. Palmer (third row, center) served as a volunteer fireman for the Torrington Fire Department for 15 years, starting in 1901, when William Dayton was chief. After a paid department was formed in 1916, Palmer served as assistant chief under Edward J. Kelley and John Claxton, then was appointed chief in 1922. One of Torrington's longest-serving firefighters, Palmer was still fire chief when he died in 1936.

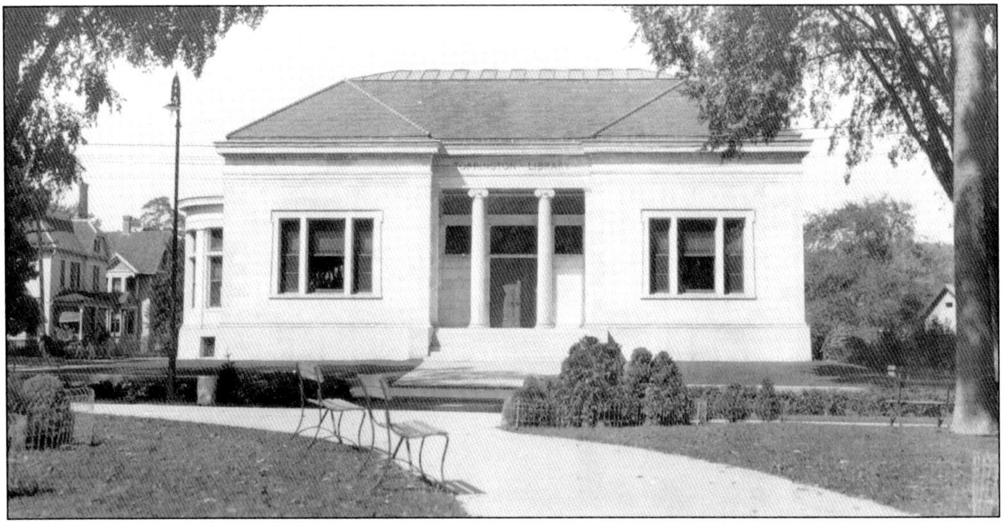

The Torrington Library, designed by architect Ernest Greene, is a simple, dignified white marble building in the Neo-Greek style, originally built with a recessed portico and Ionic columns, bronze-covered doors, and a red-tile roof. The interior woodwork was done by Torrington's Hotchkiss Brothers & Company. A gift of Elisha Turner, the building on Litchfield Street was dedicated in 1901.

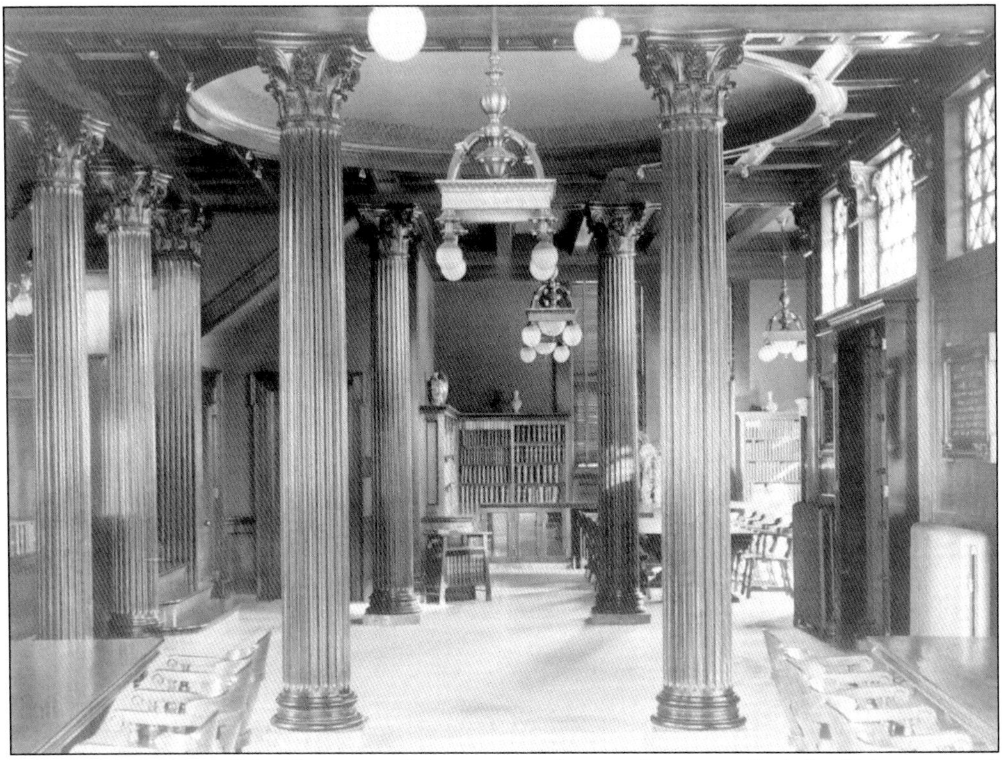

The main entrance of the Torrington Library opened onto what was called the "delivery room" (shown here), where tall, fluted Corinthian columns surrounded the ceiling's dome. The reference room, visible through the columns, was finished in quartered oak and fitted with bookcases and cupboards used to store photographs and prints.

Henry H. White (standing at farthest left) bought the *Torrington Register* newspaper in 1882 and "put his life into the paper," according to the *Torrington Register Souvenir Edition*. He moved the offices to Water Street, constructed the two-story building shown here, and purchased the best up-to-date printing equipment. By 1897, the newspaper was an eight-page daily that retailed for 2¢, had a staff of 13, and was a member of the Associated Press.

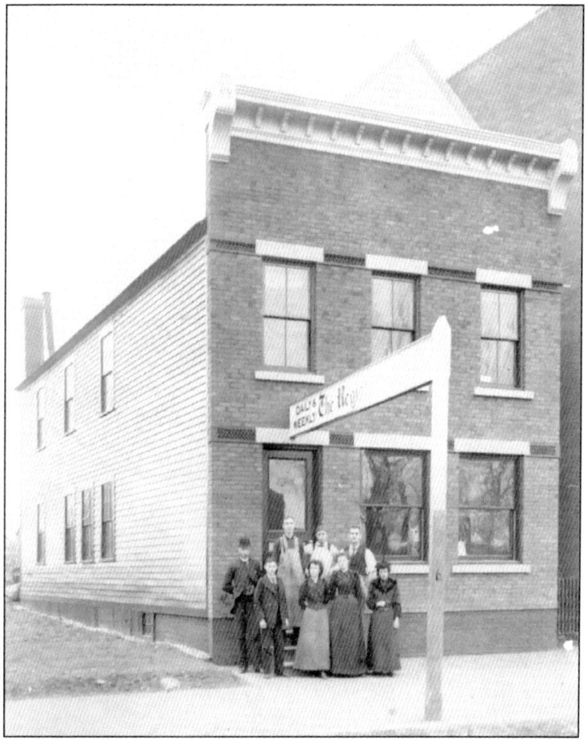

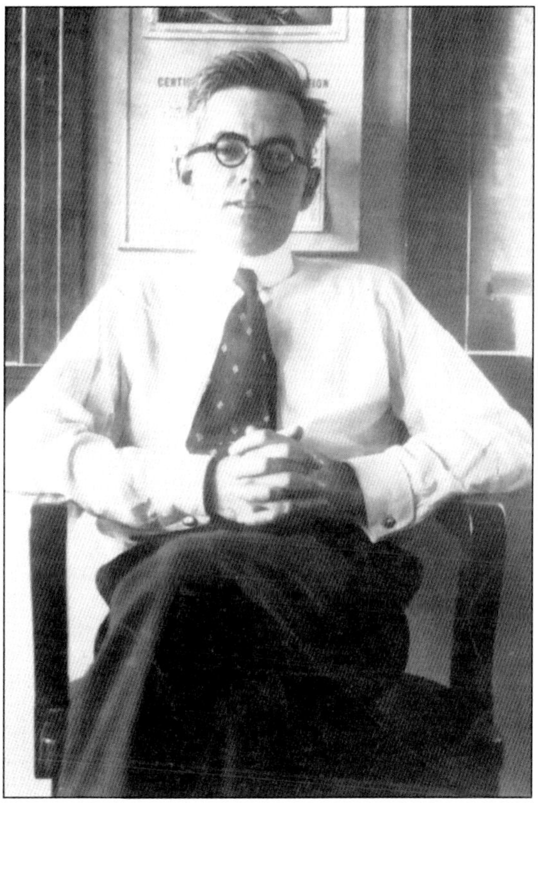

Brooklyn-born John Thompson, hired by the *Torrington Register* as a substitute reporter in 1909, worked his way up to editor-in-chief by the time of his unexpected death in 1949. His popular column, Read-It-or-Not, drew letters from around the country for years. One of the Torrington Historical Society's founding members, Thompson also compiled a 22-volume pictorial history of Torrington that remains an irreplaceable resource.

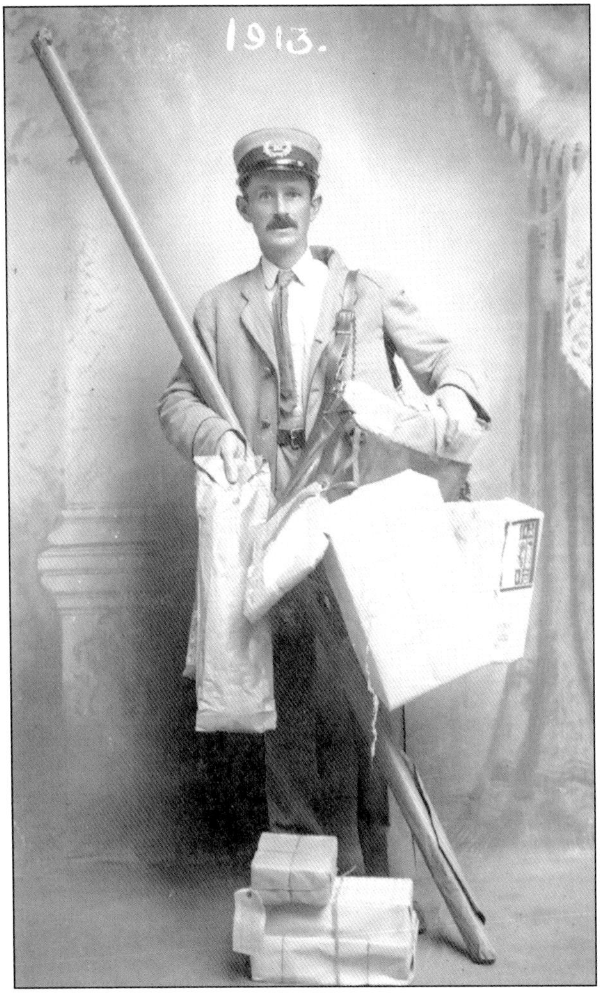

A 1912 *Evening Register* article recalls "the pleasure that was felt in having mail actually brought to the doors of the houses." This 1913 photograph shows parcel post deliverer E.C. Smith laden with packages.

In June 1905, Torrington's post office, which had moved many times, settled in for a 30-year stint at the corner of Prospect and Water Streets. This was the first federal office building erected in Litchfield County. The post office was relocated to Church and Main Streets in 1936 and then to East Elm Street in 1978. Note the "Stop and Go" sign on the corner; Torrington's first traffic light was not installed until 1927.

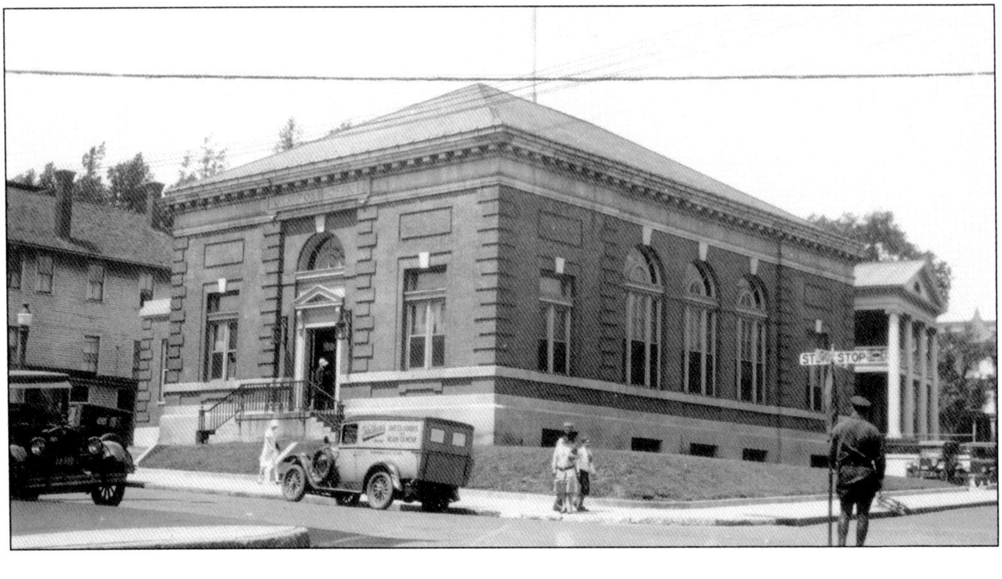

In April 1891, the Young Men's Christian Association (YMCA) opened its doors on Main Street in downtown Torrington. The YMCA was built by Hotchkiss Brothers & Company for $12,000 on land donated by Elisha Turner and located north of the Conley Inn. The state-of-the-art facility had a gymnasium, baths, a reading room with six daily newspapers, evening classes, a boardinghouse directory, and a lovely parlor with a piano for visiting ladies.

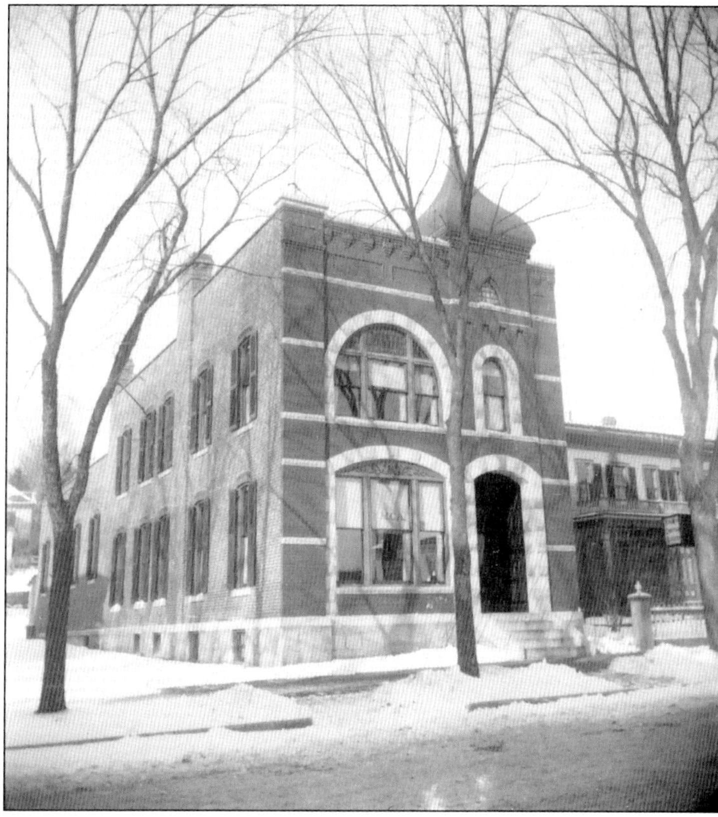

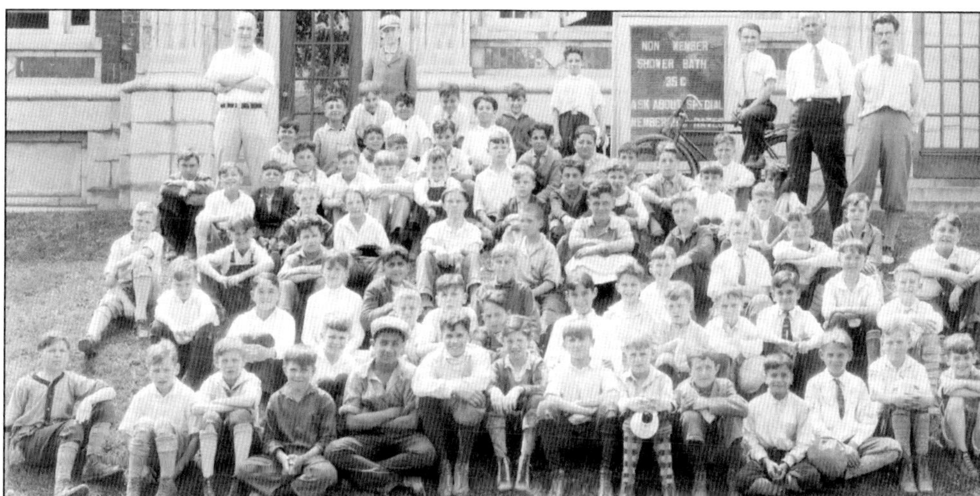

By 1923, the YMCA had outgrown its Main Street location and a new facility was dedicated at 259 Prospect Street, where it still operates today. The YMCA gradually included girls in its activities; this large group of boys is posing on the YMCA lawn around 1928. Baths at the YMCA, which were available for a small charge, must have been quite a draw at a time when some residents still bathed by filling tubs with water heated on the stove.

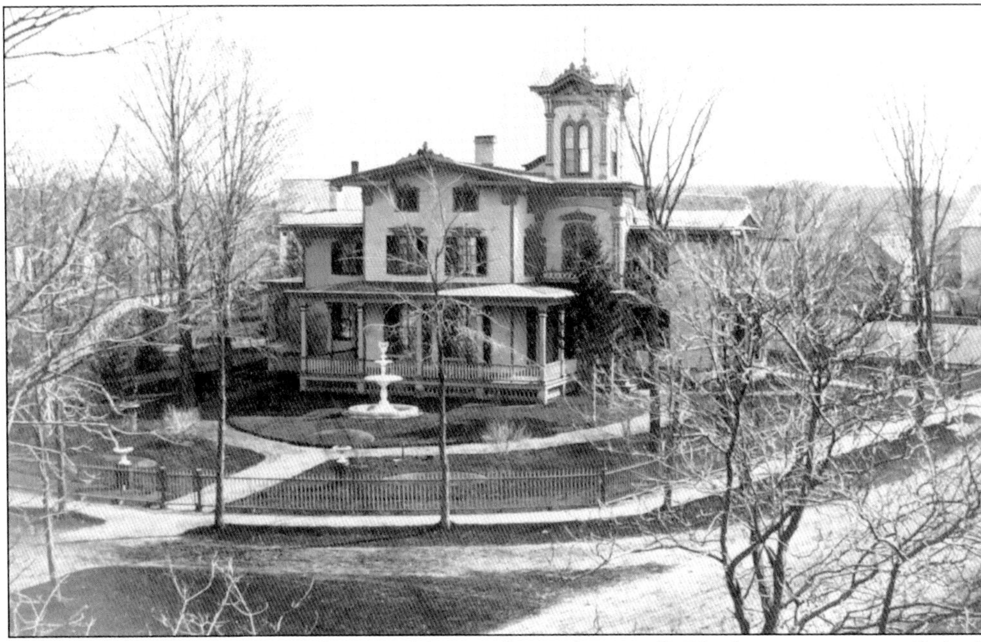

Coe Memorial Park was once the site of the Coe house (pictured). The house was originally built by John and Charlotte Hungerford, who sold it to Lyman and Eliza Coe in 1863. By 1906, both Lyman and Eliza had died. Their children donated the house and grounds to the town for a park in memory of their parents, "who loved Torrington and its people." A condition of the gift was the removal of the Coe house. Torrington hired the Olmsted Brothers firm to design Coe Memorial Park, but contract problems led to their dismissal. Nevertheless, Olmsted Brothers wrote that the park should have shade and broad walkways. The picture below, which was taken after the park opened in 1909, shows both of those features as well as the commercial buildings that used to line South Main Street.

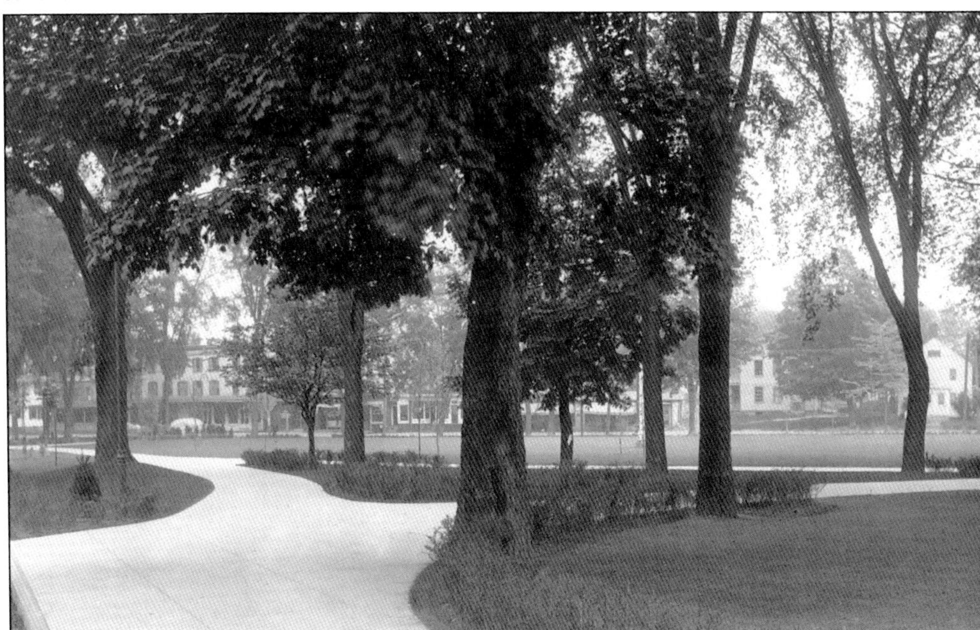

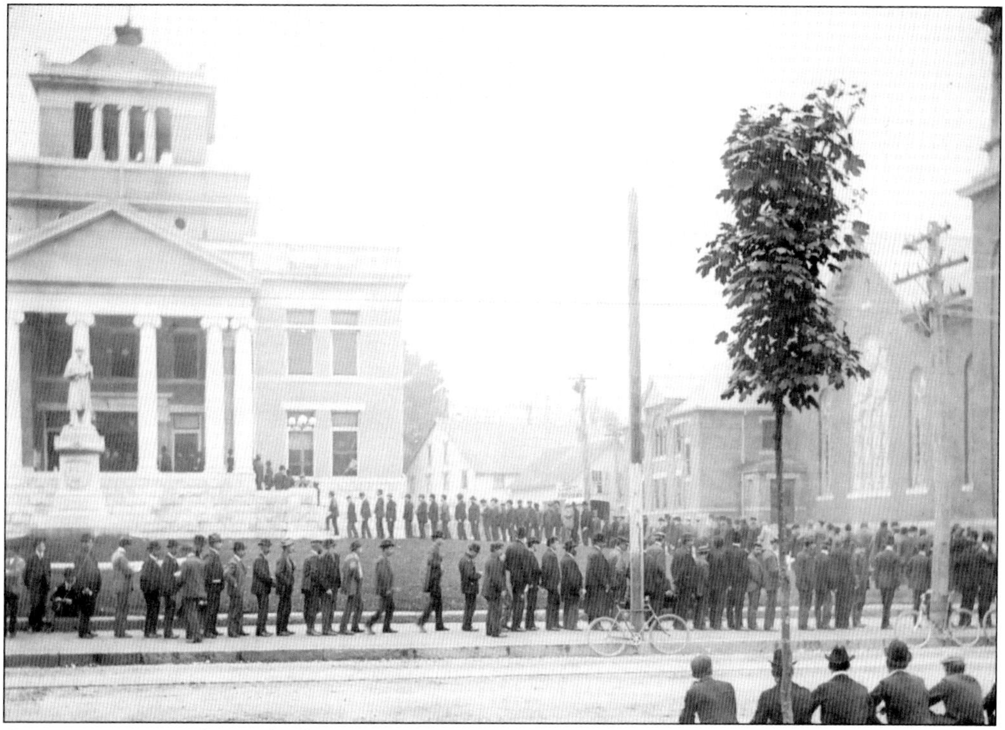

Torrington's second town hall was built by Hotchkiss Brothers & Company in 1898. Constructed of buff brick with marble trim and a copper dome, the building was described as a "chaste beauty," by the *Torrington Register*. It housed courtrooms, the police department, the town clerk, the men's and women's jails, and even a room for tramps. In this c. 1900 photograph, men are lined up to vote on whether to make Torrington a dry town.

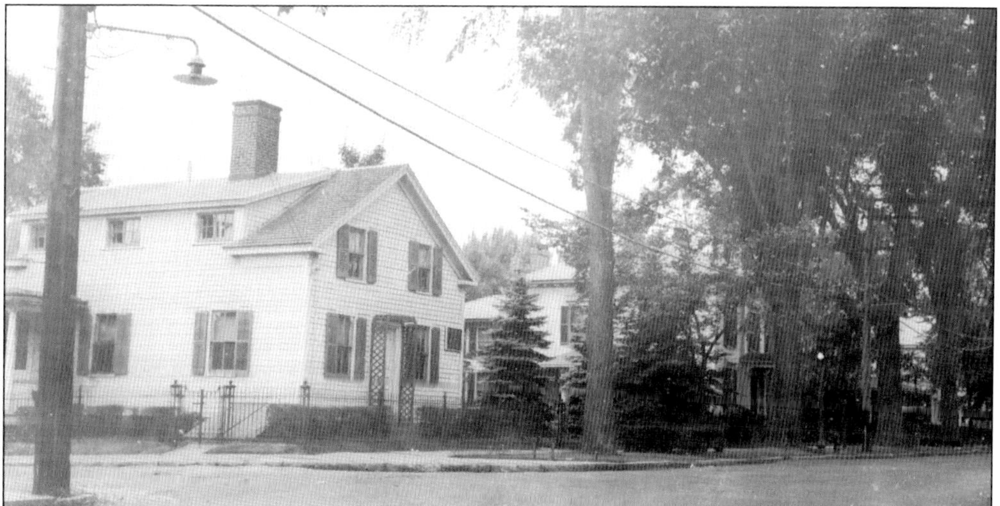

The Maria Seymour Brooker Memorial was founded in 1918 through a gift of Charles F. Brooker in memory of his mother. Started as a day nursery, the organization has expanded its services and footprint throughout the decades and now includes a children's dental clinic established with the support of the Temkin family in memory of local doctor Abraham Temkin. Brooker Memorial is located on Litchfield Street on the site of the original Brooker family homestead.

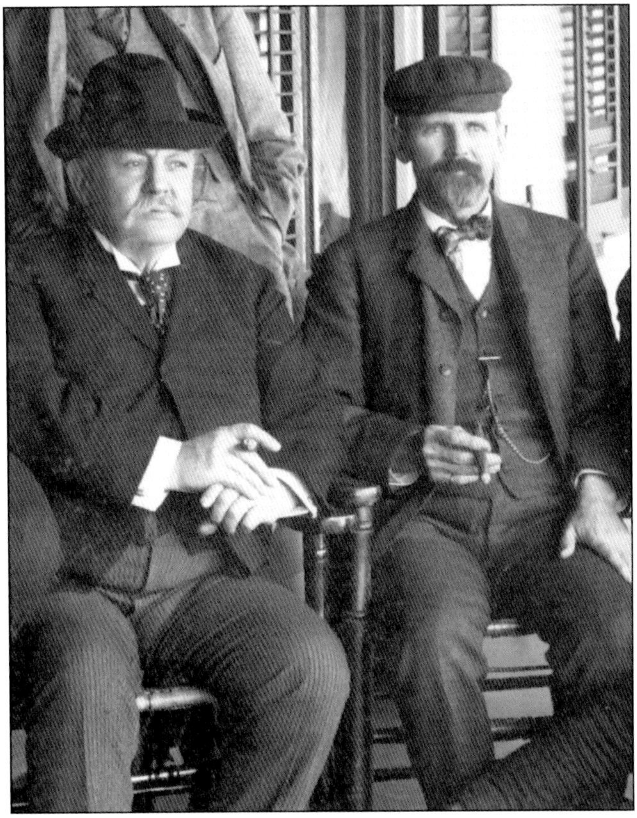

Uri Hungerford (left), who made a fortune in copper and brass, maintained close ties to Torrington, where his civic-minded mother, Charlotte, lived. Inspired by her example and persuaded by his close friend James Doughty (right) not to wait until his death to bequeath money, Hungerford gave the city $500,000 in 1910 to "buy a suitable site and build an adequate hospital."

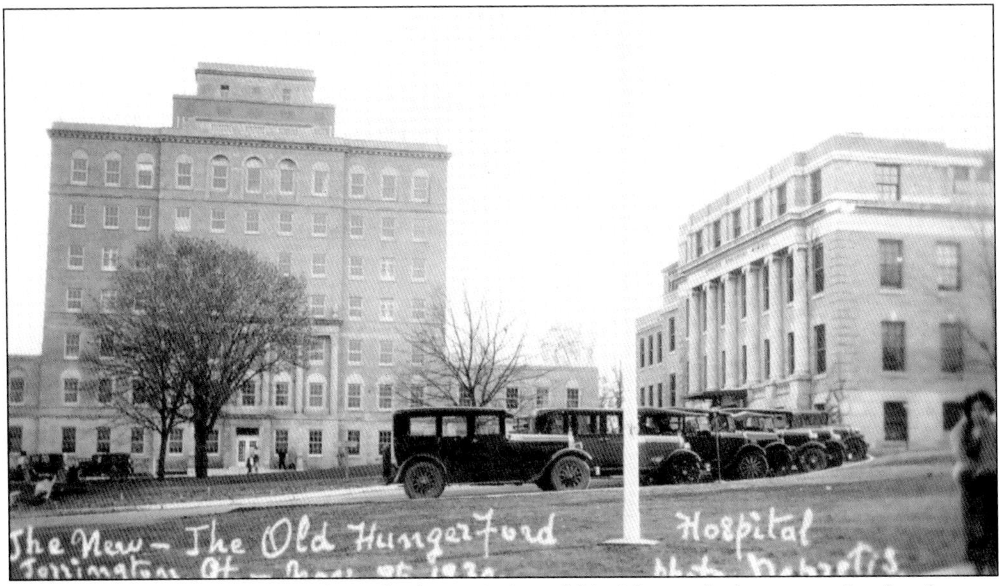

Charlotte Hungerford Hospital was built in 1916, and Uri Hungerford supported it for the rest of his life—and beyond. A major bequest when he died in 1926—and another when his wife died the following year—allowed the hospital to undergo a needed expansion in 1930, tripling its capacity. The hospital has continued to modernize and improve to meet local needs in the 21st century.

Grace Coe married Dr. Hiram Pulver, a local homeopathic physician, in 1890, then obtained her own medical degree in homeopathy. After Hiram was killed in a tragic runaway horse accident in 1901, Grace continued their Main Street practice even after losing an eye from a patient-related infection. Grace Coe Pulver is one of a long line of dedicated local female physicians, nurses, and midwives dating back to the 1700s.

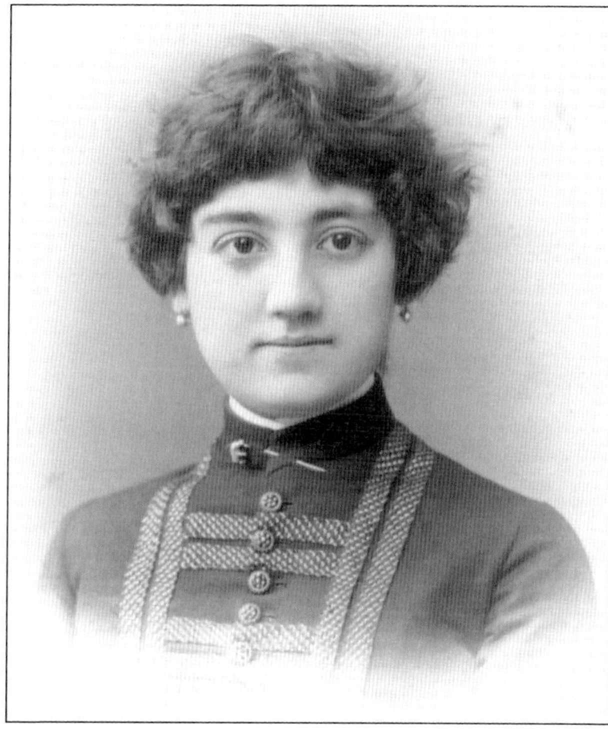

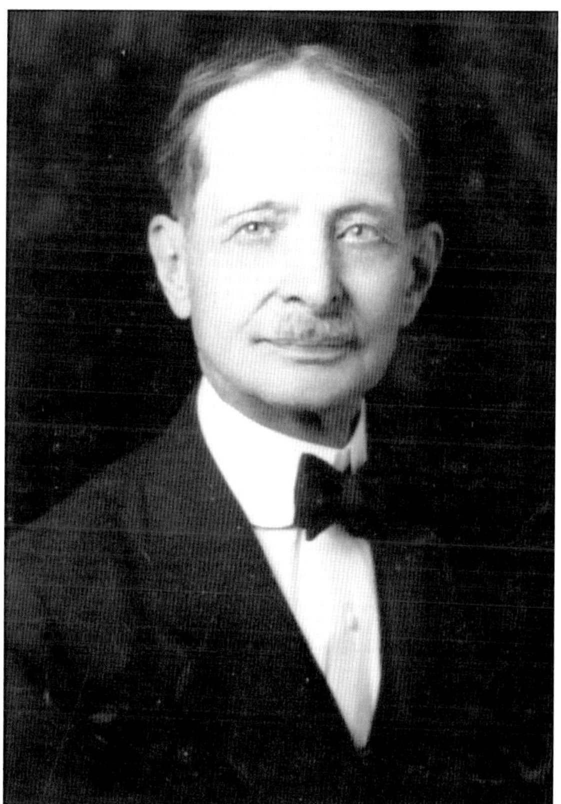

As Torrington's first health officer, Dr. Elias Pratt dealt with epidemics of typhoid, smallpox, and diphtheria and worked to introduce laws and ordinances to limit these outbreaks. He was the first doctor appointed to supervise the city's schools, and he established the first vaccination clinics in 1922. Dr. Pratt also championed the construction of Charlotte Hungerford Hospital and was its first medical director.

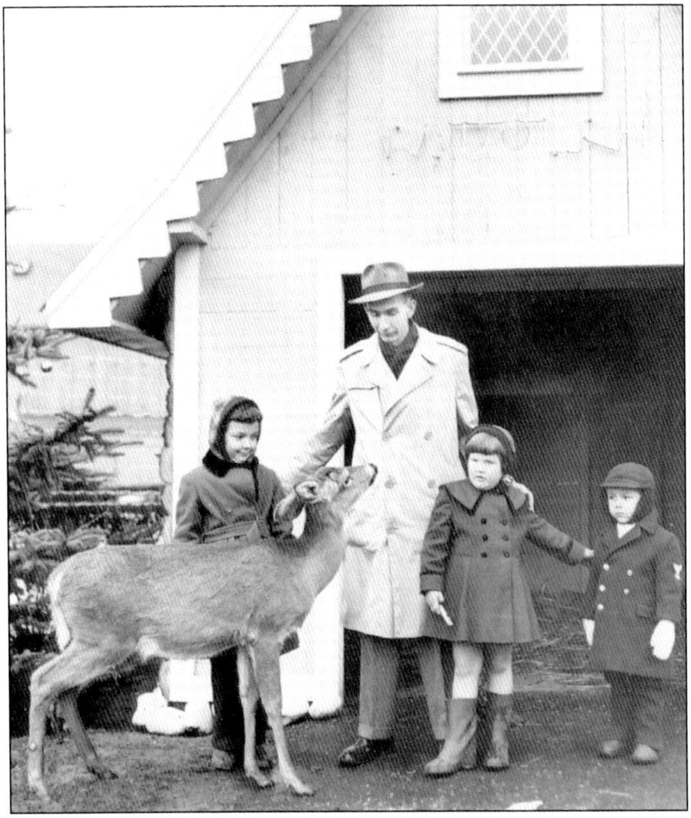

Carl Bozenski poses with some young friends and Rudolph in this undated photograph taken at Christmas Village. While bedridden far from home in a tuberculosis sanitarium, Bozenski had imagined creating a Christmas wonderland. Upon his return to Torrington in 1946, he put his ideas into action. With help from the recreation department, local clubs, businesses, and volunteers, Christmas Village opened in 1947 and was an immediate success.

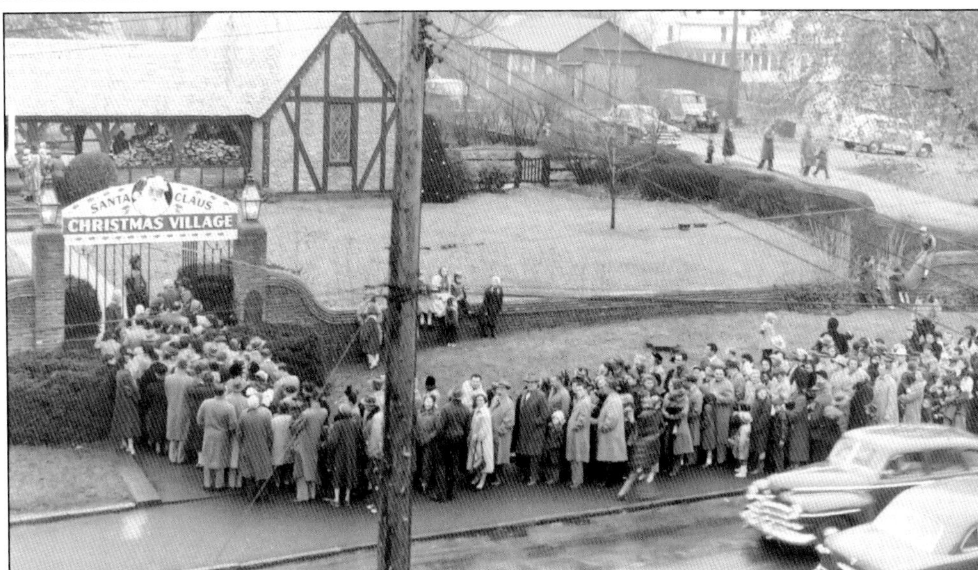

Christmas Village, located at Alvord Memorial Park, is commercial-free, has no admission charge, and attracts thousands of visitors each year. Here, visitors line up on Church Street in 1949 as they wait to enter the two small Tudor-style houses that were converted into Santa's North Pole home and his workshop for several weeks each year. Fred Short won the contest to design the Christmas Village sign.

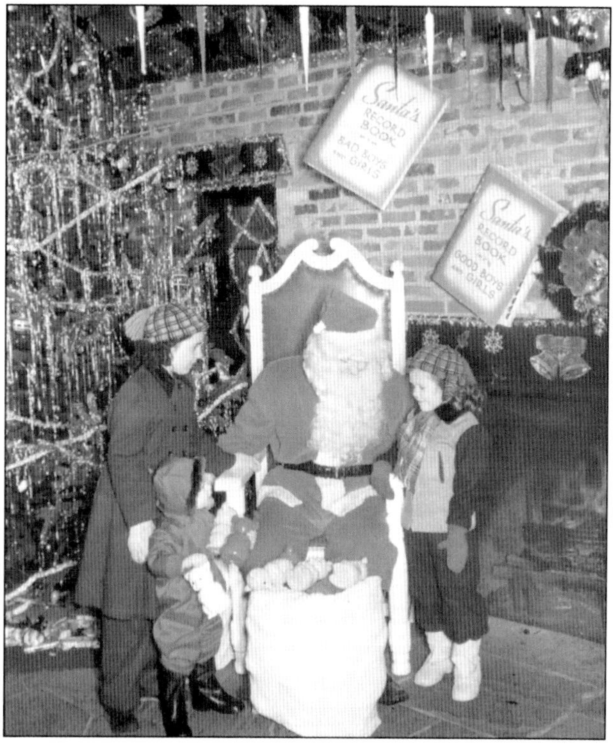

Sitting on a magnificent throne, Santa Claus welcomes young visitors. With toys stacked to the ceiling, a roaring fire in the fireplace, and yards of festive tinsel, the setting at Christmas Village is magical for children and adults alike. Each child receives a small gift made possible through the generosity of local residents.

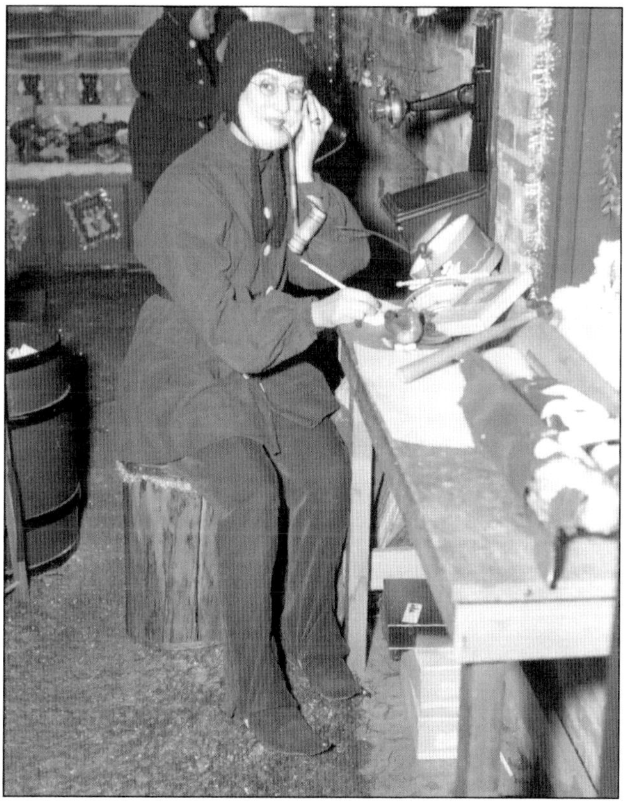

Before the new toy shop was built, guests made their way through a covered passageway to another little house—Santa's workshop. Several elves worked in a room crowded with toys while bubbles floated, music boxes played, and a toy train circled the room. Here, elf Tippy (Roberta Valli) is hard at work. The rustic wooden stool was designed by Paul Freedman.

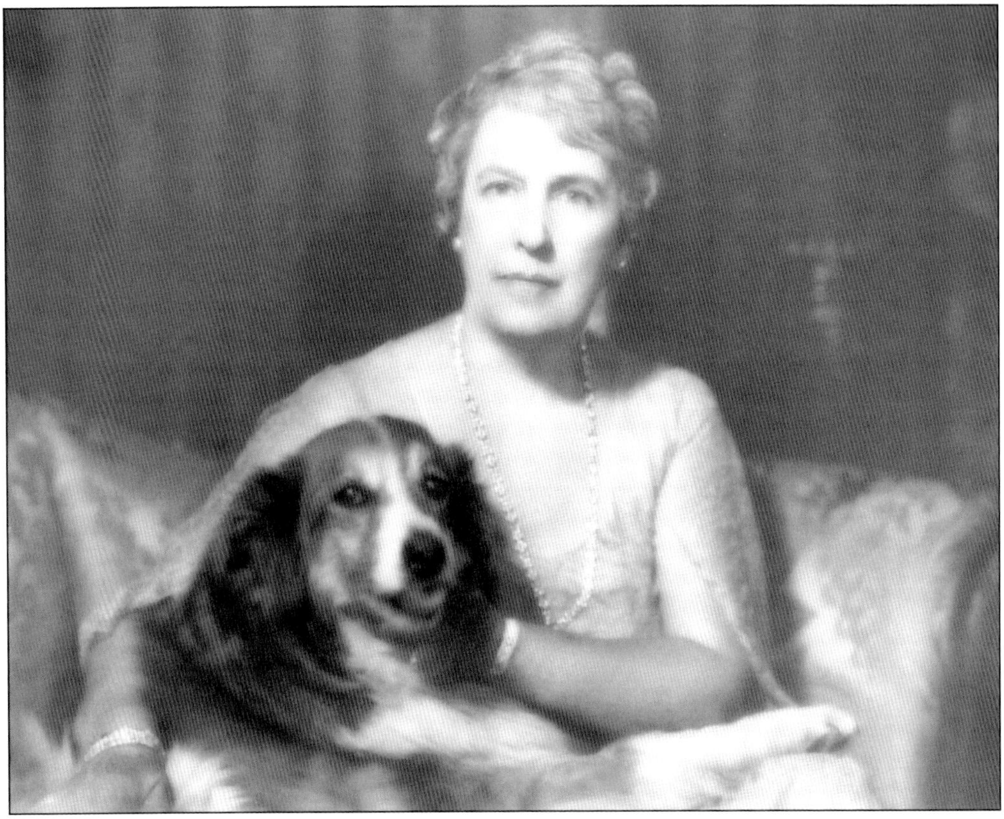

Gertrude Fyler Hotchkiss (1868–1956) was one of Torrington's great philanthropists. She is shown here around 1935 with one of her beloved dogs. Hotchkiss lived at 192 Main Street in a home built by her parents, Orsamus and Mary Fyler. When she died in 1956, her will established a trust for her home and designated the Torrington Historical Society to operate it as a museum. Her gift has allowed the Torrington Historical Society to have a place where it can share Torrington's history with people from near and far. The sign pictured below highlights the cultural treasures that have a permanent home as a result of Hotchkiss's gift to the community: the Hotchkiss-Fyler House Museum, the Torrington History Museum, and the John H. Thompson Research Library.

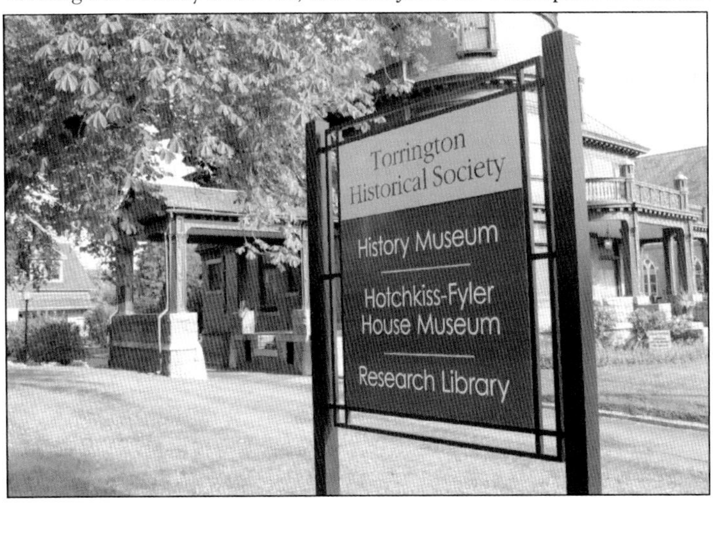

About the Torrington Historical Society

In his first edition of *A History of Torrington*, John H. Thompson, the first president of the Torrington Historical Society, writes that he was once asked: "Why bother studying about Torrington and its history?" Thompson answered with another question: "How can a man or woman attain the highest degree of citizenship without knowing something about the community in which he or she lives?" Thompson's response continues to define the work of the Torrington Historical Society and inspire its mission "to build a sense of community through an understanding of our shared past."

Founded in 1944, the Torrington Historical Society, under Thompson's guidance, began to collect documents, artifacts, and photographs that chronicle the history of Torrington. In 1956, Gertrude Fyler Hotchkiss bequeathed the use of her Main Street estate as a headquarters for the society in memory of her parents, Orsamus Roman Fyler and Mary Vail Fyler, and her husband, Edward H. Hotchkiss. Over the years, many new benefactors have given generously to preserve the history of the community.

As a result, the collections started by Thompson and the society many years ago have been steadily growing and now include a remarkable collection of photographic prints, negatives, and digital images covering all aspects of Torrington's history. These collections have been mined to create this book, which seeks to make us better citizens as envisioned by Thompson 74 years ago.

Torrington Historical Society, a private, not-for-profit organization, relies on the generosity of the community to advance the vision of John H. Thompson and Gertrude F. Hotchkiss. Without community support, it would be impossible to continue the work of collecting Torrington's history, preserving it, and making it available to everyone through exhibits, programs, publications, and research. For citizens wishing to help with this work, there are many opportunities. These include donating historical materials, becoming a member, making a bequest, or simply lending a hand. With your support, we can continue to preserve Torrington's unique history and make this a stronger community.

Torrington Historical Society
192 Main Street
Torrington CT 06790
http://www.torringtonhistoricalsociety.org
(860) 482-8260